A WIND ON THE HEATH

A Memoir

A WIND ON THE HEATH
A Memoir

KENNETH McDONALD

Epic Press

Belleville, Ontario, Canada

A WIND ON THE HEATH
Copyright © 2003, Kenneth McDonald

National Library of Canada Cataloguing in Publication
McDonald, Kenneth, 1914-
    A wind on the heath / Kenneth McDonald.
Includes index.
ISBN 1-55306-558-1.--ISBN 1-55306-560-3 (LSI ed.)
    1. McDonald, Kenneth, 1914-. 2. World War, 1939-1945—
Personal narratives, British. 3. Great Britain. Royal Air Force—
Biography. 4. Authors, Canadian—Biography. I. Title.
PS8575.D652Z53 2003   C813'.54
C2003-901632-3   PR9199.3.M31144Z47 2003

For more information or
to order additional copies, please contact:

Epic Press
www.essencebookstore.com
1-800-238-6376

Epic Press is an imprint of *Essence Publishing,* a Christian Book Publisher dedicated to furthering the work of Christ through the written word. For more information, contact:
20 Hanna Court, Belleville, Ontario, Canada K8P 5J2.
Phone: 1-800-238-6376 • Fax: (613) 962-3055
E-mail: publishing@essencegroup.com
Internet: www.essencegroup.com

Printed in Canada
by
Epic
Press

To Ruth, my beloved wife.

BESIDE THE DESK

There's night and day, brother, both sweet things; sun, moon, and stars, brother, all sweet things; there's likewise a wind on the heath. Life is very sweet, brother; who would wish to die?

GEORGE BORROW

Do not go gentle into that good night,
Old age should burn and rave at close of day;
Rage, rage against the dying of the light.

DYLAN THOMAS

Remove far from me vanity and lies: give me
neither poverty nor riches; feed me with food convenient
for me:
Lest I be full, and deny thee, and say, Who is the Lord? or
lest I be poor, and steal, and take the name of my God in
vain.

PROVERBS 30:8,9

▓ TABLE OF CONTENTS ▓

◼ PREFACE ◼

The quotations at the side of the desk are about life and death. Just as George Borrow reminds me that sun, moon, and stars are all sweet things; that there's likewise a wind on the heath, and that life is very sweet—who would wish to die?—so does Dylan Thomas admonish me in my old age to burn and rave, to rage against the dying of the light.

If birth, life and death are the great themes, between each man's covers are three phases. The first, from school's end to early manhood, however long it may seem, is short—rarely longer than five years. During this time, he grapples with all the world's problems he has met in his readings, is persuaded by other readings how easily they might be solved, and is impatient with institutions that persist in falling shy of his mark.

In the second phase, marriage, career and children occupy his time and energy: the institutions are there and he works within them as best he can. It is during the third phase, when the children have left home and he has time for reflection, that he returns to the problems, not with any great confidence of solving them, but at least with some knowledge of what moved mankind to do the things it did while he was around.

How long the third phase lasts is partly a matter of heredity, partly one of how he conducted himself, but for those who saw active service in World War II, the fact of having reached even the first and second phases is above all a matter of luck.

Upon exceptional men, survival imposed a duty to give thanks by devoting the rest of the life that was spared to the service of others, as Leonard Cheshire did.

Upon most, I suspect, survival imposed no duty other than to get on with the business of living the second phase that the war had interrupted. Among the many I know personally who are in their third phase, there are three characteristics. First is gratitude for survival, not with any sense of achievement or particular skill, but accepting the luck. Second is the modesty that stems from that acceptance, and third is a readiness to work among the myriad organizations outside the orbit of the State which depend on volunteers for vitality. Common to all, and given reasonably good health, is a refusal to think of themselves as old.

But the fact remains. Once past eighty, what to do with the time is different from when you had to provide for the family and get the children educated. No time then for other occupations. Even though by reading you might escape into poetry or literature, you knew the escape was temporary, that you were out on parole and shouldn't really be escaping when there were reports to write.

On the longer flights across the Pacific, or to South America, or following the ancient caravan routes eastward from the Levant that the airlines still trace, usually alone, the only good thing at those altitudes was poetry. You stared through the window at the immensity below, argued with yourself as to whether marks on the ocean were islands or the shadows of clouds, thought on the whole very little (unless you were homeward bound) about what awaited you at the destination, and were uplifted by the words of the poets.

Poetry, too, is right for hospitals. In 1981 and 1982, I had a brush with cancer, discovered after surgery for an enlarged prostate, and spent altogether six weeks in the Toronto Hospital. Part of the time I was in a ward with three other men, but that was also when I was in the midst of editing Verne Atrill's book, so that I had plenty to do with the proofs for it and for the newsletters I was writing for the National Citizens Coalition.

It was when I was in a private room that the poets came for company, not only the formal ones but also those anonymous masters of English who translated the Bible and wrote the *Book of Common Prayer*.

When you think that perhaps you're not going to make it for

very much longer, it's no use fretting about past mistakes. Too late for that. You look not so much for reassurance as for tranquillity. For you it will be a new experience, yet one you are about to share with the host that forms the greatest majority of all. So you turn to the Venite, to the Collects for Peace and for Grace, to Nunc Dimittis, to Ecclesiastes and Isaiah 55, and I Timothy 6,7, and to Proverbs 30:8,9.

It comes back to what ought you to do as the time grows shorter. If you're lucky enough to have a talent that you enjoyed putting to use and that also earned you a living, probably you will go on doing it until you drop. Winnett Boyd, I'm sure, will be thinking of new and better ways to do things right to the end. Both engineer and inventor, he personifies what I see as the best in Western man: following Nature's course, as Warren Blackman noted, in seeking economy of effort.

Verne Atrill was of the same company. Ranged against them are that curse of mankind, the professional politicians of which the twentieth century spawned more than its share. Lenin, Stalin, Hitler, Mao Tse-tung, Pol Pot, Castro—what did any of those tyrants do in their lives other than promise to raise up the masses they were instrumental in murdering?

Not in the same league, but still an ever-present threat to the body politic are our own professional politicians. Most dangerous are those with their personal vision of what they want to turn Canada into. Pierre Trudeau, who led that particular field, did damage to Canada's social and economic fabric that will take more than a generation to repair.

Inevitably you run out of friends. They die, or get sick, or move to retirement homes, and you catch yourself sizing up the ones who are left for signs of decay. If you enjoy good health, you may even feel detached from the process and think, with the Pharisee, that you are not as other men are—until the others have gone home. Then, doing your nightly exercises, you see again the wrinkled skin on thighs and upper arms, and the liver spots on the backs of the hands, and remember that time is growing shorter for you in the same way as it is for them.

You get the sense of having taken part in a performance wherein you played a number of roles. Although you were always on stage, only very rarely were you the principal; the roles ranged from bit player, to walker-on in the crowd scenes, to chorus, to prompter.

You recognize, in many of your actions, Ouspensky's description of the man-machine doing things mechanically, recognize also the physical danger of letting the machine take over too much. You park at the local plaza, cannot remember whether you stopped the car at all the stop signs on the way there, and are reminded of how Ouspensky interpreted Jesus's injunction: "watch and pray" was meant literally; in the small things like driving to the plaza as well as the big things like choosing between right and wrong.

You notice you are taking things a bit easier, still irritated by politicians' hypocrisy but certainly not losing any sleep over it, and wonder if this is another sign that you are starting to detach yourself from the world. The idea for an article that today's newspaper prompts—that formerly you would have felt bound to write—is savoured for an hour or so, and then discarded as not being worth the trouble of writing.

You wonder what effect all the articles had—whether anyone thought them worth clipping, or whether they were read and shrugged at, and passed by, and then, one morning when you have been cajoled into turning up at a breakfast meeting and are about to take your leave, the man who arranged the meeting volunteers the admission that he was of the liberal left until he came across your columns and they changed his way of looking at things.

At the time of Munich, when bombs were being hung on the Harts and all the world waited to see what Hitler would do the following weekend, you knew the war was coming and worked quite hard at filling every minute with what you thought you wanted to do before it was too late. Much of that feeling stayed with you during the war, inclining you toward excess in a mood of sustained desperation.

But when it was over, and the threat of sudden death was lifted, you stopped thinking about death: you were only thirty-one, and a seemingly indefinite future stretched ahead. Even when men you knew were killed in flying accidents, although you were sorry they had gone and remembered with gratitude what fine fellows they were, the circumstances were unlike your own: your life was not threatened.

When cousin Alan died at fifty-nine, the event was remote

and, once you had brought yourself to think about it, not unexpected. It is only now, when the mortality rates have taken on a personal flavour, that you begin to pay attention to the time.

No use regretting, but what ought you to have done with your life, and who was to say? Now you remember the bad times, not bad because uncomfortable, like Rivers or the menage behind The Bull, or dangerous, like some of the flying, but bad because you drank too much, or didn't pay enough attention to the children, or were unkind to Ruth, or were foolish and careless about stocks and lost money, or were rude to people.

A selective memory allows you to gloss over those things, even to persuade that you learned from the mistakes and became a better man for having made them, when you know at heart that if you had tried harder and listened inside to the small voice—watched and prayed—you might not have made them, or at least not so many of them, or so often.

A bit late to strive for perfection. Man is imperfect, and the gravest harm is done by those who claim he is perfectible if only he can be made to follow their precepts for corporate behaviour. The works that repay study are the ones that address him as an individual, and that offer him, this moment, glimpses of salvation. You have studied them and are imperfect, yet the modes of conduct they teach are plain enough and quite easy, when you are alone and reading, to follow.

It is when you quit the study and mingle with all those other imperfect people that the trouble starts. You share their prejudices, and enlarge on them in company, lie a little—social lies, you tell yourself—and gossip when the voice inside is trying to tell you that you should never say anything harmful about another person, or even think it, because thoughts carry just like the spoken word.

This brings you back to politics, which is about behaviour and how people are to be treated, and to the recognition that you can disagree strongly with a politician's views while crediting him with sincerity. He is mistaken, but he is still a good man.

What to do, then, about the ones who are not sincere, whose motives you think are venal, who seek not only advantage for themselves, but who seek also to mold the community in their image? You have to fight them, because what they are trying to do is wrong.

Even today—especially today—when moral relativism is

about its business of blurring the old rules, the verities are still there. Some things are good and right, some evil and wrong. In your old age, you can see the difference and you know that you have to fight for what you believe to be the right.

You know it is wrong to steal, and lie, and cheat, and you know that individuals do those things, because you have done some of them yourself. It is when governments do them that wrongs are piled upon wrongs, until whole societies are infected.

Nor is this another circular argument. Just as man the individual seeks a perfection he knows is unattainable in this world, so does man the citizen who must live in it seek protection against the sins of his fellows. That is the justification for government: to let each one employ his talents without infringing upon anyone else's ability to employ theirs.

The men and women who form the government know the difference between right and wrong, and if the fashion of the times leads them into shading the distinction, you and every other citizen have a duty to set them straight, or at least to try.

On a good day, the tide may seem about to turn, and you have to remind yourself that nothing is fixed. If you are nearing the end of a voyage, many more are venturing on new ones.

"The race is not to the swift, nor the battle to the strong... but time and chance happeneth to them all." The question returns: what did you learn? Where did Mr. Senior lead you, or Mr. Vallins, or O.J. Robertson, or H.M. Tomlinson and all the multitude of writers and poets, or your mother and father, or Leonard Cheshire, or Ruth?

In his essay on "Crabbed Age and Youth," Stevenson wrote: "Old and young, we are all on our last cruise. If there is a fill of tobacco among the crew, for God's sake pass it round, and let us have a pipe before we go!"

The pipe is still there in the cabinet we were given as a wedding present. Engraved on the stem is "Charatan's Make, London, England, De Luxe." In my hand, it becomes again the companion of years, bulging in pockets, knocked out on the heels of shoes, filled with smoldering aromas, projecting the image of manly reflectiveness, a prop for the role, and discarded thirty years ago.

But not forgotten. From across the years, the mind recaptures two singular smells. One is the intensely personal smell of the oxygen mask, the other that of the first puff of St. Bruno Flake when you had fished the pipe from that awkward inside breast pocket of the battle dress tunic after dropping from the hatch of the Halifax onto Yorkshire soil again.

Today even some tobacco manufacturers admit the stuff is addictive, and there's no doubt that busybody governments have made it expensive, but who can forget the peculiar fragrances of Nosegay and St. Julien, Gold Block and Three Nuns, or the sight of enticing jars of special blends in the windows of Bewlay's, and Astley's, or Fribourg and Treyer?

In the village of Pavenham, where in the thirties a friend from Bristol days and I stored a canoe for excursions on the Bedford Ouse, Arthur Tucker and his wife welcomed the world to The Cock. There of a summer morning, the first guest was Jim Middleton, who delivered the milk and whose hobnailed boots I can still hear as they clatter on the cool, tiled floor of the bar—and hear the clink and gurgle as Arthur Tucker draws the first pint of the day from the barrel down the three steps to the cellar. Nosegay was Jim's smoke, and I can smell that, too.

The players parade before me in the attitudes and with the voices I remember, three-dimensional snapshots as real now as the players were then. The Stuckeys, my parents, aunts Kit and Rose, Treca and Ada, schoolmasters and school friends, OJR and the Captain, Wheatley and Boris, Peter and Proc, Desmond McGlinn, Tim McCoy and Clare Dilworth, Doc Reynolds, Jock Stewart, Peter Walker and Wilf Cambridge, Ramsan and Mr. Wan Chik, Al Lilly and George Keefer, Colin Brown and Winnett Boyd, Verne Atrill, Bill Bolt and Bill Gairdner, Brian Rogers, and our own children.

And Ruth.

A dozen years ago, I rewrote an early novel—one of the famous unpublished seven of my first shots at writing. It was a romantic adventure set in Singapore in the mid-1920s, and I called it *The Giant Sapphire*. It didn't fly, but a literary agent, Matie Molinaro, thought it might do as a miniseries for television. She tried unsuccessfully to interest one or two film companies, and I put it aside until the fall of 1991, when I hooked it out again and approached three film companies myself.

At one of them, a helpful woman explained I would have to turn the book into a screenplay before any company was likely to be interested. Through Bill Bolt, I met George Salverson, a retired writer of screenplays who read the book, liked it, and offered to educate me in the business. A year later, many of George's ideas had been incorporated in a screenplay that did the rounds before expiring, but my reason for mentioning it is that, like all such pieces, it consisted of three acts: the Set-up, which introduces the characters and gives you an idea of what might happen; the Confrontation, which supplies the action; and the Resolution, which pulls the threads together.

Just as birth, life, and death are the great themes, so has my life consisted of three acts. The Set-up lasted from birth through school and joining the air force to meeting Ruth; the Confrontation from marriage until the children's departure; the Resolution from then on.

When I say that marriage takes a lot of work, it is with the benefit of hindsight. For years I took marriage and Ruth for granted, as if both were for my advantage, new props to the solo performance. I had acquired a second pilot, but there was no question as to who was in charge. My embrace of Canada and Canadians included her, my relish of new experiences blinded me to the possibility that the new experiences she was drawn into by marriage might be difficult or even unwelcome. That I, from England, should enjoy Canada excluded the possibility that she, from Canada, might not enjoy England.

If it is true that over the years we learned from each other, it is I who had most to learn. Wives and mothers bear the gravest responsibility, that of raising the children. But they also bear a lesser that grows in importance as the children mature, and it is to civilize their husbands. If I am more thoughtful of or sensitive to other people's feelings than I was thirty years ago, it is because Ruth showed me the way.

Yet she would be the last to accept the award. Two people could hardly be closer than we who have shared so much. We read one another's thoughts without speaking and revel in the tumult of recollected experience. But we cannot share everything. Some thoughts of hers are hers alone, as are some of mine.

It may be that, just as I have learned to head off and suppress negative thoughts, she has come to do the same. Or it may be that wives and mothers who indulge children's weaknesses as they strive to correct them indulge their husbands' weaknesses also in the knowledge that correction must wait upon example.

The thoughts we keep to ourselves are peculiar to our essential differences. The husband and wife who avoid recalling events or circumstances that were a source of strife between them have learned such avoidance for the sake of harmony. But the thoughts they keep to themselves are a man's and a woman's, ever hidden from both.

Some of mine are written in the chapters. Modest ambitions were realized more by luck than application, yet acquired habits of thought had something to do with it. The impulsiveness and lethargy that bred mistakes were modified by an acquired habit of taking things in their turn that imposed order upon impulse and stirred lethargy into action. If lethargy made me less susceptible to the sins of covetousness and anger, it embodied the one of sloth— and although lust was submerged in the discipline of marriage, it was not so much conquered as eroded with age. Yet if, as I believe, I was subject neither to gluttony nor envy, how can I escape the charge of pride?

Of all seven deadly sins, pride is the hardest to reconcile with any of the seven virtues one might reasonably expect to merit by suppressing it. Sherlock Holmes noted that when you have eliminated the impossible, whatever remains, *however improbable*, must be the truth. Thus if we align deadly sins opposite cardinal and theological virtues, we might oppose lust with prudence; anger with temperance; sloth with fortitude; covetousness with justice; envy with faith; and gluttony with charity. However improbably, this would leave hope to face pride. Pride in achievement is pride still. Hope transcends pride by eliminating the personal contribution: we hope that circumstances, and help from the inner voice, will favour the outcome we desire.

After many years, I acquired private means but was hardly diligent in practicing virtue—unless some of the writing sowed a good seed, and who is to say? Well along in the Resolution, a certain involvement in current affairs, a commitment to the Aircrew Association and the Bomber Harris Trust, helping friends or acquaintances with the mechanics of writing, simple repairs about the house—these are as unremarkable as they are undemanding. Even the book John Ferguson and I put together about a simplified system of taxation—although we believe the fundamental principles we advocate returning to would, if adopted, conduce to the general prosperity—even that was reflexive, journeyman's work near the end of the day.

And it is not enough. The light may be dying but there is still ground to be fought on. The principalities and powers that Colin Brown fought are gaining strength; as Chesterton warned, the sky grows darker yet and the sea rises higher. Freedom is no longer of but for a press that slips comment into reports and slants the news by selection and omission. Television propagates a view of events that admits no rejoinder from the audience. Majorities have been led to believe not only that rights can be legislated, but demanding they be satisfied at their neighbours' expense "can be demonstrably justified," as Canada's Charter of Rights and Freedoms asserts, "in a free and democratic society."

In short, Canadians have been clamped into a redistributive process described by Bertrand de Jouvenel as "far less a redistribution of free income from the richer to the poorer than a redistribution of power from the individual to the State."

It is government as referee that makes the game worth playing, but the State as player that spoils the game for everyone. Failure to make that distinction, and to stop the State's relentless growth, led tens of millions to their deaths in the past century—yet, because the Canadian State presents a tolerant and welcoming face to the world, Canadians believe themselves immune to its malignant influence.

What my contemporaries look upon as "our war" was a struggle for individual freedom against the State's arbitrary power that culminated in the Nazi tyranny. In 1939, when young John Ferguson enlisted in the Royal Canadian Naval Reserve, he did so as an individual who knew that a great evil was abroad. Like Colin Brown, he fought his fight in destroyers on the North Atlantic and rose after six years to the rank of lieutenant commander. We have known each other a long time, but it was not until 1993, when a reference of mine to the CBC's revisionist film *The Valour and the Horror* took us back to the war, that he mentioned his ramming a U-boat and how the foredeck of the destroyer was engulfed in flames.

Our branch of the Aircrew Association comprises a membership of former pilots, navigators, bomb aimers, wireless operator/air gunners, flight engineers and air gunners whose wartime service reached into every command and theatre of operations. Some interrupted schooling to enlist, others left promising careers, and all put their lives on the line for an idea worth fighting for.

When we meet together, for a few hours we are no longer elderly men retired from a variety of careers, but men who fought in the air for an idea that, however vaguely formed at the time, has become clear to us. The fight we entered in 1992 against the cultural arms of the Canadian State was not only to tell the truth about the business we were engaged in fifty years before, but to honour the memory of friends who gave their young lives in the cause of good against evil. When we stand for a minute in silence, we see and hear them as they were, and as they are still in our hearts.

And we know that the fight continues.

Chapter 1
▣ 1914—1936 ▣

The use of camcorders will deny future generations the luxury of seeing themselves through the indulgent eyes of memory. The camera doesn't lie, and that is the way they looked—whereas my own memory started when there were few cameras about and I have to rely on fading snapshots for an idea of what I looked like when I was very young, or what my parents looked like before I was born.

I put the start of my memory at age two, by which time Dad had left Bristol for the Great War, Mother was doing his job of selling the dairy products of a Southampton company (Auguste Pellerin) to grocery stores and small hotels in Gloucestershire and Somerset, and most of my days were spent with Alice Stuckey in the semi-detached house at 30 Alexandra Park that she and her husband, René, had bought before he went off to war with Dad in the Rifle Brigade. However, it was Mother who took me to the bedroom window and pointed to a Zeppelin in the distance, which the record shows to have been in 1916, and consequently the basis for starting my memory then.

The Stuckeys were childless. Alice became "Auntie Alice" to me, and my sole rival for her and Mother's attention was the Stuckey's Airedale dog, Michael. Alice and Mother were much of a size, about 5 ft. 4 in. and slender, Alice's hair prematurely grey and Mother's light brown. They were similar in temperament, both with a lively sense of humour, and although in retrospect Mother seems the more serious of the two, she was also doing

Dad's job on top of her responsibility for bringing me up.

She was born Eva Harriet Balston in Southampton on January 6, 1888—a bad year for the family, according to a letter written in 1949 by her older sister, Ada (which also traced the Balston family to a place called Tytherleigh on the Devon/Dorset border in 1108). Ada wrote:

> I think it was in 1888 that my grandfather lost a big fortune on change. He was then advised to file a petition for bankruptcy: this he refused to do; paid everyone 20/- in the pound and so ruined us all. For years my dear parents and their children had to endure great privation and there were times when I think I hated life and everything in it!! It was not 'til my father's stepmother died that things began to improve a bit for us. Then, all my grandfather left had to be shared amongst his seven children.

Mother, too, was one of seven, a boy and six girls. They were raised in the little house at 134 Milton Road, of which I have two recollections. One is of Grandmother Balston busy in kitchen and scullery or laying and clearing the table, the other of Grandfather Balston sitting in his high-backed wooden armchair, by the fire in winter, by the window in summer.

Two of the girls married sailors—two others, businessmen. Of the two who were unmarried, Ethel spent her life teaching at a private school near Pietermaritzburg, in South Africa, and Ada, who lost her hearing at the age of eleven, lived at home. The boy, Harry, went to live in the United States before my time.

Mother was the youngest daughter, and like Ethel, a teacher. Even though she taught closer to home—at Hartley Wintney, some forty-five miles from Southampton near the intersection of Hampshire's borders with Berkshire and Surrey—the facts of her making the effort and then finding somewhere to live in a strange place at a young age while supporting herself all bear witness to an energetic and independent spirit.

I have to guess how my parents met. Since they lived in different parts of Southampton, they are unlikely to have attended the same church. It might have been in Hartley Wintney, or on train journeys to and from Southampton after Dad started travelling for Pellerin's.

In one of the few pictures from those days, they are standing together as part of a group somewhere on the Isle of Wight, Dad in a jacket and white flannels, and Mother wearing a high-waisted dress. In another, they are at a post-christening event, Dad with a pipe in his hand, and Mother wearing a cartwheel hat.

How to do justice to her? I lived at home for twenty-two years and cannot remember a single instance of a raised voice, certainly not a raised hand, yet I must have provoked one or both many times. That it was a happy marriage, I have no doubt, for she made the different homes the way they are supposed to be: where you feel safe. She read to me, taught me to read, was so careful of spelling that it has never bothered me, and accustomed me to dictionaries by her habit of testing me from the copy of *Collins's* pocket version that she carried with her.

I think of her setting out from the house with Dad's order book in her purse, walking to the corner of Alexandra Park and along another road to the brow of the hill, where she would go down the steps to Redland Station.

That part of western England and south Wales was served by the Great Western Railway. The carriages were painted chocolate and cream, and were pulled on the express runs by mighty engines with names like Caerphilly Castle. Local traffic, however, chuffed its way around Devon and Somerset and parts of Gloucestershire and Wiltshire behind short, squarish, anonymous engines, at least one of which has been restored to play brief roles in films of the period.

If she was torn between her responsibility for me and the newer one for doing Dad's job, my guess is that the former gave way to the latter soon after walking round the corner of Alexandra Park. Perhaps everyone welcomes new experiences, but I suspect the feeling is also heritable. It is surely more instinct than imagination that allows me now, sixty years after she died, to see the young woman setting out on her journeys and to feel the excitement, not so much of what was going to happen later in the day, as of what was happening while she walked to the station, sat in the trains and buses, and let her mind savour the fact of being alone with her thoughts.

The Stuckeys were Bristol people. René sold the meat products of Harris's, and I assume he and Dad became friends in the course of business. Before they decided to enlist, they had to work out how their wives could keep the home fires burning while they were away. Mother and Dad rented the house, 8 Cornwall Road, where I was born. It made sense for Mother and me to move to 30 Alexandra Park which was larger, with three bedrooms: whatever the two men could send from their pay would supplement Mother's earnings. Harris's might have continued to pay part of René's salary to Alice.

At all events, Mother made the switch from schoolteacher to commercial traveller, while Alice kept the house and looked after me and Michael until the end of the war and the men came home.

Both were lucky, posted not to the Western Front but to Salonika, in Dad's case, and to the Near East in René's, whose picture shows him outside a building near Bhatoum on the border of Georgia and Turkey. Dad, wounded by a piece of shrapnel in the left shoulder, was transferred to hospital in Malta before being invalided home in the last year of the war to the convalescent hospital at Netley, not far from Southampton.

It would have been he who took the snapshot of me on Mother's knee on Netley's beach, because I can remember seeing him in hospital blues. He kept the piece of shrapnel, with the date of the wound engraved on it, on his watch chain. The wound was in his left shoulder and he would favour it, in the first year or so after the war when we were on holidays at Weston-super-Mare and throwing a ball to each other, by pretending to feel the pain and calling "My left" in a jocular way I suspect was not all in fun. One of my clearer memories of him is standing on the sands of Wentworth Cove and throwing the solid rubber ball high in the air for me to run and catch.

I had reached an age when friends of Dad's began to ask me what I wanted to be when I grew up. What I wanted to do was not discussed at home until near the end of the school years, and my one inclination, toward the stage, came no closer to realization than did my stock answer (join the Navy) toward finding out how to prepare myself for, or indeed how to set about entering, the senior service.

The naval influence came from two films of the period. One, with Milton Sills, was about naval warfare in the Mediterranean during the Great War. Called *Mare Nostrum*, its pictures of gallant four-stackers breasting the waves were accompanied when I saw it by the pianist's rendering of Mendelssohn's *Hebrides Overture* (Fingal's Cave). The other was called *The Battles of Coronel and the Falkland Islands*, in which Admiral von Spee's squadron destroyed Admiral Cradock's off Coronel and, a month later, was tempted to shell the wireless station on the Falkland Islands, unaware that two battle cruisers under Admiral Sturdee were coaling there. Four of von Spee's five ships were sunk.

When the war was over, Mother and Dad found a ground-floor flat at 8 Tyne Road. My formal education began at Miss Patterson's, in a row house at the foot of Tyne Road, and then at Brighton House, far enough away off Whiteladies Road to justify my getting a bicycle. I was there for four years, until Mr. Senior, who taught English and Latin, History and Arithmetic, and took us for gym and games, started his own school, Belgrave House facing the Downs at the top of Blackboy Hill. He persuaded Mother and Dad to send me there until I was eleven and able to go to the Cathedral School in the centre of the city.

Mr. Senior is the first non-relative other than the Stuckeys to appear, and stay, on my stage. He was then in his late forties or early fifties, with a fringe of white hair round the edges of his head, very upright and energetic, striding purposefully before us, cap and pipe firmly in place, walking stick out and down, out and down, as we hurried to keep up with him on the way to the Downs or the gym.

My propensity for showing off made a sort of bond between us; on his side to make points for the class, and on mine to impress him with performance or cheek. Thus, when he was describing life in Saxon times, how they dried their hands by waving them in the air, and how the Normans used linen napkins instead, it was as natural for him to make the point by asking "Which would you have done, McDonald?" as it was for me to answer, "Waving them, Sir," while doing so to the accompaniment of rewarding giggles from the class.

My enduring memory of him is in the sitting room of the house he shared with his sister, and which became Belgrave House. There, as we sat around the polished wood of the table at the start of the school day, he would put on his silver-framed glasses and read the Second and Third Collects, which never

27

failed to comfort me that I would fall into no sin neither run into any kind of danger.

For those short moments, I was transported into a state of holiness that would return from time to time in many different circumstances like Wordsworth's intimations of immortality. Soon they were to be reinforced during my year at the Cathedral School, and afterwards, when we had moved to Croydon, at that historic borough's Parish Church, flashes compounded of organ music and plainsong, stained glass and vaulted transepts, and the words of those anonymous masters of English I mentioned before.

Although Mr. Senior plays the dominant role on my early stage, he is not alone. At the Cathedral School, he shared it briefly with my Form master, "Auntie" Cook, so named for his theatrical gestures and use of both percipience and sarcasm to keep discipline. He noticed, and made me conscious of it, by remarking that a boy who made room for me on one of the benches when I joined the Second Form did so to the exclusion of another boy who had been his friend. On another occasion, he pointed to a boy whose mouth was open and explained, as he swept his gown around him, that it was the indelible mark of an empty mind.

I was in the school choir, which came under the care of Mr. Tyrrell, the Fifth Form master, who taught Physics and Maths. He was a hunchback and, no doubt partly because of that, a man of considerable presence in our eyes. Unlike the other masters, all of whom—even Dr. Watts, the Head—came in for some banter among us, Mr. Tyrrell was genuinely respected, and no one thought of poking fun at his deformity.

Standing before us on the tiled floor of the chancel as we ranged ourselves in the choir stalls, he would exhort us to reach the high notes by raising his arms above his head so that the gown was raised too, as if he were indeed uplifted by the combination of our modest efforts with the grander notes of the organ that accompanied them. He rode a bicycle to school and I saw him once on his way home, toiling grimly up one of the city's many hills in low gear, and in no way diminished without his gown.

My enjoyment of the Cathedral School came to an end when Pellerin's decided to open an office in London and offered Dad the job of managing it. I've no doubt it was put to him as the opportunity for personal advancement that is the way of companies, and Mother and Dad must have talked it out before deciding, but I think it was a mistake.

Dad exchanged the relatively placid life of Bristol, where he and Mother had good friends, for the rush and stress of London, where they knew nobody and the people they did come to know were not in the same league as the Stuckeys or Burpitts. Dad was forty, Mother thirty-eight, I was twelve, and my brother, Tom, just a year old.

For me, the important thing was school. The nearest to where we lived was Whitgift School, the next was Whitgift Middle—both of these named after the sixteenth-century Archbishop of Canterbury—and the third, Selhurst Grammar, was about three miles away in the direction of the Crystal Palace. Whether my marks weren't good enough for the first two, or there weren't any vacancies at short notice, I don't know. At any rate, I went to Selhurst, where I got a good education, but at the price of missing the atmosphere and tradition of the Cathedral, which might have been duplicated in Whitgift Middle's medieval buildings.

Selhurst was quite new. It was built about a year before the Great War (towards the end of which it was used as a hospital), to replace the Croydon Borough School near the town centre (former pupils were Old Croydonians). Alongside it on The Crescent was Selhurst Grammar School for Girls, the two red brick buildings a monument to some forgotten councillor. They stood in their own grounds, each surmounted in the centre of two wings by a modest belfry.

At the time, the five years I spent at Selhurst seemed very long indeed. Academically I showed some aptitude for Maths, Latin, and French (for which I was given a prize at the Cathedral School), and for Eng.Lang.Litt., which got me the prize in the Fifth Form in 1930. I won a senior scholarship in 1928 which helped with the fees, and showed no aptitude at all for Physics, Chemistry, History, Geography, Art, or Carpentry. Classes were graded: 1A, 1B, 1C, all the way to the Fifth, but boys who didn't reach the Fifth faded away to the workforce or a technical school.

I joined after term had begun and went into 2A under John Wedd, who was also the French master, dressed well, and was interested enough in the theatre to organize trips during the next three years to the Old Vic and, on one occasion, to the Coliseum to see *White Horse Inn*. School dramatics, however, were handled by the Music master, and this gave me the chance to show off in three productions: *The Private Secretary, The Pirates of Penzance,* and *Admiral's All*.

In the last, for which Mother made my frock-coat and epaulettes, I played Collingwood, forgot my key line at the end, and managed to contrive some business that edged me close enough to the wings to hear the prompt. In *The Croydon Times* review, I got a favourable mention from the Old Croydonian who wrote it.

I matriculated in 1930 and stayed for a year in the Sixth to take Commerce and gain the Higher School Certificate, largely through an intense effort of memory in the days before the exams. Two or three of my contemporaries went on to university, and that is about the measure for those days: you went there if you showed exceptional scholastic ability, or were intended for teaching or the Church. Otherwise, it was the civil service or the business world. One of my close friends went to Cambridge. Another, who was consistently first or second in the form, took the civil service exams and passed directly into the executive class (he was killed during the war, a navigator in Bomber Command). A third, an average scholar like me, left school from the Fifth to work for a trading company in London and joined the RAF with a short service commission in 1935. We lost touch during the war, but I found out from a man who was in the same squadron that he survived and went to live in Rhodesia.

Outside the classroom, I was a fair enough centre three-quarter to get into the 2nd XV in the Fourth Form, and the 1st for the last two years, a fair enough bat and off-spinner to get in the school eleven in the Fifth and captain it in the Sixth, and fair enough on the field to win the high jump and 110 yd. hurdles. I was beaten on points in the school heavy-weight finals, and came well behind in the swimming events. I was made a prefect in my final year (1931).

I had been a Wolf Cub in Bristol, was old enough for the Scouts by the time we reached Croydon, and it was with the 42nd Troop that I was initiated into the rituals of camping. For weekend camps, we went to Selsdon, about three miles from Croydon, where we pitched our tents in a sloping field, at the top of which were thick woods.

At night we sang songs around the campfire, and on the last night, new recruits were required to pass a test which consisted of being sent, one at a time, to the far side of the woods, from where they had to make their way in the dark through the trees to the edge of the slope and back to the campfire—an eerie business I can remember to this day.

In the summer of 1927, we went by train from Euston to Glasgow, most of the journey at night, changed trains for Ardrossan, and boarded a splendid steamer to sail across the Firth of Clyde to Brodick on the Isle of Arran. Campsite was in a field above Corrie, some six miles north of Brodick, on the lower slopes of Goat Fell—at 2,866 feet, the highest point in that part of Scotland. The next two weeks were marked by rain so steady as surely to constitute a record of some kind, even for Scotland's west coast.

Since we were camped on the side of a hill, the tents, too, were on a slope. After a few days, when I lifted the edge of my groundsheet, there was the water, trickling down on its way to the sea. The Rovers managed to get the fires going to cook food and make hot cocoa and soup, and we must have been quite damp, but I don't remember having any trouble sleeping. Our beds were made by folding a blanket and fastening it down the side and at the bottom with blanket pins like giant safety pins. Pillow was one's pack with a towel over it.

Cocoa and soup were heated in dixies slung by their handles over the fire, and water for washing and drinking came from the burn that raced down the hillside at the edge of the field—cold, clear water whose taste I can still recapture. This was in August, so the temperature despite the rain must have been somewhere in the fifties during the days, sometimes higher, and although I don't remember the cold particularly, I do remember the contrast one day when we went for tea to a place where there was a fire and I felt the blessed warmth from it on my knees. While we stuffed ourselves with bannocks and jam, the daughter of the house sang for us in a gentle, sweet voice, the song I remember being "Ye Banks and Braes of Bonnie Doon," haunting and sad like so many Scottish songs.

We gave in to the weather before the end of the two weeks, and were taken down to a boathouse for a final night to sleep in its dryness and relative warmth after being administered a tot of whisky by the Rovers. My cousin, Alan Maxwell (Treca's only son), who had joined us for the holiday, came down with pneumonia when he reached home. Still, we had seen something of Scotland, and made two long train journeys and two crossings of the Firth of Clyde—not bad for twelve- or thirteen-year-olds in the 1920s.

Two years later, a group of us went to France, where we camped in the grounds of a school not far from Fontainebleau, engaged in scouting pursuits during the days, and went in the evenings to the local *estaminet* where we played French billiards and were introduced to grenadine, my first alcoholic drink since the dram in Scotland. In Paris, we stayed two nights at l'Hotel Soufflot, near the Panthéon, and did most of the usual tourist things: Eiffel Tower, Notre Dame, Sacré Coeur, Invalides, Galeries Lafayette, Louvre, Champs Elysées, Arc de Triomphe and, not least, autobuses and the Metro.

Experiencing Frenchness at first hand was a good deal more fun than French lessons, and although we enjoyed the camping, the village and Fontainebleau, it is Paris that stays in the mind, especially vivid to us who knew London well and automatically drew comparisons as we went along.

The second figure to enter, and stay on my stage was Selhurst's English master, G.H. Vallins, co-author with another master (H.A. Treble) of an English textbook, *An ABC of English Usage*, and later, other books. Mr. Vallins imparted his love of the language not so much by what he said as by the expressions on his face when he was reading favourite passages. He was then in his late thirties, about five feet eleven, with fair hair that hung over the other side of his brow from the parting, and although his eyes, through the steel-rimmed glasses, looked unfocussed and some-what vague, he was never laughed at; he kept order without any apparent effort, and I think it was because the boys could sense the dedication to what he was trying to inspire in us.

I trace his lasting influence on me to two episodes. The first, which extended over a number of lessons while we were studying Milton, was rooted in his selection, recitation, and subsequent dis-cussion of the passage in *Lycidas* from "Alas! what boots it with uncessant care..." to "of so much fame in Heav'n expect thy meed." I was in the Fourth Form, fifteen years old, and the matter of fame being the spur towards earthly reward and somewhat vain in consequence impressed me so much that seventy years later I can still recite the passage.

The second episode was nothing more than Mr. Vallins's favourable comment on an exercise in what would now be called creative writing: write a short story based on the adage "Promises, like piecrusts, are made to be broken." He wrote on my effort that it was the best work I had done and, as you can see, I haven't forgotten it.

I see now that the two episodes were complementary; the first towards tempering my cockiness with the odd dash of humility, and the second toward writing as an avocation. The fact that I had to wait forty years before I could afford to turn it from avocation to career merely attests to two other facts: that it was a modest talent, and that I lacked the courage to put it to the test of trying to live by it.

About that time, I came across advice attributed to an ancient Greek I've been unable to identify who urged me to acquire private means and practice virtue. I had little prospect of acquiring the first, but it still appealed to me as a sound maxim. Only later did I realize that by virtue he meant not so much the kind associated with haloes and stained glass as the kind epitomized by Leonardo da Vinci and Thomas Jefferson.

To Mr. Vallins I owe a lasting enjoyment of good writing, an introduction to English literature that encouraged me to delve further and, not least, the words of George Borrow from his novel *Lavengro* that are propped up beside the desk.

Nevertheless, work had to be done and it turned up in the haphazard way that was inseparable from my lack of ambition for a particular calling. When I left school at the age of seventeen, although aspirations for the Navy had foundered on the inactive side of my character, I was still interested enough in the idea of a career at sea to try my luck at the offices of shipping companies in the City and the West End. This was the optimistic side taking over in the face of insuperable odds: what prospect was there, two years after the start of the Great Depression, of a company offering work to a youth who hadn't taken the elementary steps of finding out what seafaring entailed or how to qualify himself for it? Motivation, had I thought about it sooner, might have come from acquaintance with the historic ports of Bristol and Southampton, the facts of two of Mother's sisters having married sailors, and of Grandfather McDonald's having been a master mariner.

On July 3rd, 1880, Thomas McDonald, twenty-five, Bachelor, Mariner, of Trinity Road in the Parish of St. Mary, Southampton, son of Thomas McDonald, Engineer, married Kate Victoria Marsh, twenty-two, Spinster, of 25 Glebe Road in the same parish, daughter of Joseph Marsh, Tailor, in the presence of Joseph and Lilly Marsh and licenced by W.W. Perrin, Curate.

By the time I came to know him, Grandfather Mac was retired and living with Grandmother at 124 Graham Road, where the front door sported the brass plate "Capt. Thos. McDonald" from the cabin door of his last command. Its picture was in the dining room, on the wall across from the fireplace: S.S. Maresfield, of the Field Line (built 1910, by J.L. Thomson & Sons of Sunderland, 4,176 tons, steel screw steamer with three boilers, schooner rig, London registry), single funnel nestling amidst the sails. On the mantel, a clock inside a glass dome struck the hours and quarters of the Westminster chime.

While I was still at school, I went sometimes in summer to stay with Aunt Treca or one of Dad's sisters in Southampton. I remember, when Grandfather Mac took me to the County Ground to watch the Hampshire side, sitting in the sun beside the bearded man in the Panama hat and watching the white-clad figures moving across the grass.

Grandmother Mac was rosy-cheeked and silver-haired ,and my memories of her are mostly in the long kitchen at the foot of the four steps that led from the hall, or in the scullery adjoining it, from which a door led to the garden where there's a picture of me sitting on a wooden engine. She kept her purse on the dresser in the kitchen and understood little boys' need for pennies to spend on aniseed balls and licorice sticks.

Although Grandfather Mac lived until 1936, I missed getting to know him in his last years, when I had left school and might have learned more about his life. I do know that his seatime—under sail for the greater part of his career—took him to the Far East, because we still have the ivory carving of a Japanese fisherman he brought home from a trip. Latterly he was on the North Atlantic run, but it was Grandmother Mac who told me about the time when she had the premonition that his ship was in danger, and wrote down the date and time. When he came home, he confirmed it: that was when they were close to foundering in a mid-Atlantic storm.

None of this heritage pierced the armour of inactive optimism that shielded me from applying myself to the task of finding a job, and Dad came to the rescue by arranging for me to see an executive of the brokers who insured Pellerin's office in London. He invited me to have lunch with him in the City, an occasion I prepared myself for by washing my hair, shaving very carefully, and donning my best suit and shirt, with the maroon-and-silver-striped silk tie to which I had become entitled as a prefect. After passing this unexpected test, I accepted employment with the Sun Insurance Office Limited ("Founded 1710, the oldest insurance office in the world"), at its Charing Cross branch on the south side of Trafalgar Square, for an annual salary of sixty-five pounds.

The Scouts, the school, the church: these were the dominant influences outside the home. Croydon Parish Church traces its origin to the tenth century. There I was confirmed and attended services regularly until after I left school. It was through the church that I and my contemporaries made the contacts with girls that the English education system made so difficult.

I still thought of Joan Burpitt, an impossible 120 miles away in Bristol and later Cardiff, as the girl to whom I should be loyal. This coloured my tentative associations until I was sixteen, when I met Mollie Luke, a year younger, and we saw a good deal of each other until just before I joined the RAF. We both enjoyed acting, belonged to two amateur dramatic societies, went to dances organized by church groups, often travelled to and from London on the same train (Mollie had a good job with Imperial Chemical Industries), and were as much in love as circumstances permitted—notably, that marriage on my salary was out of the question.

An inclination toward the stage was indulged perennially in school plays, in amateur dramatic societies, in lecturing as a young officer and later at the Staff College, and in sales presentations for Canadair at home and abroad. Yet, the desire for applause and approval that surged before and during the performances never rose beyond desire to the craving that presumably draws people to acting as a career. I put on the show, endured the self-criticism afterwards, and then lapsed into the conflicting array that P.D. Ouspensky calls waking sleep.

What sort of a life it was for Mother I can only imagine. We had a telephone (FAIrfield 5783) for her to order the groceries. Milk and bread were delivered. She washed the clothes and linen, hung them to dry on a clothesline in the back garden or, in winter, on the clothes "airer" suspended in the kitchen, where she also ironed them.

For other items, she must have walked to the nearest shops, about a five-minute walk, or taken the trolley bus to West Croydon. When she and Dad went to the Davis Cinema in the High Street, they walked, leaving me in charge of my brother Tom. I can see them now, arm in arm, walking up the far side of the road, very close, as they were all the time, content to spend the time together, reading by the fire in winter, in the garden on deck chairs in summer.

No car (the firm offered Dad one, but he chose not to drive), no radio, visitors very rare and then mostly relatives, no close friends, no social events that I was aware of other than Dad's occasional donning of a dinner jacket for attendance at Masonic lodges, their joint appearances at school plays, sports days and prize-givings, and Sunday morning service at the Parish Church. Dad would take two weeks off in the summer and the four of us would go to Worthing or Bognor to stay in a boarding house on the front, making the best of the weather.

Dad travelled first class in the train, always a smoking carriage, and Mother and I grew aware of the stresses he underwent in the business, struggling to get his much smaller firm's product lines into the big restaurant chains and hotels against the giant Unilever which eventually took Pellerin's over after he died.

Soon after I left school, he began to suffer from what he and the doctor thought was indigestion. The cause was put down to his teeth; he underwent a series of trips to the dentist, which culminated in extractions and the fitting of false teeth, which then didn't fit very well and were in their turn diagnosed as contributing to the indigestion, requiring further trips to the dentist.

This was a rotten time for Mother and Dad. He was worried about the business, worried about his health, and of course, Mother was worried for him and frustrated by the doctors' failure to find a cure. Today, the cause would have been diagnosed— ulcers at first—and cured either by surgery or internal medicine, and he would have lived another twenty or thirty years. In which case, Mother would have lived too. Instead, he got steadily worse and by the time one of his sisters—Auntie Kit—came on the scene to insist on his going to a London specialist, it was too late.

He was buried in Mitcham Cemetery, far from Southampton and Bristol, still I'm sure in Mother's mind the man she first came to love on those trips to the Isle of Wight, and in mine, then as today, a good man and a good father. After the funeral, when we were walking away from the grave, a man who had known him during and after the war said to me that he had never looked at another woman. Although this struck me at the time as an odd thing to say—why would he?—it was entirely consistent with what Dad would have been embarrassed to hear me call a nobility of character that was compounded of honesty and devotion to home and work, of the ordinary things that distinguish right from wrong, good from evil. For many years, a man he had served with in Salonika sent a Christmas card inscribed to "Mac, the White Man," which did embarrass him, but which I, immersed in Ballantyne and "Sapper" and the *Boy's Own Paper*, attached a proper value to.

By nature, and no doubt as a gift from my parents, I'm an optimist—which makes for a placid temperament, but has the unhappy knack of changing suddenly into a desire for action. The interplay of the two emotions has often led me to sit back when I should have been doing something, in contrast to the even more frequent times when I did things impulsively that would have been better unattempted.

These contrasting strains have dogged me through the years, and if I have learned anything from first coming to recognize and then trying to moderate their effects, it is that innate characteristics are very hard to change. To hear someone's action or reaction explained by "He (or she) is like that" is no less than the truth. In matters of right or wrong, guidance is available from the inner voice, but in the loose change of daily affairs, instinct governs. Mistakes repeated in different forms or circumstances are repeated still.

In youth, the strains were buried in the cocoon of self-absorption. The world was there to be impressed by the facial expressions and attitudes I spent a lot of time shaping for it to see. It was the fashion not to show emotion, to keep a straight face when saying things I thought were funny, and to cultivate traits made popular by film actors, stage and wireless performers, and novelists. What *The New Yorker* once called everyday histrionics came close to dominating my thoughts, and it was a rare shop window that failed to attract an admiring glance at my reflection as I strutted past it.

As soon as I left school, I started smoking a pipe—regarded at the time as the activity that stamped one as at least a spiritual companion of South African farmers, Australian gold miners, or the writers of adventure stories (rattling good yarns) set in the Scottish highlands. These romantic associations were exploited by tobacco manufacturers, who lured me into buying Afrikander Mixture, Digger Flake, and Tam o'Shanter to match changing moods, while the makers of pipes responded in turn with Lovats, Petersens, cherrywoods and meerschaums.

At Charatan's, in The Minories that runs from Tower Hill to Aldgate High Street, where pipes were made to order, I had two pipes made, both of straight grain Algerian briar. The bowl of the first was at such an oblique angle to the stem as to provoke the attention I desired and it cost me 7s 6d. The second pipe, a year or so later, had a larger bowl only slightly oblique to the stem and cost 10s 6d.

For me and my friends, this manly activity—together with drinking beer, playing cricket or rugby according to season, and going for long walks in the country—occupied Saturday afternoons and evenings and occasional Sundays. In my cocoon I drew inspiration not only from dramatists and poets, and from Belloc and Chesterton, but from contemporary writers, among whom the most influential was J.B. Morton.

At the time I began working in London, he was a regular contributor to *The Daily Express* of a column under the pen name of Beachcomber, in which he displayed both a sense of humour and a talent for pricking pomposities that appealed to me. He was also the author of three slim volumes of essays, eighty-eight in all, gathered into one book under the title *Vagabond.*

In it, he wrote in the first person of his companions, Johnny O. and the Bard, Twelvetrees and Streen and Tom Three, chronicling their adventures on vacations and weekends in the Home

Counties, France, and Spain, in the 1920s. They had survived the Western Front and were feeling their way into careers, not embittered by the war of which they rarely spoke, but keeping in spite of it the romantic spirit that enlivens the essays. If there are extravagances, they are the extravagances of youth, and even though allusions to a classical education that was clearly superior to mine left me somewhat abashed, I luxuriated in visions of myself in their company.

During those first years after leaving school, it was the custom to rejoice in bachelorhood and to look upon and speak of girls disparagingly, conceits mirrored by Morton's stories. Bound to work also, we shared the distaste for commercial activities that interfered with the real world of pipes and ale and chance adventures, of impromptu songs and verses as Morton and his friends strode with their stout walking sticks over the Downs.

It never occurred to me, and neither Mother nor Dad suggested, that I might contribute some of my meagre income to upkeep of the household; it served to pay for a season ticket from Croydon to London, for my lunches, and for spending on beer, tobacco, and the activities associated with consuming them.

Although there were some pleasant people at the Sun, and although the work was certainly undemanding, the business of insuring against fire and accident never appealed to me as a career. One of the more senior clerks, who was himself a Fellow of the Chartered Insurance Institute, encouraged me to study for the Institute's exams, which I did desultorily of an evening during the first winter at a dreary office in Fenchurch Street.

But attempts to enliven construction and related matters by picturing early eighteenth-century apprentices passing leather buckets filled with Thames water from hand to hand to burning buildings marked with the Sun's metal insignia—these failed to overcome my boredom with the topics and I retired myself from the course.

What moved me to cast about for more interesting work was a setback to my optimistic side after I had succeeded to management of the Renewals department. The manager I replaced upon his promotion to another department was O.J. Robertson, who merits a place on the stage for his sterling qualities as a man and for having taught me two lessons of lasting value.

Then in his early forties, of medium height, with a round face, a neatly trimmed moustache, and black hair cut short and thinning, dressed always in black jacket and waistcoat and striped trousers, he held himself erect and walked with the precision derived from service not so long before as a wartime captain in an infantry regiment.

At school, I had gone about class work in the Pavlovian way of average students—answering questions as best I could, reading what I was told to read, and swotting up material for examinations from the relevant syllabi. Now, as I answered telephone inquiries from other branches or the company's agents, occasionally even from customers, I was participating in my small way in a business enterprise. The questions came out of the blue and even though the answers called for little more than looking up dates or sums of money in the big ledgers that were stacked, together with the correspondence files, either in the main office or down below in the cellars, I had to get them right.

O.J. taught me to be methodical. "Write it down, Mac," he would say, in reference to some inquiry I had answered after drawing a correspondence file. "Write it down in the file with the time and date. If you don't and you were run over by a bus tomorrow, no one would know that conversation had taken place." As part of being methodical, he taught me to do one thing at a time, a lesson that expanded over the years into a habit that forced me to tackle things in sequence, including—especially including—the tasks I found least congenial.

The other thing he taught me was the idea of service. Until then, it hadn't occurred to me that I had any responsibility beyond doing the work that the job called for. I did it, took the pay, and spent what was left over from essentials solely for my own enjoyment. Even my stints in the Scouts, and for a short period after I left school as a Sunday School teacher, were things I chose to do because I expected to enjoy them. I grew out of the Scouts, soon tired of trying to keep order among children who were no more orderly or receptive to Bible stories than I had been at their ages, and returned to my own pursuits.

But O.J. was an enthusiastic member of the Special Constabulary, attached to "C" Division of the Metropolitan Police headquartered in Great Marlborough Street, and although he didn't push me to follow his example, the obvious civic usefulness of the work combined with the evident satisfaction he got from doing it persuaded me to join.

The uniform, of navy blue serge with a round service cap, didn't fit very well, and the truncheon stowed in the special pocket inside the right trouser leg bumped awkwardly as I made my way from the house to Waddon station and thence to places of duty on the public holidays or other occasions when Specials were called upon to support the regulars.

Indoctrination took the form of lectures followed by practical experience in the company of a regular—this in the evenings where I would go straight from the office to Great Marlborough Street and get something to eat in the canteen before accompanying my mentor on his beat. I had hoped this might involve me in one or another of the experiences reported in the crime columns of the popular press, such as catching a thief or ordering disturbers of the peace to move on, even racing after a runaway horse and dragging the frightened animal to a halt.

None of them happened to me. The vision I had, of cornering a criminal and saying as confidently as I could that I was arresting him in the name of the law, only to have him ignore me and simply walk away, did not materialize. As we strolled—the regular majestic in helmet and middle age, I a good deal less so in ill-fitting uniform and transparent youth—along the streets south of Great Marlborough Street, nothing disturbed our even way save a prostitute whose territory had been infringed by a competitor.

However, on the Sunday when I was detailed for point duty at the junction of Coventry Street and the Haymarket, I was on my own. As I mounted the traffic island, the regular merely stripped off the white sleeves, handed them to me, and sauntered away toward Great Marlborough Street without a word or a backward glance.

I had been working in London for three years, yet not until I was confronted by successions of them bearing down upon me from Piccadilly Circus did I appreciate the size of the city's double-decker buses. Relief at their obedience to my tentative signals was spoiled by travellers invading the island to ask me how to reach places I knew by name but was too harassed to think of how to get to them. The first time, I nodded to the Haymarket, told the traveller to "take a number nine down there," on the theory that by the time he got to the stop, he would have asked someone else, and it worked for the rest of the afternoon.

The last duty I was called to was also the most impressive: lining the route in Pall Mall opposite St. James's Palace for the funeral cortege of King George V.

To return to my unhappiness with the Sun, by the time I took over the department from O.J. Robertson, my salary had risen to ninety pounds, and since I knew he had been getting about six hundred, I looked forward with some confidence to the following January when raises were announced. But the slip that authorized me to draw a revised amount from Drummond's Branch of the Royal Bank of Scotland showed an annual rate of 113 pounds—an increase no doubt in the company's eyes of 25 percent, but in mine wholly unworthy of a comer with three clerks (female) and one junior (male) under command.

I made this point to the branch manager, who arranged for me to see the personnel chief in the head office at 63 Threadneedle Street. He received me in the board room under the gaze of more than two centuries' worth of governors and explained that, although ability was recognized, so were diligence and hard work: if I pursued my studies in the Institute, I might well in due course aspire to become a branch manager.

I wanted a quicker result and began searching the papers for job opportunities. It was about that time that O.J. showed me the announcement, in his copy of *The Times*, about the proposed establishment of a Metropolitan Police College at Hendon. "That's the thing for you, Mac," he said, adding that if he were my age, he would have jumped at it. By then, I had seen enough of police work to realize it wasn't for me, and soon afterwards, the Royal Air Force's advertisements for pilot training on short service commissions gave me the opportunity I was looking for.

Not that the time at the Sun was wasted. The short stretch of what is more commonly spoken of as Whitehall, from Great Scotland Yard to Trafalgar Square, is called Charing Cross, from which the branch took its name. The Cross, last of those marking the cortege of Eleanor of Aquitaine on its journey from Lincolnshire to Westminster Abbey, was demolished in 1647, but the name survives, and in its place is the equestrian statue of Charles I.

Double doors of glass with bronze frames opened on a short flight of marble steps, at the top of which, through another double door, was a tiled vestibule flanked on its right-hand side by the counter that constituted the boundary of the office proper.

Immediately behind it, at upright desks, sat the female clerks who kept track of renewal notices and issued receipts to cash customers. Behind them were three rows of double desks, six in all, shared by the clerks responsible for the different kinds of business—fire, accident, burglary, third party liability and reinsurance. In a corner office, the chief clerk surveyed the rows of desks, while beyond them he could see the National Gallery on the north side of the Square.

Next to his cubicle, a glassed-in office of quite respectable size housed the branch manager, while beyond it, and out of sight of customers in the space whose windows looked out on Admiralty Arch, were desks for the accountant and his three female clerks. On the floor above, reached by a rather fine marble-stepped curving staircase, were three rooms: a large one for the typists; a smaller one for the three inspectors of properties already insured or owned by prospective customers of the Sun; and a cubicle for the telephone operator.

One of the inspectors had been a major in his army service and kept the rank, as did the telephone operator who had been a captain, was then in his sixties, and used the switchboard as a means of indulging his prejudices. His dislike for one of the senior clerks was reciprocated. When the latter rattled his receiver to get attention, the erstwhile captain would wait, grinning evilly at the signal on the board, before slamming the switch so that it screeched in his enemy's ear.

From these pleasantly situated premises I would sally at the lunch hour to that part of the West End which included, within my radius, such delights as the National Gallery, the Tate and the Wallace Collection, the shops of the Strand, Piccadilly and Regent Street, and the bookstores in St. Martin's Lane and Charing Cross Road.

Sometimes I would stay in London for the evening to see a play, which could still be done for 6d after waiting in line to get a seat in the gallery—"the gods." I saw Shakespeare and Tchekhov at the Old Vic, and most of the ballets and operas at Sadler's

Wells. Once or twice, a girl of my age who worked at the Sun came with me, but this arrangement fell foul of stringent circumstances and most of the time I went alone.

The hankering for the stage persisted in the nebulous way I ought by then to have recognized as a characteristic, and though I made a few attempts to write scenes which I would then offer to Mollie's criticism when we rode together in the train, it never occurred to me to educate myself in the business by drawing "how to" books from the library.

The books I did draw, and devoured during the thirty-five minute intervals at each end of the working day when the Southern Railway took me to and from Charing Cross, were chiefly novels and plays that appealed to me, but also many that I felt a duty to read. In his plays, I chuckled at Shaw's wit, but it was the Prefaces that made a profound impression. For years afterward, until I learned more about its inherent fallacies, I was persuaded not merely of the inevitability of Fabian socialism but also of its essential *rightness*.

Yet I made no attempt to read my way into authors who might have given me opinions different from Shaw's, and although the newspaper I usually bought to read in the train was the middle-of-the-road *Morning Post*, I fell under the spell of Kingsley Martin's *New Statesman* for its good writing and reviews. I was, in short, typically young and idealistic, conscripted in the army of the political Left under the banners of social justice, and sharing the wealth I was manifestly unable to acquire on my own.

A friend recommended H.M. Tomlinson's book, *All Our Yesterdays*, about his experiences in the Great War. This led me to an enduring appreciation of his writing. Tomlinson wrote in *The Telegraph*, and it was his work, especially in *Gallions Reach* and the book of essays *Gifts of Fortune*, that filled me with a longing to travel. One of the essays, called "Hints for Those About to Travel," contains this passage:

> Travel, we are often told, gives light to the mind. Consider the sailors. They see the cities of the world, and the works of the Lord and His wonders in the deep. And—well, do you know any sailors? If you do, then you may have noticed that not infrequently their opinions seem hardly more valuable

than yours and mine. Yet it must be said for them that they rarely claim an additional value for their opinions because they have anchored off Colombo. They know better than that. They know, very likely, that all the cities of the world can no more give us what was withheld at birth than our own unaided suburb. As much convincing folly may be heard at Penang as at Peckham....

Tomlinson lived in Croydon (as did Malcolm Muggeridge, who went to Selhurst a dozen years before me), and he wrote about it in another essay:

Our suburb seems raw and loud. Yet in recent years [*Gifts of Fortune* was first published in 1926, the year we moved to Croydon] it acquired an area where a shower of bombs fell from an airship. History at last? No, we have some history which is earlier than the airship, though less remarkable. We have some scholarly local insistence on Clive, who went to school near, and on Ruskin, whose grandmother kept a public-house near the High Street. We have a Fellmonger's Yard, and a Coldharbour Lane, a tavern which can claim a Tudor reference, and a building, mainly of the fourteenth and fifteenth centuries, and known to us as the Old Palace....

Re-reading Tomlinson reminds me of what RLS wrote about Hazlitt: "Though we are mighty fine fellows nowadays, we cannot write like Hazlitt." Tomlinson shows his feeling for the world beyond the senses in these lines about *Moby Dick*:

As in all great art, something is suggested in Melville's book that is above and greater than the matter of the story. Upon the figures in Melville's drama and their circumstances there fall lights and glooms from what is ulterior, tremendous, and undivulged. Through the design made by the voyage of the *Pequod* there is determined, as by chance, a purpose for which her men did not sign, and which is not in her charter.

Tomlinson wrote movingly of Joseph Conrad, whose book *The Nigger of the Narcissus* he picked up one day in a hurry for a train. Next he read *Typhoon*, and, it was plain that this writer, who was a Pole, I was told, had added to the body of English literature witness to a period of British ships and seamen which otherwise would have passed as unmarked as the voyages of the men of Tyre and Sidon.

They met first in the offices of the *English Review* a few weeks after Tomlinson had reviewed one of Conrad's books. He was nervous in consequence. Two of the editors were present, and when they began to speak of other matters, "Conrad then came over, and stood beside me. He touched my arm, apparently as nervous as I was myself. 'Thank you very much for what you said about my book. You do think I am genuine, don't you?'"

By travel, I did not mean Europe or North America. South Africa was on the list, but where I wanted to go was the Far East. Ternate, Surabaya, Celebes and Macassar, Labuan and Penang— the names that dripped so casually from Tomlinson's pen haunted me to the point where one night, late home, I tried to reach him by telephoning *The Telegraph*—a rather sad example of my conflicting strains at work again. He wasn't there, and what would I have asked him—"How do I get to Penang?" It took me twenty years to find out.

Our conceits of bachelorhood and disparaging the company of girls were partly for show, but chiefly from necessity. None of us could afford to marry, and despite the twin proddings of penury and unrealized yearnings, we made no attempt to better our circumstances in ways that today are commonplace. Not once did it occur to me that I might take on other work in the evenings or at weekends. Any such thought would have stopped short at the snobbery attached to working in offices "in the City" or "the West End," which maintained against all evidence that the salaries paid, as distinct from the wages of manual workers, were more than enough to keep us in comfort.

The snobbery was so pervasive that I wasn't conscious of it at the time, and I think now with shame at the way I and my friends laughed behind his back at a companion who had left school early to work in a garage. He made enough money to buy and drive a second-hand Riley, in which he generously drove us around while we winked and later joked about the grime he couldn't get out of his fingers.

While they waited for the train at East Croydon station, fellow clerks would treat one another to condescending glances that took in the wearers' hats, ties, suits or topcoats, shoes and umbrellas and newspapers, by which they were judged, as if the observers—who had emerged from near-identical semi-detached or row houses not long before—were in fact so clearly superior as to be barely able to suppress their surprise at finding themselves in such company.

But the true heroines were the women. Although some, like Mollie, were enterprising enough to get and hold good jobs, many more were like the typists at the Sun: paid less than the men, most of them maiden ladies (the convention was that once married, they were no longer entitled to take a paying job), forced to keep up appearances on their meagre salaries, and living out their days between the crowded, stuffy typists' room and bed-sitters in Balham or Pinner.

Once or twice I stayed after work to accompany the telephone operator to some of his pubs in the City, where he was recognized variously as the Captain, the Major, or in one place the Colonel. In preparation for these excursions, at lunchtime he would draw from Drummond's a number of crisp pound notes, one of which he would lay with a flourish on the bar at each establishment for the first round.

He was a little over six feet tall, with twinkling eyes in a smallish face on which he wore a moustache that he would trim in front of a hand mirror in between bouts with the telephone. A regular at one pub was a woman who read palms as a hobby. She predicted that I would not marry the girl I expected to (Mollie, at the time), and that I would travel abroad; safe enough guesses about the future of a young fellow of nineteen or twenty.

What I remember most, however, about those excursions was the silence of the streets as we walked by the great gloom of St. Paul's to Cheapside and Poultry past the Mansion House and the Bank, the rush for trains long past and the City withdrawn into its evening quiet, empty save for an occasional bus or taxi or a solitary constable.

Throughout this period, although I thought of myself as gregarious and worked hard at becoming popular, what I enjoyed more than anything else was my own company. My copy of William Hazlitt's essays, *Table Talk*, shows no publication date, nor did I write the date after my signature on the flyleaf, so I can't be sure when I first read *On Going A Journey*, but the opening sentiment was mine entirely: "One of the pleasantest things in the world is going a journey; but I like to go by myself."

Croydon is in Surrey, less than five miles from the Kent border and a short bus ride from starting places such as Coulsdon to the south, West Wickham to the east, and Sutton to the west, from where a ten-mile walking radius would take me by roundabout routes to Merstham or Westerham, Ashstead or Oxshott, savouring the air and striding to a rhythm inspired by a mental picture of myself, for a few hours master of my fate and captain of my soul.

Shoes were important—the stouter the better, always brown, and preferably with, in addition to the regular tongue, an extra one that hung outside over the laces and was associated with Norway. An alternative, much admired, was made by Lotus and called Veldtschoen, guaranteed waterproof, and suited by definition to a smoker of Afrikander Mixture. The only adventures to come my way, as I strode the lanes or stopped for bread and cheese and beer at lonely pubs, were in the mind: visions of myself as a character of Maurice Walsh, alone in the highlands, breasting a rise to see, nestling in the glen, my cottage with the smoke from its peat fire curling up to welcome me.

Sometimes, Mollie and I went together. Without a car, the countryside in good weather afforded us the chance to be alone with our concerns. Not least of these were the natural ones that convention denied us opportunities to indulge. Virgins both, we sought copses where we might hug and kiss while muttering endearments and imagining, in my case at least, a peat-warmed cottage with Mollie inside it.

Her father was an engineer who owned a cinema in Redhill, and his hobbies were golf and tinkering with a home-built wireless set of fearsome complexity. He smoked St. Julien pipe tobacco—an aromatic shag that I found tasteless compared to St. Bruno, but smoked from time to time to curry favour with him. It was all we had in common.

While I was absorbed by these appurtenances of growing up, Mother and Dad had problems of their own. Dad rarely brought his troubles home, but I remember the occasion when, after years of persistence, he had finally got a foot in the door of the giant

Lyons corporation only to have Pellerin's head office in Southampton mess up the order. Whether they did so by failing to deliver or changing the quote I don't know, but I heard Dad on the phone to Southampton and he was desperately disappointed.

That may have been the start, as it was certainly a contributory cause, of the decline in his health, but added to it was concern for my brother Tom, whose propensity to fly into rages was a continual source of worry—especially to Mother, who had to face it all the time. Dad managed to get him as a boarder into the Royal Masonic School, but Tom ran away twice and, after a spell on a training ship in the Hamble River—which, when he described it to me many years later, sounded like a duplicate of the *Bounty*—he worked at a number of jobs before setting up shop as a newsagent, and afterwards as owner of a residential hotel in Portsmouth.

Because of the eleven-year difference in our ages and the fact that I left home at the time he went away to school, we were never close, but I was too selfish and wrapped up in the new career to be of any practical help to Mother. I did send her money from my RAF pay, but she moved on her own to Southampton and my only other contribution was to make the case to the managing director of Pellerin's, which had no pension scheme, for some recognition of Dad's thirty years' service.

The new career began with my application for a short service commission in the Royal Air Force (four years, with a gratuity of 300 pounds at the end), and during the weeks that followed, I indulged my capacity for self-dramatization to the full. Hitler had come to power three years before, the summer of 1935 saw the Nazi riots in Berlin, and it seemed every time we went to a cinema, Movietone News would show mass rallies of well-armed and disciplined soldiers marching before the gaze and outstretched arm of the dictator. War was certainly in the air. Mollie and I were at an impasse, and I remember standing with her at the gate of her house after we had spent the evening together, looking gloomily at the sky and predicting that my life would probably end in a fatal descent from it.

The waiting period ended with the summons to an interview and I presented myself, complete with bowler hat, rolled umbrella and dark blue pin-striped suit to Adastral House at the corner of

Holborn and the Aldwych. There I joined a handful of other applicants in a waiting room before facing a board of officers in civilian clothes and answering questions of which the only one I recall was from a red-faced man: "I see you boxed at school. Have you kept it up?"

Fortunately, I passed the medical, and in due course fell upon the brown envelope from the Air Ministry to find that my application had been accepted, that joining instructions would follow in due course, and that in the meantime I would do well to purchase from His Majesty's Stationery Office a copy of A.P. 129, *The Flying Training Manual* and study it.

This gave me the opportunity, during train journeys to and from the Sun, to hold up the book in such a way that fellow travellers could see the sort of chap they were sharing the compartment with. Some of the finer points were hard to understand, and I decided to buy a short ride at Croydon airport, where the pilot might be prevailed upon to explain the odd detail. I paid my half-guinea, climbed into the cabin, and watched carefully as we took off, made a leisurely circuit of the vicinity, and landed. I couldn't see the rudder or the elevators, but the ailerons, which I had expected from my reading to waggle a good deal, seemed scarcely to move; and, as the lordly pilot stalked away without a backward glance (like the regular at the top of the Haymarket), I was no wiser apart from discovering that flying seemed to be OK.

At the Sun I was presented with two fine leather suitcases, engraved with my initials (they lasted until 1986, when they were damaged in our flood of that year and had to be discarded) and, on Sunday, July 12, 1936, after Dad had shown me how to pack my dinner jacket, I took the train for Southampton and Hamble.

ABOVE: *Kate Victoria Marsh McDonald*

BELOW (L-R): *May, William, Katherine and Rose McDonald*

William Marsh McDonald

With Granddad and Grandmother Mac

124 Graham Rd.

51

ABOVE: *Katherine Smith (Auntie Kit)*

BELOW: *Granddad Mac at Avenue House, Southampton, 1930*

52

ABOVE (IN CENTRE): *Mother and Dad*

BELOW (ON RIGHT): *Mother and Dad*

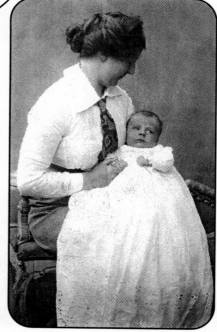

LEFT: *Eva Harriet McDonald*

RIGHT: *Mother and K.J., 1914*

ABOVE: *With Mother and Dad*

RIGHT: *K.J., May 1917*

55

ABOVE: *8 Cornwall Road, where I was born*

BELOW: *8 Tyne Road, ground floor flat where we moved in 1919*

30 Alexandra Park, the Stuckey's home, where Mother and I lived from 1916 until 1919, when Dad and René came home from war

ABOVE: *77 Longmead Avenue, we lived here from 1925-1926, when we moved to Croydon*

LEFT: *Bristol Cathedral School. I cycled here from Longmead Avenue*

Photos taken by Martha in Sept. 2002

René Stuckey (L) and Dad (3rd from L) 1916-1917

René Stuckey (L) and Dad (R) 1917

ABOVE: *René Stuckey in Batoum, 1919*

LEFT: *Dad at Malta Hospital (3rd row, 4th from L) December 1918*

With Mother, Netley Beach, 1918

With Mother, Alexandra Park, Bristol, May 1917

Ruth, at 69 Maple Avenue, Barrie

Auntie Mac and Uncle Frank Church

Auntie Mac (widowed) married Bill Paul, here with his two sons

K.J., 124 Cromwell Road, Bristol

With Tom, Bristol, 1926

With Auntie Mac and cousin Peggy, Ryde, IOW, 1928

LEFT: *With cousin Peggy, Seaview, IOW, 1931*

RIGHT: *Cousin Alan and Auntie Ethel (Mother's elder sister from South Africa)*

LEFT: *Ruth's Mother, Lucretia Craig, with Jack (centre), Ruth (right) and a friend. At the cottage, Big Bay Point, 1918*

Chapter 2

▨ 1936—1939 ▨

The Royal Air Force differs from the other two services principally in the way command is exercised. The soldier's loyalty is to his regiment or corps, part of a family within the army's corporate whole that sustains him with its particular history, its heroes and their exploits. The sailor at sea is always conscious that he and every member of the crew must pull together if they are to withstand the perils of the deep. Soldiers and sailors alike see the object of their loyalty as something immediate and comprehensible.

But the airman's attitudes are shaped less by realities than by abstractions. He is loyal to his squadron while he serves in it, but it is merely part of the greater endeavour that air power signifies. Thanks largely to the inspiration and doggedness of Hugh Trenchard, the RAF embraced from its start in 1918 the idea of the offensive use of air power as the dominant component of military strategy. The doctrine boiled down to this: keep your guard up, knock the enemy's guard down, and destroy his capacity to wage war. Fighters and bombers and combinations of the two are the vital elements of victory, and their success depends entirely upon the men and women who maintain and supply the aircraft and weaponry.

Thus, in the Second World War, the RAF's offensive arm— Bomber Command—was in continuous operation from September 3, 1939, when Flying Officer A. McPherson, Commander Thompson, RN, and Corporal V. Arrowsmith first crossed the

German coast in Blenheim N6215, until the night of May 2/3, 1945, when a force of 179 Mosquitoes attacked airfields near Kiel in advance of British and Canadian ground forces. For three years, until the United States Army Eighth Air Force began to grow in strength, Bomber Command was the sole means of carrying the war to the German heartland.

This is not to depreciate the vital roles of the other commands (Fighter, Coastal, Transport, Training, Maintenance, and the tactical air forces over Europe and in overseas theatres), but rather to make the point: the airman partakes of the element in which he flies; where he strikes is at his choosing, not his enemy's. On June 5, 1944, the night before the Normandy landings, Bomber Command flew 1,211 sorties—its greatest total in one night and almost all in direct support of the landings.

From then until mid-August, as *The Bomber Command War Diaries* reports:

> Operations consisted of a multitude of small or medium-sized raids. Sometimes aircrews flew two sorties in twenty-four hours. By day, they might be bombing targets only a few yards from the battle lines in Normandy; a few hours later they could be bombing an oil refinery in the Ruhr.

Nowhere was this more forcefully stated than in the post-war report by Adolf Hitler's former armaments minister, Albert Speer (*Spandau; The Secret Diaries*):

> The real importance of the air war was that it opened a second front. Unpredictability of the attacks made the front gigantic; every square metre of our territory was a kind of front line. To defend ourselves against air attacks, we had to produce thousands of anti-aircraft guns, stockpile tremendous quantities of ammunition all over the country, and hold in readiness hundreds of thousands of soldiers, who also have to stay by their guns, often totally inactive, for months at a time.

Like every successful leader, a good squadron commander leads by example. In peace, he instills the importance of training by demonstrating the professional competence that training confers. In war, he elects to fly in the most challenging conditions. Flight commanders do the same. But the more junior officers—the generality of aircrew who man the force, except that they also aspire to competence—are denied the chance to lead in the way a subaltern leads his platoon or a lieutenant commands his small ship.

Pilot officers and flying officers, even flight lieutenants, given an acquired ability in the air, must look for reputation elsewhere—in sport or other activities that accompany service life. This is a product of the flexibility that distinguishes air power. The need to apply both flexibility and concentration of force requires command to be exercised remotely from the squadrons that do the work.

A squadron commander in any one of the operational commands may develop tactics that later are adopted by other squadrons and later still as doctrine; but these are exceptions to the rule that the doctrine, once adopted, stands until some other exceptional commander improves on it. Yet this apparent thrust to conformity, which might be expected to discourage initiative, has the opposite effect.

Denied their military and naval contemporaries' opportunities to lead, the RAF's junior officers must look for other ways to express their individuality. In this, the service has found means to help them. Between the two world wars, the Schneider Trophy competitions, long-distance flights, and aerobatic displays brought flying officers and flight lieutenants into the public eye while experimental and test flying of new or improved aircraft types and flying under hazardous conditions in the Met. Flight established reputations for the pilots concerned. In more recent times, aerobatic displays draw large audiences, competitions against allied air forces bring recognition to individual participants, and the RAF's contribution to both national and UN-sponsored air operations affords scope to aspiring leaders.

For the first fifty hours of flight training, embryo pilots were sent to civilian-operated flying schools. Air Service Training Limited ran the one at Hamble much on the lines of the RAF establishments in which most of the instructors had served on short- or medium-service commissions before taking their gratuities and turning to flying instruction as a career.

My instructor was a retired flight lieutenant of middle height, sturdy frame, and rather too short a temper for the job. Your successful flying instructor has much in common with successful teachers anywhere, including patience and understanding, the power to impart information, and—of course—professional competence. But he is also engaged in a business that puts him and his charges at risk from a number of sources.

Taking off and landing an aircraft call for a nicety of judgment that can hardly be expected of a beginner until he has several hours of practice behind him; the nicety must be exercised by the instructor in deciding how close to disaster he can let the student go before making the vital correction. Even at a safe altitude he can never relax, for the student might mistake an instruction, get the aircraft into a dangerous situation, and then freeze onto the controls. Always present are the risks of structural or mechanical failure, and the airman's perennial enemy—the weather.

My instructor exposed us to the risk of mistaking an instruction by directing me to "try a flick roll" when I had only a few hours experience and none of aerobatics. A flick roll sounded to me as if the thing to do was to shove the throttle forward, jam on full left rudder and haul back on the stick, a manoeuvre that had the immediate effect of forcing us outward against the straps as the aircraft performed an inverted spin and I heard the instructor's strangled cry through the speaking tube—"I've got her!"—as he took over the controls. Afterwards, he told me what had happened and that it was a first for him as well.

AST was equipped with the Avro Cadet, an open cockpit biplane driven by a Genet Major engine of 135 h.p. Communication between instructor and student was by means of Gosport tubing, named after the Royal Naval Air Service aerodrome where the device was first installed during the Great War. Short rubber tubes dangled from the helmet's earphones to meet in a metal Y-piece. In the front cockpit, the instructor's Y-piece was connected with the student's speaking tube. In the rear cockpit, the student connected his listening tube to the instructor's speaking tube that passed from front to rear.

There were thirty-two of us on the course: twenty-two, like me, civilians off the street; the other ten were regular airmen selected for pilot training, who were that much ahead of us in general service knowledge as well as knowledge of their particular trades. During the next two months of a good summer, we flew fifty hours, learned the elements of navigation, airframes and engines, familiarized ourselves with local pubs, and made, in my case, friendships with four special people of whom two survived the war. Peter Murdoch, Boris Romanoff, Mervyn Wheatley and Arthur Proctor— all five of us struck sparks off each other and blossomed in one another's company for the ten months we were together.

Monday was spent in collecting manuals and flying kit. Tuesday was the great day when flying was to start. The half-guinea ride at Croydon airport was forgotten as I waddled out, parachute banging against the backs of my legs, to the Avro Cadets in their neat row on the grass.

Picture yourself, on that warm summer day, with the breeze stirring the long grass under the fuselage and the fresh scents of sea and country giving way, as you draw near the aircraft, to the smells of fabric dope and engine oil. You are moving with difficulty in fleece-lined boots, zippered flying suit, silk gloves inside zippered leather gauntlets, and helmet with goggles attached. You bring the hanging part of the parachute harness up between your legs and pass the other two straps through it before clicking their ends into the quick-release fastener in front of your chest, so that you are in a crouched position as you lift a foot to the step and climb into the rear cockpit.

The four straps of the Sutton harness are fastened across your chest, and you see before you the dials of the instruments. The instructor attaches the Y-piece from your earphones into the rear-cockpit end of his speaking tube, climbs into the front cockpit, and you hear his voice, distorted by the tube, in your ears. He is telling you to look at the instruments, while he describes them, and to feel the controls, which he waggles from his cockpit so that your hand on the stick and your feet on the rudder pedals are shaken in turn.

Next you hear his shout to the mechanic, standing in front of the propeller: "Switches off." The mechanic repeats it and pulls the propeller around to suck in fuel, then stands at an angle to the arc of rotation with one hand grasping the raised end of the prop. He repeats the instructor's shout of "Contact," and swings the engine into life.

Now the cockpit is filled with noise and movement as the needle rotates on the RPM counter and the oil temperature and pressure gauges start to register. At the instructor's wave, the mechanic pulls away the chocks, and with a surge of the engine, you are moving forward quite roughly as the tail skid bumps over the hard ground. Your feet on the rudder pedals are jolted back and forth as the instructor steers a zigzag course to keep a clear view ahead.

You stop at an angle to the wind, the fore and aft trimmer is adjusted, the voice in your ears says "Off we go," and after a turn into wind, you feel the throttle lever thrust forward. The engine roars, the slipstream brushes the top of your helmet as the thing picks up speed, the tail comes up, and bump, bump, bump, you are skimming over the grass.

The voice says it is keeping the nose down to gain speed, and then the stick comes slowly back. Out of the corner of your eye, you see the ground falling away and you concentrate desperately on the voice. The altimeter needle crawls around to 2,000 feet, the throttle is eased back, the voice invites you to feel the controls and you grip the stick, your feet pressed firmly against the rudder pedals.

The thing was straight and level when you began, but you realize the air is not smooth—a wing dips, you overcorrect, the nose goes up, you push the stick forward, the thing starts to dive, and you feel pressure on the controls as the voice says "I've got her." The voice shows how easy it is to keep the thing straight and level. You try again, nervous now at the thought of repeated failure, and your tenseness communicates itself to the controls. The thing seems to be balanced on a needle point, defying the frantic jerks of your hands and feet as they respond too late to the signals from your brain. Your view of the horizon takes in the instructor's helmeted head and you see, fixed to one of the centre section struts, a mirror through which cold eyes are watching you.

The time drags on. You have taken a dislike to the instructor, sitting there with all his experience and snatching control just when you were about to correct. But gradually, the intervals between his corrections lengthen, and instead of staring ahead at the horizon, you begin to look down, as well, at the boats dotted in the Hamble River and the ships ploughing up Southampton Water.

The instructor takes over for the approach and landing, and you sit idle, your confidence returning, as you watch the airfield grow bigger. The voice is silent now, the engine is throttled back, and as you glide toward the boundary, you sense for the first time the buoyancy of the thing, the realization that even without the engine it will fly, down, but forward as well. The aircraft crosses the hedge, the wheels skim the grass, the stick jerks back into your lap, and with a bump, you are down.

After a week, and with by then nine-and-a-half hours' experience, I was given a short test by the chief flying instructor and cleared for my first solo—a flight, according to my log book, of five minutes that contrived to crowd in a host of sensations: joy at being alone in the cockpit, taxying out, taking off, climbing to 700 feet, shouting and singing and making faces in the mirror, and turning in for the glide, over the hedge and then holding, holding, smelling the grass as the Cadet's wheels rumbled on to the field.

One of the more enjoyable exercises was the forced landing, in which the instructor simulated engine failure by closing the throttle and inviting you to choose a field which you would then approach in a series of S turns, timing the last so that you could lose the last bit of height by sideslipping over the hedge before straightening out and opening the throttle to climb away.

Choosing the field was a challenge because, in the few seconds after the instructor closed the throttle, you had to remember the wind direction from when you had taken off, look out for trees and power lines, guess at the condition of the ground, and start your glide. After about twenty hours, we were authorized to do advanced forced landings, which called for an actual landing in the field set aside for the purpose a few miles from Hamble. Here, you throttled back at 2,000 feet and made your quiet turns until you were over the hedge, slipped off the last bit of height, and landed.

On one or two occasions after landing, I remember throttling right back, so that the engine was just ticking over, and climbing out to lie for a few minutes on the grass, listening to the larks, before getting back into the cockpit and taxying to the edge of the field for the takeoff.

For me and the other civilians, Hamble was our introduction to the Royal Air Force. Although there was no marching, the service atmosphere was pervasive. From the commandant, a retired group captain, down to the former NCOs who taught the elements of airframes and engines, the staff exuded their accumulated experience. We became conscious of the difference between ourselves, who aspired to become commissioned officers, and the regular airmen who aspired to become sergeant pilots. We were allotted private rooms and were served our meals in a mess where we donned dinner jackets for dining-in nights.

The British preference for amateurs over professionals, which contributed to the Empire's decline and fall in the face of competition from professionals the British had often trained, worked for us. Graduates of interviews by our peers and acceptably educated, we were stamped by the English class system as the superiors of leading aircraftmen (LACs) who had five or six years' experience of the service. One of them—who was commissioned in 1940 and was shot down in February 1941, in an outstandingly courageous daylight attack at mast height on the German cruiser *Hipper* in Brest harbour—made the point in a letter to me many years after the war:

> By this time I had received my commission and served my four plus years [as a prisoner of war] in, probably, more comfort than our NCO colleagues.

My own amateur status was composed of a certain fluency derived from the teachings of Mother and Mr. Vallins, as well as practice in the school's debating society and on the amateur stage; an introduction to the ideas of discipline and service through membership in the Special Constabulary; and a brushing acquaintance with engines gained from having learned to drive a car. Set against this, our LAC colleagues had been taught how to maintain and repair the structure of an aircraft in the trade of rigger; or to maintain and repair engines in the trade of fitter; or to apply the principles of cataloguing and inventory-keeping in the trade of Clerk/Equipment (known as store-bashing); or to become familiar with King's Regulations and Air Council Instructions and the Manual of Air Force Law in the trade of Clerk/Admin. Still, attaining the ambition to fly which had motivated them to join as boys of fifteen or sixteen was no doubt reward enough to restrain them from parading these obvious advantages. They might be required to treat us as superiors, but that was entirely within the tradition of forbearance accorded all officers by the NCOs who actually make the three services work.

When fresh experiences are shared, the participants have something more than humanity in common. If they are much of an age, and the experience includes a present or future element of danger, they are likely to remember both the experience and the people for a long time. Add to this similar backgrounds and a sense of humour, and the makings were there for the friendships I formed at Hamble.

Four of us were twenty-one or twenty-two years old. Wheatley, whose older brother, Terry, was just completing a medium service commission, was twenty-six. We were attracted to the RAF for the same reasons: boredom with the jobs we were doing, the excitement of flying, a sense that war was on the horizon, and, not least, if war didn't break out, the promise of an interesting four years and 300 pounds at the end.

We took the lead in the kind of escapades that occur naturally among congregations of young men, and which I was conditioned to promote. The cockiness was due partly to self-confidence, partly to a degree of sophistication acquired during the years in London, but chiefly to a facility for trotting out remarks that were well-received by the others. A modest talent for repartee and impromptu speaking marked me for delivery of the address on behalf of the course at the final guest nights both at Hamble and Netheravon afterwards. Cockiness is showing off, so it had to be my chamber pot that was seen to repose at the top of Hamble's wireless mast where I had climbed to hang it after the guest night.

Peter Murdoch invited me to his home in Bournemouth for a weekend. His father had died not long before, and I remember his mother as a slender, fair-haired woman who made me welcome in a house very similar to ours in Croydon. An older brother was a lieutenant in the Tank Corps. Peter and I were about a size. He had the long thighs of a sprinter and was an accomplished rugby player, but his forte was boxing. Later that year, we drove to Oxford to watch him compete in the Flying Training Command championships. He won his weight and we marvelled at the left he produced, it seemed from nowhere, to knock his man out.

He was clean-shaven, had a long upper lip that gave him the appearance of being about to smile, as in fact he often was, and wavy, dark brown hair that was parted slightly to one side of top dead centre. I know he was a good pilot, because later at

Netheravon, after we had got our wings, we were authorized to take passengers. We flew together as pilot or passenger on eighteen different exercises for a total of 12 h. 45 min.

His generous nature came to the fore when we had left Hamble for the two-weeks indoctrination into service discipline at the RAF Central Depot Uxbridge. Dad died just as the Hamble course was ending, so that I left before the others and joined them again at Uxbridge. Peter came into my room to offer sympathy, an awkward moment for both of us that was also lightened by the shared loss.

Arthur Proctor was twenty-one, a couple of inches under six feet, thickset, clean-shaven with black hair and an oblong, reddish face on which he wore a jovial expression that changed almost to a splutter when he broke into a laugh. His parents lived in Kenya, but he was educated in England, had worked like me in a London office, and was also a Special Constable. He and I were drawn against each other in the preliminary boxing trials at Netheravon, in the course of which he broke my nose for a third time, the first two having been in the gym and on the rugby field, both at school. As often happens in the curious chemistry of sport, this formed a bond between us.

Boris Romanoff was also twenty-one, six feet tall, broad-shouldered, with fair hair, a close-clipped moustache and regular features. His sports were soccer and boxing, but his true love was the stage. At Netheravon, he organized a dramatic society and both directed and acted in two plays while we were there. It was his hope at the end of the four years to take up acting as a career. His habitual expression was serious and determined, so that when you made him laugh, the transformation was all the more rewarding, but his seriousness was genuine; he had a strong faith and was concerned about the human condition.

Mervyn Wheatley, the oldest at twenty-six, was a little over six feet, with ruddy features, his black, wavy hair tinged with grey, and eyes that were quick to reflect the cheery outlook he brought to affairs of the day. He was imaginative, an instigator of escapades and off-duty activities generally, and possessor of an offbeat sense of humour that stimulated the rest of us. His sports were golf and fly-fishing.

We were typical of the hundreds of young men who responded, between 1935 and 1939, to an expanding RAF's need for pilots. Our images of war in the air were formed from films like *Dawn Patrol*, in which white-scarved pilots rode their Camels and SE5s against the Albatrosses and Fokkers of enemies still governed by the tradition of chivalry in single combat. If we spoke of war, it was by mocking it to the accompaniment of gestures and facial expressions copied from the films, a play like other plays that happened to someone else. We were engaged in a serious business we refused to take seriously, an extension perhaps of the amateur tradition, but also a defence against what the news from Europe seemed to presage for us.

After we had put in our two weeks of square-bashing at the RAF Depot under the eyes of uncompromising flight sergeants and got ourselves measured for and fitted with uniforms by the authorized tailors, we joined graduates from other civil schools at Netheravon.

The practice of using civil schools as relatively inexpensive means to filter out the unfit was self-evident. Of the survivors from Hamble and other schools who made up the forty-seven acting pilot officers (A/P/Os) and Leading Aircraftmen (LACs) of No. 4 Course at Netheravon, only one failed the flying (he was transferred to armoured cars), and there was only one fatality, when LAC Lofty Barrett flew out of cloud into Sidbury Hill.

Netheravon was the home of No. 6 Flying Training School, perched at the west end of Salisbury Plain about 800 feet above sea level, a grass field of dips and hollows alongside which were the hangars, office buildings, messes and quarters that had served the same functions for our Royal Flying Corps predecessors flying aircraft very similar to the Avro Cadets we had left behind at Hamble.

Now, however, we were to fly what the chief ground instructor had intrigued us by referring to as His Majesty's sports models: the Hawker Hart, and its derivatives the Audax, the Hart Special, and the single-seat Hawker Fury. The Hart had entered service only five years before. Many light bomber squadrons were still equipped with variants of it, and we were suitably impressed. It was big, its shiny streamlined engine nacelle gave it the racy look expected of an advertised 184 mph top speed, and it *felt* businesslike.

The Rolls Royce Kestrel engine was almost four times as powerful as the Cadet's Genet Major, the rear cockpit of the Audax was surrounded by a Scarff ring to traverse a Lewis gun, from the front cockpit the pilot controlled a Vickers machine gun that fired through the arc of the propeller, and the light series bomb racks could carry 520 lbs. of bombs.

My instructor was Sgt. Falconer, a calm professional who bridged the nominal gap between sergeant and acting pilot officer with the tact born of long practice, while leaving me in no doubt of who was in charge and imparting to me as much of his piloting skills as I was competent to absorb. He taught me two things in particular. After a guest night when some of us had ended up in the sergeants' mess and were late to bed, he took me up for instrument flying, when a blind-flying hood was pulled over the student's (front) cockpit, and engaged me in a series of entries into and recoveries from spins that cured me forever of mixing alcohol with flying. The second thing was through a failure on my part.

At the end of the first term, when we were awarded our wings, the graduation ceremony included a flying display in which I was detailed to do the solo aerobatics. Sgt. Falconer briefed me to fly into wind so that the manoeuvres—a slow roll followed by a loop, and then a roll off the top of a loop—would be done pretty much within the perimeter of the airfield and thus well in view of the spectators. However, when I went to the flight office to sign the authorization book, the flight commander was there, and he told me to fly the other way. Instead of standing up for my instructor, I said "Yes, sir," and although the manoeuvres were OK, the effect was spoiled and I let Falconer down.

The flight commander taught me something else. He walked with head bent forward from having broken his back some years before, when he taxied on to the line of takeoff just in time to get himself landed on by an aircraft he hadn't seen. This taught me to look both ways and behind as well as in front—not only in airplanes, but also in cars, all to good purpose so far, especially when the traffic lights are green.

At Christmas, Wheatley and I decided to go to Paris, and since he hadn't been there before, I flaunted my experience and booked us into the Soufflot. We went by boat train from Victoria to the Gare du Nord, and spent two days and nights practicing our French, drinking German lager from *formidables*, seeing the sights, including Josephine Baker at le Moulin Rouge and, on the second afternoon, being enticed into a brothel, where in a large room walled entirely with mirrors we were plied with champagne by an array of naked women of whom one was black, and counted ourselves lucky to get out again at the cost of the champagne.

On the way back from Paris, while I was staying with Wheatley at his parents' home in Eastbourne, he took me to a house party at Robertsbridge, some fourteen miles north of Hastings: half-timbered house standing well back from the road, oak floors and comfortable furniture and wide, well-filled fireplaces, women in long dresses and men in tails. After dinner, during a pause from the dancing, I was prevailed upon to relate our recent experiences in the City of Light to the accompaniment of laughs and chuckles from as appreciative an audience as you could wish. Funny how you remember these things.

The man I noticed who wasn't laughing was the one who claimed a proprietary interest in the girl I had been dancing with more than once. I never saw her again, but pictured her from time to time, married to that sullen-looking fellow and thinking of what might have been.

After we got our wings and were authorized to take passengers—we also threw a dance in the Mess to which Boris and Wheatley invited Evelyn Dall, a much admired musical comedy actress of the day—I experienced the first of only two forced landings in twenty-one years of service.

Wheatley and I were detailed to do a war load climb, for which lead weights were attached to a bar passed through the fuselage to simulate a bomb load. We took off, A/P/O Wheatley as pilot, at 12.10 and climbed as instructed to 16,000 feet, the Audax's effective ceiling, when he called through the Gosport tube, "Let's see how fast it will go," and stuffed the nose down. He called out the air speed readings, which reached 240 mph before he levelled out at about 500 feet, only to see puffs of overheated coolant passing by the cockpit. He called again that he was going to put down in a field. I peered over his shoulder to see, just in time, high tension cables ahead which he had probably just seen as well, and screamed "Pull up!" through the tube.

We missed them and he made a good landing in a rather small field near Mottisfont. The farmhouse was close by, and after we had telephoned the airfield, we were entertained to a splendid tea in a bright sitting room—cretonne-covered settee and chairs, latticed windows with deep sills, vases of flowers—until one of the instructors arrived with a van and a driver to take Wheatley back to Netheravon while the instructor flew Audax K 7345 out of the field with me aboard as before.

The last three weeks of the course were spent at Penrhos, the new airfield near Pwllheli at the top of Cardigan Bay, where we actually fired the guns and dropped bombs using the bombsights we had been learning about. Welsh nationalists objected to the intrusion and had been busy painting slogans in green paint as well as burning down a hut at the edge of the airfield.

This was Armament Practice Camp and there was a holiday atmosphere. We were near the end of the course, we were by the sea, it was spring, there were no parades, and the flying was fun. We made (forward-firing) Vickers gun attacks on a towed drogue, or on ground targets. We aimed practice bombs from 6,000 or 10,000 feet at the offshore marker after squeezing down past the folded seat in the rear cockpit to lie full length below the pilot's seat, aligning the grid wires of the bombsight with the target, and watching the white shape make its way down until we saw the puff of smoke, usually at some distance from the target. There's a picture of me from *The Daily Express*, hanging a practice bomb on the wing rack of an Audax, grim, determined, for the civilian audience.

In spite of that, I don't remember making the obvious connection between what we were doing at Penrhos and the whole purpose of the Royal Air Force. Amateurism prevailed, and when one of the younger officers showed genuine enjoyment in the air firing details we told each other smugly it was bad form. (He was also very good at it and did well as a fighter pilot in the war.) Not long before, five Audaxes, flying in formation from Ternhill to Penrhos, had flown into one of the Welsh Hills, a salutary reminder of the need to know what we were doing.

Yet a year later, when Wheatley wrote to me from 105 Squadron to say he had upbraided airmen who were lounging about instead of checking the bomb-release mechanisms of the squadron's new Fairey Battles by reminding them "This is to prepare us for war!" he still meant it as a joke.

Not that the equipment we had was of much use in the airman's perpetual battle with the elements. When we left

Netheravon for squadrons, the aircraft were either the same as we had been flying—the light bomber squadrons were equipped either with Audaxes or the slightly more powerful Hawker Hinds—or with equally dated successors of Great War types. Thus, Peter Murdoch went to Old Sarum to fly the Hector (a Hart with a Napier Dagger engine to replace the Rolls Royce Kestrel), Boris to Mildenhall, where the Fairey Hendon had just arrived, an all-metal monoplane bomber with two Kestrels and a top speed of 155 mph at 15,000 feet, and Proc to Dishforth and the Heyford, which (Proc told me) "did everything at 80 mph—climbing, cruising and approach."

Wheatley and I went to the newly opened Harwell, where both squadrons—105 and 107—were equipped with Audaxes. Our navigation aids were maps, the naked eye, and drift readings taken by the observer, who aligned the bombsight's drift wires with objects on the ground and calculated the wind velocity at the height flown.

All this was fair enough in clear weather. However, when we flew above cloud, as we often did in formation after climbing up through it—an eerie business, keeping station with the leader, silver dope and roundels showing through the wisps of vapour—we were dependent on the leader's Dead Reckoning calculations, worked out from a pad on his knee using the Met. forecast wind. Although flying above cloud in bright sunshine after having left a dreary day below was almost worth the trip, you had the uncomfortable feeling, as you followed the leader down again through the clag, that his DR might be out, or the cloud base might have lowered, and that you might be keeping station en route to a spot of high ground, like Lofty Barrett .

Behind the scenes, new aircraft were being designed. Soon they began to come into service: Handley Page Hampdens, Fairey Battles, Bristol Blenheims, Hawker Hurricanes, Armstrong Whitworth Whitleys, Vickers Wellesleys and Wellingtons, Westland Lysanders and Supermarine Spitfires. 105 Squadron was slated for Battles, but the first squadron to get them was 63, at Upwood, in May, 1937, and an entry in my log book shows me ferrying one of 63's old Audaxes to Harwell for B Flight.

It was about that time that a man on 107 Sqn. came back from a short navigation (sn) course at Hamble. Mother was living in

Southampton and two months nearby at Hamble seemed to be a good way to spend the rest of the summer while we were waiting for the new aircraft, so I applied. It hadn't occurred to me that sn courses might be held at other establishments until the notice came through attaching me to the School of Air Navigation at Manston in Kent, to which I drove in my second-hand Singer 9.

Its predecessor, my first, was an Austin 7 with a sunshine roof—a tiny car that used no oil and did about fifty miles to the gallon for the two months I owned it. With four passengers, its top speed was thirty-five miles per hour—just the thing for pub crawls (often with one man standing, with head through the sunshine roof, to lead the singing on the way home). The Singer was bigger, had four forward gears, and would go quite fast. Wheatley and I took it for a few days' leave to a village in Devon, where he fly-fished while I walked the countryside and we spent the evenings playing darts.

At Manston I made some new friends, learned quite a lot about navigation, and spent some cheerful evenings in Margate, Ramsgate, and Minnis Bay, where it must have been Bobby Seale, from Newtownards, who took the picture of David Martin-Barrett, Ken Doran, Leslie Smallman, Kevin McCrudden and me (with the Charatan pipe). Barrett was one of the few pilots I met—Willie Tait was another—who really knew about aircraft engines. Most of us took an absurdly cavalier attitude to them, as if they were the sole responsibility of the lower orders who proclaimed them service-able for us to take off with.

Thus, Barrett's car was a serious one, a new Fiat, and he liked to root around garages in search of vintage cars. I went with him once to a place on the North Foreland where we discovered a 1929 Vauxhall, with fluted bonnet, low windscreen, wire wheels, and leather upholstery, in a garage that boasted an RAC sign. The owner let us take it out and David got it to fifty-five in second gear before changing up and taking it to eighty.

One evening, Ken Doran broke his arm when I was driving the Singer back from Ramsgate. His arm was half out of the window and an oncoming car forced me to the side, where Ken's arm hit a telephone pole. Two years later, he won the first DFC of the war and was embarrassed to be identified in the audience of the theatre he'd gone to after getting his gong from the Palace, and being hauled up on to the stage. Afterwards he won a bar to the DFC and retired as a group captain in 1961. Barrett and McCrudden were shot down early on, but survived the war. Seale did not, and Leslie Smallman was killed in an Anson in New Brunswick in 1941, searching for another aircraft that had crashed. (His wife, Mollie, and baby, Peter, reached Canada after being rescued from the *Athenia* when she was torpedoed off the Hebrides on the first day of the war.)

At the end of the Manston course, when I had expected to return to Harwell, I was posted instead to No. 2 FTS at Brize Norton as an instructor. One of the course assignments had been to give a lecture on a subject of our own choosing. I picked the new gyro-driven instruments (artificial horizon and directional gyro), went to Sperry's in London to get sectional diagrams, and swotted it all up for the lecture.

Lecturing, after all, is a form of acting, and I enjoyed it for that reason. I spent two months at Brize Norton to learn the routine from another pilot officer, but senior to me, who was the Station Navigation Officer. During the expansion, it was quite common for pilot officers to command flights, to serve as squadron adjutants, and to fill the station jobs in charge of ground sections— Armament, Transport, Signals, Intelligence, Photography—which later became the prerogative of specialist officers.

Flight lieutenants even commanded squadrons; our first CO of 105 was Flt. Lieut. Roger Maw, and B Flight was commanded by P/O Dickie Wall. Dickie mortgaged his 300 pound gratuity in a rakish 1931 Lagonda that he spent hours polishing and tinkering with behind the mess at Harwell. Barely above the minimum height, he said he needed to stow an ammo box on the seat to see over the wheel. Dickie sported a fierce moustache which gave colour to his story about the convert at the Salvation Army meeting who, standing before the band and after admitting to coarse habits of old, would contrast them with his present condition and declare: "But now that I've been saved, I'm a changed man. I'm 'appy, that's what I am. I'm so 'appy, I could put my foot right through that fuckin' drum."

Brize Norton is near Burford, in the Cotswolds, where the houses and churches are built of stone that shows a hint of gold even on dull days, as if it remembers the sun and is merely waiting for it to come out again. Nearby is Minster Lovell on the Windrush, surely one of the prettiest names, and one of the prettiest villages, in England. At that station, I met a flight lieutenant not long back from India, who had me envious with descriptions of Kashmir, and another who lived in one of the married quarters and whose wife invited me to dine with them, my first introduction to what was known as the married patch.

In the short time I was at Brize Norton I flew a number of students on navigation tests, but one flight proved to be a test for me. On December 10, the station commander decided to go to Penrhos, where the senior term were doing the armament practices that we had done while seniors at Netheravon, and I was detailed to fly him there and back in a Hart.

The outward flight was uneventful, but after lunch the weather began coming in from the Irish Sea and I didn't much like the look of it. However, the group captain said he was game if I was, and we took off. Quite soon the cloud base lowered. I wasn't going to get mixed up in cloud over the Welsh Hills, so we followed the coast down to Aberaeron, where I figured we could get through the gap west of Brecon Beacons (2,907 ft.). This worked out reasonably well, but the visibility was poor. It was getting dark when we came out over the Bristol Channel, already close to two hours airborne and running short of fuel. By all sorts of luck, and with me frankly lost, I recognized Filton, circled until they got a flare path out, and was able to put the thing down (2 hr. 20 min.).

The station sent a staff car and someone else brought the Hart back the next day. Low flying in good weather is fun, but not late on a December afternoon, in the back seat of a Hart, with a bare 230 hours experience, with wisps of cloud floating under the wings and the knowledge that higher ground is about.

After two months I was posted from that delightful place to another FTS, where I spent four weeks of which not one cheerful memory survives: a dreary station on the edge of a railway town, staffed with grumpy senior officers whose names I've gladly forgotten, one of whom gave me a rocket for fraternizing with the pupil pilots at a pub in the town where I had driven one evening in desperation to escape the dreadful mess.

Relief came with a posting to No. 11 FTS at Wittering, not far away in a neighbouring county, but otherwise in a different world—a permanent station built in the 1920s, with married quarters, a comfortable mess looking out on well-tended grounds, and as cheery a crowd of officers as you could wish to meet.

Among them was Wheatley's older brother Terry, who had completed a medium-service commission and was re-employed as Assistant Adjutant. He drove an MG Magnette and gave me a ride to London once or twice when I went to stay at the Hendon mess for a night in the West End with Wheatley or Boris.

Terry and his wife bought two adjoining cottages at Saxmundham and knocked out the common wall to make a decent-sized sitting room with the chimney piece standing proud in the centre, so that you could sit on either side of the fire. It was about a dozen miles inland from the Suffolk coast, not far from Martlesham Heath, where Terry had been stationed in the Met. Flight. He and I flew there for a weekend at the beginning of April, when daffodils were out and primroses were in the hedgerows where we walked the lanes.

The Met. Flight was a dangerous game which called for climbing in all weathers to the service ceiling of the aircraft—single seat Furies, and later, Gauntlets—to take temperature readings before letting down on a radio bearing. Terry didn't talk about it, but I found out from other sources that it called for two flights a day, early morning and noon, taking temperature readings at every 50 millibars of decreasing pressure up to 22,000 feet. The only aids were an ultra-sensitive aneroid to register height above the airfield and a standard TR9 transmitter/receiver for air-to-ground communication. This was generally regarded as one of the toughest flying jobs in the RAF, and the enemy, as always, was the weather. Squadron Leader D.H. Clarke, DFC, AFC, in his book *What Were They Like to Fly?* described one incident:

> That particular morning there was a thick mist which merged into a low cloud-base. The visibility was no more than twenty to thirty yards. I conducted [Warrant Officer Bill] Bailey to the take-off point by running at his wing-tip and steering, when necessary, by dragging or pushing on the wing; I found the boundary fence, checked the faint breeze by the feel on my cheeks, and turned him into wind. His head ducked into the cockpit as he set the wind on his com-

pass; then he waved, the Mercury's burble changed to crackling power, and he was gone—the mist swirling and curling in the slipstream.

To bring Bailey down again, Clarke stood in the middle of the airfield and stationed airmen at 30-yard intervals back to the flying control office. As soon as Clarke heard Bailey's engine, his shouted message—"He's to the northeast, about five miles"—was relayed via control to Bailey, and revised until he was judged overhead. From that point, it was up to Bailey. Knowing his speed and altitude, he performed a timed approach by means of Rate One turns and reducing height to land through the mist. All this was in a Gauntlet biplane fighter, and Clarke added, "The preparations for ensuring his safe return were almost impossibly crude—*and yet it needed only four months to the declaration of war!*"

Two things happened at Wittering, both to do with flying. The first was when Desmond McGlinn, another instructor, took off for a weather test in a Fury. I happened to be on the flight line and watched him disappear into cloud at about 150 feet. Then I listened to the sound of the Kestrel and pictured him, eyes glued to the turn and bank indicator, altimeter and compass, while the Kestrel's snarl faded on the descending turn from the downwind leg and the Fury reappeared, fish-tailing to lose speed, and landed on three points about halfway along the grass field.

When I asked him about it, he said it was simple: you watched your rate of turn, you knew your air speed, there was no wind near the surface, you timed your downwind leg, watched your turn again, slipped off some height, and there was the field in front of you. Desmond was the only pilot I knew who had an Exceptional rating in his log book (he didn't tell me—I saw it once in the book).

The other occasion was a visit from three German Air Force officers on a training mission. I was too junior to join in the formal discussions, which I would think were pretty guarded, but close enough to the group in the ante-room to hear how good their English was and to see how easily, apart from the different uniforms, they could have passed for RAF officers. One was Ernst Udet, an ace from the Great War who did some interesting things between the wars, including designing a kind of flying bomb, but whom Goering put into a senior staff job that didn't suit his talents. He made a botch of it and shot himself on November 17, 1941—a case of what KR & ACI called Officer Unsuitable For His Posting.

In April 1938, the school was moved to a safer location at Shawbury, in Shropshire on the Welsh border, where we were under canvas until quite late in the year, late enough to find frost on our beds the odd morning. North American Aviation had a hangar on the far side of the field where Harvards were assembled and tested, subjecting the quiet countryside to the peculiar propeller whine of that famous trainer.

Two USAAC officers—Capt. Burton, i/c production, and Lieut. Wilcox Wild, the test pilot—were the first Americans I had met, and Wild particularly was a fine ambassador in that conservative English county. He and his blonde wife lived in one of the new married quarters and introduced us to the barbecue and other facets of America's hospitality. He sported a Kirsten pipe, an aluminum-stemmed device I had seen advertised in *Esquire*, and we had friendly arguments about its vaunted merits vs. the old-fashioned kind.

However, Wilcox wasn't smoking when he decided to test a Harvard one night when we were night-flying. I didn't like to ask him if he'd flown much at night; at any rate, when he'd been airborne for more than an hour, I began to worry—especially because, as station navigation officer, it would be my job to lay on a search. I had visions of wreckage somewhere in the hills to the west. To my relief, about thirty minutes later, we heard the familiar whine. Wilcox landed alongside the flare path, taxied around to the duty pilot, and shouted "Where can I buy some gas? I've got to get back to Shawbury tonight."

Flying in those days had its advantages. There was no radio. Even if you weren't sure where you were, no one else knew, either. You could land, if you felt like it, in a field. You could also, in that pleasant pre-war flying club, drift off to have lunch with friends at their messes or borrow one of His Majesty's sports models for a weekend, as I did to Southampton a number of times, to Finningley once to stay with a friend from Bristol days, to Driffield to see Proc, and to Cardiff for Joan Burpitt's wedding. (On the way back from Cardiff, the cloud base lowered when I was following a valley and I had to do a smart-stall turn to get out again.)

For special occasions, we would lay on formation flying and aerobatic displays for the local populace, nine Harts at a time in formation and Desmond McGlinn doing the solo aerobatics in a Fury or a Gauntlet. The Hart cruised at 120 mph and stalled at about 55, and the worst place to be was wing man in a line-abreast formation.

When the formation was flying straight and level, all you had to do was keep abreast of the man on your left (if you were at the right end) or right (if you were at the left end), and you could also see the others in line to keep you straight. But when the formation turned, two things happened, both to the wing men. Let's say the turn is left. Numbers Two and Three on either side of the formation leader in the centre see his helmeted head nodding left and start their turns, followed by Number Four, formating on Number Two, while Number Five formates on Number Three, and so on, along to the ends where Number Nine, at the left end, formates on Number Seven, and Number Eight, at the right end, formates on Number Six. Now, the whole line of nine aircraft is tilted at about forty-five degrees on its side. At the right (top) end, Number Eight has his throttle well forward, struggling to keep his position, seeing the line below him and the ground below that, and feeling suspended by a hair from falling on to Number Six. Meanwhile at the bottom, Number Nine is throttled back, feels as if he is hanging on his prop, and is looking *up* at the line (and the sky beyond) that seems to be falling on him. After that, landing in formation was a piece of cake—as well as being, on a grass field that allowed plenty of room for nine at once, rather a pretty sight.

It was all open-cockpit flying, mostly by day, sometimes at night, when map-reading was made easy by the lights of the towns. When, too, if you were Duty Pilot, you stood at the downwind end of the flare path, holding the Aldis lamp to flick red or green at the aircraft in the circuit, and then watched as they came, in turn, low over the hedge, holding, holding, to land on the right-hand side of the paraffin flares. Especially at an FTS, you were never so close to the feel of flying as in that moment before the touchdown when you saw the instructor, goggles and helmeted head over the side of the rear cockpit, tensed and ready to take over if things went wrong. Anyone who has taught flying will remember—that was when you were really paying attention.

Open-cockpit flying had its drawbacks, but on a fine day, flying low over the Welsh border country or the Yorkshire Moors and watching the greens and browns passing below the wings, there was nothing to touch it.

Shrewsbury was our nearest town, seven miles away, and although there were some villages round about, social life for young officers was pretty well limited to the offspring of whoever among the local gentry chose to call on the mess. Since I was Mess Secretary, seeing that mess calls were returned was one of my jobs. These led eventually to the odd tennis party and hunt ball, in the course of which we met some nice people and even one or two closely guarded girls. Shropshire was army territory, and this was brought home to another man and me when we made one of the calls. While we balanced teacups, smiled a good deal, and chatted desultorily, our hostess, who I noticed had been staring at us, suddenly asked me, "Mr. McDonald, what is your *rank*?"

"Flying officer," I said, and seeing her puzzled expression, added, "like a first lieutenant." The frown gave way to a look that contrived to mix comprehension with a nice touch of disdain as she said, "Ah! But the air force isn't quite *army*, is it?"

By this time I had exchanged the Singer for a second-hand Ford 8. It came equipped with a reconditioned engine which required running in at thirty miles per hour for 500 miles, and I was able to cover the balance of those by driving to Wheatley's wedding near Lewes, where his bride, Joan, lived. Driving back after the wedding, I stopped at a pub for a sandwich, got into conversation with a pleasant fellow who was heading for Badminton in Devon, and gave him a lift as far as Salisbury—during which he talked me into lending him five pounds I could ill afford to lose, but, when my subsequent letter to the address he gave me came back undelivered, did.

Wheatley was still at Harwell, now equipped with Battles. Peter's 16 Squadron Hectors had been replaced by short-nosed Blenheims, Boris was flying Wellingtons in Suffolk, and Proc was in Yorkshire, flying Whitleys. In the messes and pubs, we spoke about the war that was coming, and at the time of Munich, everyone was on standby. We felt strongly that we should be backing the Czechs, whose thirty-five divisions and powerful defences could more than hold the Nazis at bay while Britain and France attacked in the west. Even at FTSs we hung bombs on our Harts and Audaxes, and didn't leave the stations without depositing a telephone number where we could be reached.

The Spanish Civil War was going strong and we didn't like the idea of the Luftwaffe and the Regia Aeronautica getting in all that practice. Peter and Valerie were married on April 22, 1939, Proc soon after, but it must have been 1940 or 1941 before Boris's wedding, because there's no mention of Madge in his long letter to me written from Hendon in February 1940.

On three occasions I flew to Southampton for weekends with Mother, and drove there at least twice for trips we made together to Bristol to stay with the Stuckeys at their new house on Pinecroft Avenue, and to Chard to stay with Aunt Treca, widowed by then and keeping house for her son, Alan, who worked in the National Provincial Bank there. I remember standing with René Stuckey, his grey hair turned white, drinking gin with a dash of sherry before lunch while Mother and Alice caught up with each other in the kitchen.

In Chard, Treca had a house on the main street, flat-fronted, with a passage at the side leading to a walled garden. Tom came with us on that trip. I remember driving with him to Lyme Regis early one morning and the two of us swimming well out into the bay, the sea calm as a lake.

Alan had kept up an early fascination with conjuring tricks and performed at parties in the neighbourhood. He introduced me to scrumpy, the Somerset cider which had a much stronger punch than beer, and was then 3d the pint in country pubs. One evening we took two girls out, one probably the Joan he later married, and the other whose only feature I remember was a chest of heroic proportions.

Desmond McGlinn, rather like Boris, was one of those thoughtful, serious men that it's so rewarding to say things to that make them laugh. We put in our fair share of walking in that A.E. Housman countryside. Desmond was an instructor for the senior term, and when it was the current senior term's time to do their armament practice at Penrhos, I would go there for several days to fly final navigation tests. On one occasion, I was able to demonstrate the impetuous side of my nature by flying an Audax back to Shawbury on the assumption that it was needed there. It wasn't, and the squadron leader who commanded the Advanced Training Squadron drew my attention to the telephone standing on his desk. Many years later, I re-learned the lesson from a journalist who kept a piece of paper by the typewriter with the admonition "Never assume!"

One of the navigation tests illustrated for me the part imagination plays in instrument flying, when you have to force yourself to trust the instruments despite contrary signals from the physical senses. The test was to take off on instruments, climb to 5,000 feet, and fly a triangular course of about 180 miles over North Wales. The student worked out his courses from the forecast wind and we were in clear air long enough for me to check it and give him a course correction for the first leg, which took us over the lower slopes of Mt. Snowdon, the highest point in Wales at 3,560 feet. By then we were in cloud, which persisted until I instructed him to let down and we came out over Tremadoc Bay. All this time he was under the hood, concentrating on the instruments and oblivious of the weather outside. After we landed and I told him we had been in cloud most of the way, he went white in the face at the thought of flying over the unseen high ground.

The Clarke from whose book I quoted tells of a chilling experience in the Met. Flight when he had only 170 hours in his log book. The pilot who was detailed for the morning flight was delayed getting to the airfield, and Clarke had to make it in drizzling rain and with a cloud base no more than 300 feet. At 10,000 feet, still in cloud, he lost control, got into a spin, and managed to recover just before breaking cloud in the dive at 300 feet. By great good fortune, he was in a valley with enough room to haul back on the Gauntlet's stick and tear through the tops of trees to reach the airfield. He wrote: "From that dreadful morning onwards I was never able to fly in cloud again and I must be the only pilot to survive the war who was absolutely incapable of flying blind! And for the whole of the war not a soul discovered my blind fear."

Clarke was lucky, as was any aircrew member who survived those years and the war that followed. Of the forty-seven pilots who gathered at Netheravon in September 1936, I know of only ten, including me, who survived the war. Ian Swayne, who transferred to the Fleet Air Arm before the war and took part, in 1940, in the historic torpedo attack on the Italian fleet at anchor in the port of

Taranto, was killed in a train crash at King's Cross in 1944. Gilbert Haworth, a retired squadron leader who lived in Rutland, told me in a letter: "After three years of war I was the only survivor of my 1938 course."

In the four years from the time the expansion started in 1935, young men of the British Commonwealth learned the rudiments of air warfare with the aid of inadequate equipment. Attracted to the RAF for a number of reasons, they did not deserve to die in such numbers.

Yet throughout those years, a spirit was abroad that lingers like the glow in Cotswold stone. As the young men parade before the eye of memory, they are laughing, jumping into and out of old cars, standing before the fire in messes, sitting in flight offices on foggy days, playing darts or nattering by the bar in pubs that lent their names to the time: Ram Jam; Raven; Alice Hawthorn; Haycock; Half Moon; Randolph; Shepherd's; Vaynol; Bull; Lamb; George.

It was in the Green Man at Steventon that Wheatley won a game outright with three darts in the double nineteen, but our favourite was the Harrow, standing beside a lane two or three miles from where we crossed the boundary of Harwell's grass air-field. There, early of a summer evening, we would join the sunken road that led to the pub, striding between the hedgerows and mar-velling at the swifts' superb airmanship as they swept in front of us to brush the knobbly tarred surface of the road and whirr ahead in climbing turns.

Boris was at home in the West End, where we would start off at The Cossack with Barclay's Russian Stout and work our way west. The photograph of him at the nightclub in Paris captures the atmosphere he relished. His ambition for a career on the stage after RAF service was linked with the idea of going to Hollywood to try his luck.

Peter hoped his gratuity would help him qualify as a veteri-narian. Proc spoke vaguely of farming. Wheatley's lively mind and cheerful presence would have met opportunities to match. The young men dreamed of futures different from pasts that had dis-appointed them. For too many, the future was short-lived.

Chapter 3
❂ 1939—1942 ❂

Sometime in 1938, when Desmond and I were at Shawbury, a notice in station orders invited applications for service in Australia, Canada, Rhodesia, or South Africa. Attracted to the idea of travel, we put in our names and forgot about it until the following summer when the station adjutant called us in to sign a form extending our short-service commissions from four to six years, and soon after that we were posted to Canada.

When I told him about the posting, Johnnie McKid, a Canadian who was in the graduating class, said to me: "Mac, you're going to civilization." Johnnie was also a qualified aeronautical engineer. Years after the war, I learned that he was killed on April 27, 1942, when a small force of thrty-one Halifaxes and twelve Lancasters attacked the *Tirpitz* and other German warships in Trondheim Fjord. Johnnie was then on a second tour of operations after having won the DFC on his first.

Passage was slated for the Cunarder *Ausonia*, sailing from Southampton on August 19, which gave me a chance to spend the embarkation leave with Mother. When Desmond and I boarded, we found five more pilots in the party: Flight Lieutenants Mellor and Waterhouse; Flying Officer Smallman; and Flight Sergeants Abercrombie and Willis.

We docked long enough at Quebec City to walk up to the Chateau Frontenac, and the next day we reached Montreal, where two RCAF officers—Flt. Lieut. Bill Proctor, and F/O Harvey Jasper—

had brought a Norseman on floats alongside to take us to Trenton.

This introduction to Canada was very much in line with Johnnie McKid's forecast. Moreover, since August 27 was a Sunday, we reached Trenton's mess in the afternoon to find the spacious ante-room filled with cheerful officers and their wives or girlfriends, all joining to give us the kind of welcome that Canadians are noted for.

Four days later, Desmond and I were posted to Camp Borden, Desmond as a flying instructor and yours truly to replace Joe Gutray as the station navigation officer. Bill Proctor flew us there in a Fairchild 71, and we liked the feel of the place right away: less formal than Trenton, and with its line of Bessonneau hangars from the Great War reminding me of the RFC connection that had stamped Netheravon.

When the war started, Canada made her own declaration on September 10. Camp Borden's CO, Wing Commander (later Air Vice-Marshal) Leigh Stevenson, called the small band of officers together in front of the old wooden mess, told us that the war was on, that we were officers and it was our duty to lead, and that if we saw anything that needed doing, we shouldn't wait to be told but get on with it, pretty much all in that one sentence.

Jackie Mellor and Dick Waterhouse, both of them my age but senior to me from having joined three years earlier, immediately put in applications to return to England for active service. Although I did the same, it was only for the sake of unanimity. The RAF had posted me to Canada, and when it wanted to send me somewhere else, it would do so. Nor did it seem likely that, having gone to the expense of sending us to help in setting up a mammoth training scheme, it would have much sympathy for appeals, however nobly motivated, to reverse course.

Jackie felt strongly that the RAF's job was to fight the King's enemies, that he had been trained to do that, and he renewed his applications regularly for as long as he was at Borden. When he did go into action, he did predictably well and finished the war with a DSO and DFC.

In an effort to get the most out of a limited number of aircraft and instructors, we worked 24 hours on, 24 hours off—the idea being that one shift would hand over to the next at midday, when the shift that was relieved would rest for twenty-four hours.

Instead, as soon as we had eaten lunch on the days off, we piled into cars and headed south for Toronto and the Royal York Hotel, where the fourth floor came to be set aside for the RCAF.

I remember arriving there one mid-afternoon with Jackie Mellor, and after we had stacked the dresser with bottles of Cincinnati Cream (The Handsome Waiter) and laid the remainder in the half-filled tub, we went across Front Street to Union Station and walked along the tracks to where a giant Canadian Pacific engine was hissing and grunting, with its two engineers aboard. We were in uniform, accepted their invitation to climb into the cab, and spent the next while getting some dual on the controls. By the time we got back to the room, others had arrived, and the party followed its customary course. Instructors and (provisional) pilot officers, some of them with girlfriends, would drift from room to room, talking about flying, or the war, or Toronto, or England, glasses in hands, most people smoking (Sweet Caporals, Macdonald's Export, Players' Mild, Pall Mall), until the supper dance drew the crowd to the Imperial Room. Then, because Ontario's liquor law prohibited drinking anything in public except wine or beer, bottles would be hidden under tables to strengthen the mixes from the bottles on top.

Pluto, Dick Waterhouse's black Labrador, would be there, perfectly trained to sit, if instructed, in the middle of the floor while couples danced around him. When the last waltz had been waltzed, people streamed back to the rooms and kept the thing going until the small hours, so that usually it was light by the time we headed north for Borden. None too soon, the 24-hour schedule was changed, but the parties continued as fresh courses of (P)POs savoured the delights of the city.

Until Harvards started to come through from the States—pulled across the border with ropes, at first, to avoid infringing the US's neutrality—Borden had an interesting assortment of aircraft: Fleet, Lockheed 10, Bellanca, Fairchild 71, Northrop Delta, Oxford. It was in a Fleet that I had my second forced landing, a painless affair on September 27 when Desmond and I flew to Fort Erie to collect another Fleet and were obliged to put down in a field in bad weather.

The Lockheed 10s—L 1526 and L 1529—were two of three requisitioned from Trans-Canada Airlines, and I used them a few times as aerial classrooms: students would map-read, lay off courses and calculate the winds, while I wandered up and down the aisle checking the work. On one flight, we got into cloud soon after takeoff on a triangular cross-country to Brantford, Niagara and return, and were in cloud most of the way, with yours truly working quite hard that time at the DR plot, until I gave the signal to let down, fingers crossed, and out we came slap over the airfield at Borden.

Not long after that, a newspaper wanted some publicity shots. I flew the photographer, a Mr. Barlow, in the chase Harvard, echelon right from a vic formation of three. Without radio, I had no means of knowing that Bill MacBrien, flying No. 2, would decide to do a slow roll off the final dive over the airfield. I was echelon right from him, the camera whirring in the back seat, when suddenly there was Bill, inverted and above us and on his way down to our right. Instinctively I hauled on stick and rudder in a ragged climbing turn that got us clear, it seemed by inches, but was probably a foot or two.

Waterhouse, Mellor, McGlinn and I pooled our scarce dollars (we were on RAF rates of pay, which didn't go very far even when the pay managed to catch up with us) in a 1937 Pontiac sedan and shared it on a first-come, first-served basis until Ruth and I became engaged and I bought the others out. My first solo in a Canadian car had been in Keith Hodson's Plymouth coupe when I had to go down to the hangars from the mess, and he just handed me his keys and said, "Take mine." Typical of a Canadian, but in that particular case of an outstanding officer in whose memory (Air Vice-Marshal Keith Hodson, OBE, DFC*) the RCAF Staff College library is dedicated.

The students were much like those we had known in England, many of whom were Canadians. In Canada, although there was no lack of discipline, the relationship between students and instructors was much less formal, especially off duty, than in England, where the staff had a separate ante-room in the mess and fraternizing with the students (pupils) was discouraged.

Borden's airfield was grass, as were those we had flown from in England, and when the snow came it was compacted with rollers, a typically practical Canadian approach to the local conditions in that heavy snow belt. After England's damp cold (especially *inside*), we didn't feel the cold the first winter and rarely wore greatcoats, while in messes and houses, we roasted.

The bush pilots who came through for refresher training were older and in many cases had more flying experience, certainly more varied experience, than we did. I remember asking Mac Hallatt what he and his partner did to pass the time in Canada's north when weather grounded them. He said when they got bored they would stand outside the tent and slog each other. Mac was a big, husky chap, and I remember one evening at a room in Barrie's Queen's Hotel when, toward the end, he went to the wash basin in the corner and wrenched it away from the wall.

When Ansons arrived at Borden, I used them as flying class-rooms. The bush pilots would take it in turns as first pilot while I sat in the right-hand seat or wandered about the cabin checking the logs, and it was the accepted drill that when we were on finals, the "navigators" who had nothing else to do would run back and forth in the cabin to change the trim for the man in the left-hand seat, battling with the control column.

Joffre Wolfenden (Wg Cdr RCAF Ret'd) has a story about that early period. He was a (P)P/O at Trenton when Wing Commander C.M. McEwen, the station commander (later A/V/M McEwen and commander of 6 Group), returned from Ottawa, where he was briefed about the forthcoming British Commonwealth Air Training Plan and what it would mean—expansion, of course, but also promotion. Sitting in the mess, McEwen looked around the group, nodded to a senior flying officer—"You'll probably be a squadron leader"—to a flight lieutenant—"You'll be a wing commander"—and then to Joffre—"As for you, you little bastard, you'll be dead."

Those first few weeks were filled with a sense of foreignness combined with kinship, and a daily realization of how practical and down-to-earth Canadians were. When Wing Commander Leigh Stevenson lined up the small group of officers on September 10—wedge cap above worn face, bent nose, good eyes—and told us if we saw something that needed doing, we shouldn't wait to be told but get on with it, he epitomized that sense. It was reinforced, as time went on, by the Canadian blend of service discipline and training with the expertise and management capabilities of the entrepreneurs who ran the civilian-operated schools that played such a major part in the success of the whole training effort.

The town nearest to Borden was Barrie, where I met Ruth Margaret Craig on a blind date in September, courtesy of Jean Lay, who ran The Flower Bar at the five points. Its back room was a rendezvous for many of the instructors, one of whom—Flt. Lieut. Gordie Dunlop—Jean married the following February.

Ruth and I got on well from the start, did most of our familiarization in Barrie pubs, the Royal York and King Edward hotels, became engaged in February 1940, and were married on May 17 (Desmond was best man). That is sixty years ago as I write, but I can recapture as if it were yesterday the excitement that centred on the young, fair-haired woman who always seemed glad to see me, whose eyes lit up when I made her laugh, who made me laugh in turn, who exuded an air of calmness, and yet was game for any of the activities that turned up, usually at short notice.

No doubt some of the attraction was due to the surface differences. I was from England, which was still the mother country, redolent with history and investing me and the other RAF types with whiffs of its glamorous past. Ruth exemplified the new country I was trying to understand, seeing my native differences through her eyes as did she through mine what was familiar to her. Calmness, courage, a sense of humour, the physical features that drew me to her were fortified by abiding qualities of a high order. (When I spent those six weeks in the Toronto Hospital, Ruth came all the way downtown every day, driving herself or taking public transport, so that we could be together.)

One of the advantages of being married to someone who is a true companion is that you share many of the memories; without having to say much, chance sights and sounds will trigger recollections of people and places you enjoyed, or didn't enjoy, and the shared experiences draw you closer still. Marriage, apart from being the origin of the family and the single most powerful influence for good in any community, like everything else worth having, takes a lot of work—especially at first, when the differences start to register. But as the years go on, the differences grow less pronounced, the two learn from one another. They also see themselves reproduced in the children, recognize some of their own failings, are relieved to discern a better nature than they had at the same age, or a sharper intelligence, and draw comfort from reflection that yes, perhaps the race is on the move.

Top of Ruth's and my prescriptions for a successful marriage is politeness, and that involves proscriptions. You learn not to criticize the other, especially not in public or in front of the children, avoid topics that lead toward places where you don't see eye-to-eye, and avoid reminiscing about circumstances where you didn't see eye-to-eye in the past. This doesn't mean that you won't disagree about things or argue, merely that you are careful to stop the disagreements and the arguments before they get out of hand; tactical retreats work well for both parties in the knowledge that the other will return to the charge when the climate is right, and the thing will be finessed to the common satisfaction.

Nor is this toleration. The great thing about loving your wife or husband is that you love them in spite of their faults: faults you both know you have. Nor is it dull. Loving someone and living with them every day is exciting, rewarding, stimulating. Even now, after sixty years of marriage, when one of us is sitting in the car somewhere, and the other is walking back to it, we watch, and remember all the other times and places, and think how good the other is looking, considering.

In May 1940, however, we were too taken up with ourselves to look beyond the next day. Added to the pervading uncertainty of wartime were the more immediate uncertainties of accommodation and of that concomitant of service life: the posting. Ruth's father, who had been mayor of Barrie a number of times and was consequently a figure of some renown, found us a ground-floor flat in the Bayview Apartments that backed on to the Kempenfeldt Bay of Lake Simcoe where Barrie is situated. A sister-in-law helped us get furniture together. We were there for four months, until I was posted to Trenton for the specialist navigation course. Ruth found us rooms in a boarding house in Belleville (our Barrie apartment was snapped up by a young couple in the army).

A month later, the navigation school was moved about 1,500 miles west to Rivers, Manitoba. My letter to the mayor brought word that a Mrs. Bradt would be glad to accommodate us. Five couples drove in convoy to catch the ferry across Lake Superior before freeze-up, were snowed in for three days at Dryden, and reached Rivers a week after leaving Trenton.

I'm the optimist, Ruth the realist, but it was too early in our marriage for her to discount my mental image of this apple-cheeked widow standing at the picket fence before her neat house to welcome us, so that you could understand Ruth's disappointment when we turned right from the railroad station along the main street to find, fronting on the snow at the end, a grey frame cottage to one side of which stood what appeared to be a water pump.

Our room was equipped with a pull-out couch, a side table on which was a two-burner fed by gas from a cylinder, and some furniture. Water was drawn by yours truly from the pump, but there was no water available in the basement where the chemical toilet was installed. It sat proud near the furnace, and Ruth screamed just in time to stop Mr. Bradt's feet from descending the steps when she was in possession the first day. I persuaded him to put a bolt on the inside of the door. Ruth and Dorothy Birchall spent a good deal of time at the depot within reach of waterborne sanitation.

The course included astronomical navigation and occasionally I brought a sextant home to practice, when Ruth and I would stand outside the house in the prevailing sub-zero temperatures, Ruth with a flashlight to write down the readings as I called them out. In the warmth of the house I would then use Dreisenstock's Tables to translate the readings into an assertion that we were at, or at least fairly near, Rivers, Manitoba.

When the course ended eight weeks later, I was posted to Regina, where we checked in at the Saskatchewan Hotel in company with a number of service couples who said they had combed the city for apartments without success. But Ruth went househunting on foot, and within a day or two had us installed in a second-floor corner flat of the new Grenfell Apartments. Moreover, because the flat was unfurnished, this resourceful young woman talked a Mr. Derby, who ran a furniture store, into renting us enough items to furnish the bedroom, sitting room and kitchen.

Our three-month stay at Regina was average for that period of the war, when airfields were being opened up across the country, new headquarters established to administer them, and experienced people were at a premium.

But our move from there to Portage la Prairie was a lucky one, just over a year in duration, most of which was spent, after a month in rooms, in a large house converted by the company that operated the school into the Crescent Apartments for the company's senior staff and us. Our ground-floor flat had a bay window, hardwood floors, and two six-foot partitions that split it into sitting-room, bedroom, and kitchen; the bathroom was along the hall.

My job was Chief Supervisory Officer of No.7 Air Observer School. Cy Becker, an Edmonton lawyer who had been a fighter pilot in World War I, was the Manager, Matt Berry the Operations Manager, and Scotty Moir the Chief Pilot. They and their civilian staff flew and maintained the Ansons and looked after the infrastructure, without any fuss but with great efficiency.

My first flight into Portage was in a DH Dragonfly from Regina, when the field was still frozen. My second was with Scotty, delivering an Anson after the thaw, when the field was gumbo. He put on full flap, held it with power on just above the stall, sideslipped off the last 100 feet, and landed on the hangar apron.

Another incident I remember was when one of the civilian pilots let a (non-flying) service instructor take over the controls of an Anson, and the latter made an ass of himself by flying it low over Portage. Technically, it was a court-martial offence, but Matt Berry dropped by the office with his slow, quizzical smile, and said, "Ken, why don't you have your guy in and make him wish he'd never been born, and I'll do the same with my guy? No one was hurt, they won't do it again, and there'll be no paper."

That was the spirit I remember from those days in Canada: getting on with things without a lot of fuss; in fact, taking things for granted that, as I look back on them now—the airfields, aircraft, and all that went into them—were tremendous achievements.

While we were enjoying this varied but safe existence, terrible things had been happening to my friends. The Battle squadrons of the Advanced Air Striking Force were shot out of the sky in May 1940. In Chaz Bowyer's *History of the RAF*, he reports that:

> The loss rate for May 10-11-12 was frightening—40 per cent, 100 per cent, and 62 per cent respectively. Of nearly 140 bombers serviceable on the morning of the 10th, the AASF was reduced to 72 by dusk on the 12th... In the late afternoon [of the 14th] the entire AASF's bombers made their attack on the Sedan bridgehead—71 Blenheims and Battles from 12, 105, 139, 150 and 218 squadrons—and 40 never came back, the highest loss rate ever experienced by the RAF to date...

Between May 10 and June 15 alone the AASF had lost 115 aircraft and almost as many crews—virtually the entire strength available on the opening day of the German blitzkrieg.

Our only sources of personal news were letters from home and the casualty lists that began to appear in *Flight* and *The Aeroplane*. Wheatley wrote from France, in part as follows:

...Week after week of inactivity with an occasional scare that brought us untimely from our beds to shiver on the tarmac in 40 degrees of frost waiting with mixed emotions for the order to get cracking on our first raid. Only once did I fly over enemy territory at what I thought was the comparatively safe height of 21,500 feet. The Germans resented the intrusion... puffs of HE shells appeared all round my aeroplane— so this was war! They looked so harmless and I was surprised to find myself rather enjoying the experience. The net result was two small shrapnel holes in the wing.

In December came leave and that amazing afternoon when I actually found myself on Lewes platform with Joan held so tight she couldn't breathe. So for ten halcyon days and then back again to the routine. Shortly after, a letter came round asking for volunteers for a new secret flight being formed in England. I plonked in my name and forgot about it. Then we went to Perpignan for a practice camp and dropped bombs in the Med. It was a wonderful place— snow-capped Pyrenees towered over us 15 miles away, the mimosa was in full bloom, there was no black-out, and the local brew was a pleasing wine called Muscat. On the last day but one I was standing in the sun when the squadron leader came up and said, "Catch the train tomorrow, Wheatley, and get to Heston as soon as you can!"

Three days later I was at Heston. This was on February 22 and today (March 19) I have just learned that I am to stay here indefinitely. There were ten other chaps here when I arrived and they were going to select six. The tests were mainly extra stiff medical ones and the machines we fly— Spitfires! Yes, believe it or not, old boy, I am actually flying Spitfires with a Blenheim, a Harvard and a Hudson thrown in. Unfortunately I can't tell you anything about the job because it's desperately "cloak and dagger" but you can take it from me that it's the most interesting job in the RAF today and there isn't a pilot born who wouldn't give his soul to be in my shoes.

Too soon after that letter, Wheatley's name was in the list under Missing, believed killed in action. Much later I learned that he was killed on what must have been one of the first PRU (Photographic Reconnaissance Unit) sorties, in an unarmed Spitfire (N 3069) on March 22, 1940.

Following the German breakthrough in May, there were many familiar names in the lists, including Peter Murdoch's. I learned many years afterwards that he was shot down in a long-nosed Blenheim,

> ...taking off from an advanced landing strip near Lille in May 1940... while hedge-hopping two AA batteries opened up on me at close range, engines kaput, etc. Navigator had unfortunately a bullet with his name on it. It was then I can only imagine the kitchen sink they threw at me that took the nose cone away. Somehow or other my rear gunner and I got away with it.
>
> After that it was only a question of time when a German motorized unit captured us and one Stalag or Oflag after another followed including a very severe winter at a place called Poznan in Poland. But I tried to keep mentally and physically fit and took part in some tunnelling and diversions of escape including one with Douglas Bader and another with the Wooden Horse. Finally liberated by the Russians— what an uncouth, cruel lot they were. The Americans got us out in the end.
>
> My elder brother Fred met his death in a tank battle at Lille a day or two after my disaster.

Boris Romanoff was killed in a Whitley, March 15, 1942. Just before we left Portage, a parcel arrived from Madge with a new suede zipper jacket that she thought he would have wanted me to have. After the war I learned that he was in 138 Special Duties squadron, based at Tempsford—the squadron that dropped people and supplies into occupied France.

Proctor survived the war after a series of vicissitudes that he described to me in a long letter in the 1980s ("the massive missive"), and which included crash landing a Wellington on the night of September 23/24 1940, the RAF's first raid on Berlin:

...and getting hopelessly lost on our return through a front with the radio U/S... flew through the Southampton balloon barrage, setting off the sirens, only to find the area fogbound. Petrol being non-existent, found a wee hole in the fog and after a couple of attempts landed in a ploughed field... through the fog emerged the farmer and his man behind a pair of shotguns, and I yelled "It's all right, we're English, don't shoot!" It transpired we had landed about 15 miles from Andover.

When the bombing started, Mother and Tom moved in with Treca, whose house in Swaythling was well away from the city centre and farther still from the docks. Grandmother Balston and Ada also moved there when houses on Milton Road were hit, but afterwards they went to Poole, where Grandmother Balston died in August 1942 at the age of 89. Avenue House, where Dad's youngest sister, Auntie Kit, lived, was hit. Although she had to move, she kept the office going at Avenue House with tarpaulins over the damaged parts.

Mother wrote regularly, but didn't say much about the bombing except that it was a nuisance, and made jokes about huddling under the stairs for safety. In the last letter she wrote, June 21, 1942, which caught up with me after we left Portage, she must have known she had cancer, but said little about herself.

I had flown a Ventura from Gander to Prestwick (after landing short of fuel at Eglinton, in Northern Ireland); ten hours and twenty minutes to Eglinton. We had been in Montreal for the month of June while I converted to the Hudson. After two nights in the Mount Royal Hotel and learning that I would probably be there for two or three weeks, Ruth found us a room we could afford in Mme. Trudel's house on Bishop Street, saw me off every morning in the scheduled bus that left Dominion Square for Dorval, and spent her days pretty much alone until I came back in the late afternoon.

On July 3, I took a Ventura on a cross-country to Pennfield Ridge and was fogbound there until the 6th—a rotten time for

Ruth, because we knew I would be leaving almost at once when I got back. At Pennfield, I ran across Spanner Spence, who had been a flight commander at Shawbury, was now a wing commander, and had been operating in Bomber Command. He was a portly chap with a sallow complexion, and he confided, when I asked him what it was like, "Mac, it was awful," on which cheery note I winged my way back to Dorval.

Two days later, after a forlorn parting with Ruth in Dominion Square, I took off for Gander. At the Met. office there, when I was laying off courses to match the forecast winds (since I was a specialist navigator, I was allotted a second pilot and handed a sextant), an Imperial Airways captain standing alongside asked me what I was doing. When I told him, he said, "Good Lord, I always steer 092 and it works like a charm."

Apart from the sextant's light bulb giving out halfway across, and, as I mentioned before, the fuel running a bit short, the flight was uneventful. We took on fuel at Eglinton, passed the leftover packets of sandwiches to the RAF groundcrew—the first white bread they'd seen for two years—ate and slept at Prestwick, and then went on by train to London and, in my case, Southampton, to wait for a posting.

This allowed me to spend time with Mother and Treca, as well as Tom, and to see Auntie Kit. There was a lot of bomb damage, especially in the dock area, barrage balloons hung in the sky, there wasn't much to be had in the shops, and the issue and clipping of coupons had become a major industry—for food, clothing, gasoline, and as we found out later on, almost everything to do with babies.

I was posted to No. 23 Operational Training Unit at Pershore in Worcestershire. A wartime station, its airfield was encircled by a perimeter track from which hard standings radiated at intervals to accommodate the Wellington IIIs and so disperse them against the threat of attack by enemy intruders. Although there were hangars to house aircraft undergoing major repair, it was at these dispersal points that most of the servicing was done. In the open air, in all kinds of weather, at airfields throughout the United Kingdom, fitters and riggers, electricians and armourers and other specialist tradesmen performed daily inspections of engines and airframes to prepare them for flight.

When inspections were completed, the NCO in charge of the aircraft signed the inspection sheet, RAF Form 700, and presented it to the pilot for his signature of acceptance. But that was only the formal part of an association rarely spoken of aloud, yet endemic to the business of flying: the interdependence of air and ground crews. At operational stations particularly, the servicing crews took personal pride in "their aircraft," looked to "their aircrew" to bring it back safely, were quick to repair damage from enemy action, and mourned if it "failed to return."

Bicycles were the means of transport and I bought a second-hand one, with fixed gear, that I took with me to Southampton on the first 48-hour leave. This involved changing trains at Basingstoke, where the connecting train was already at another platform, and I had to make a dash for it down steps and through the subway, carrying suitcase in one hand, bicycle in the other, gas mask swinging from shoulder, pedals catching the odd leg of fellow travellers in passage.

Mother was in a nursing home, recuperating from surgery—removal of a breast—and was as cheerful as ever, but I had not been back at Pershore long before there was a wire from Treca to say Mother had died (August 14, 1942). So I didn't see her at the end. Treca, in her no-nonsense way, arranged the funeral and burial and then told me, so that all I could do as soon as I got to Southampton was to cycle to the cemetery at Swaythling and stand there, trying to say in my mind the things I was too selfish and insensitive to say when she was alive.

ABOVE: *Hamble, July 1936—(back from left) McDonald, Wheatley, Murdoch; (back fourth from right) Romanoff; (centre, fourth from right) Proctor; (front fifth from right) Swayne*

BELOW: *#4 Course at Netheravon, September 1936—(second row fifth) K.J., between Romanoff and Wheatley, Murdoch on Wheatley's left, Swayne; (front row fourth from right) Proctor on Swayne's left*
KNOWN SURVIVORS: *Drake (row 2, #3); Kelsey (row 1, #9); McDonald (row 2, #5); Murdoch (row 2, #7); Proctor (row 1, #12); Stenner (row 3, #4); Tams (row 4, #5); Thomas (row 2, #11); Toyne (row 1, #8); Wilkinson (row 3, #9); Barrett (row 3, #5) was killed at Netheravon, flying out of cloud into Sidbury Hill.*

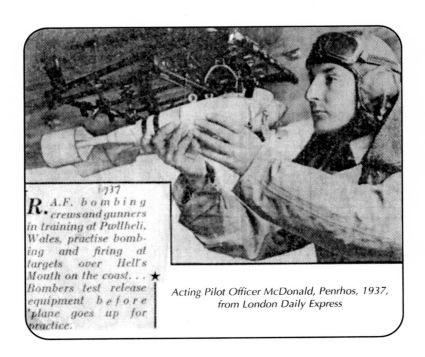

R. A.F. bombing crews and gunners in training at Pwllheli, Wales, practise bombing and firing at targets over Hell's Mouth on the coast. . . Bombers test release equipment b e f o r e 'plane goes up for practice.

Acting Pilot Officer McDonald, Penrhos, 1937, from London Daily Express

BELOW: *Netheravon, seven-a-side, March 1937*
Drake, Stenner, Fowler (RAAF), Wood, McDonald, Toyne, Wood

Hawker Audax

ABOVE: *with Martin-Barrett, Doran, Smallman, and McCrudden, Manston, August 1937*

RIGHT: *Peter Murdoch and Valerie, 1939. Romanoff (L), Peter's brother (R)*

Paris, 1940, Romanoff C.

Desond McGlinn, Barrie, 1939

Camp Borden, December, 1939

With Mellor, Waterhouse and Dupont, Camp Borden, 1939

May 17, 1940, Barrie

May 1940, Barrie

Rivers, Manitoba, December, 1940

Crescent Apartments, Portage la Prairie, Manitoba

Portage la Prairie

Leaving Portage la Prairie, 1942

Detroit Lakes, Minn. en route to Montreal, 1942

Wellington, Mk. III

*With Ruth and her parents,
69 Maple Avenue, Barrie, 1942*

*Photo, part of escape
kit if shot down*

BELOW: *Halifax, Mk. II*

ABOVE: *Halifax, Mk. II, minus M/U turret, perspex blister added beneath*

BELOW: *Air and Groundcrew, 78 Sqn., Linton-on-Ouse, March 1943. K.J. leaning on Flt. Sgt. Timms, NCO i/c B. Flt.*

ABOVE: *with Aircrew (front): Reynolds, McCoy, Stewart; (rear): Cambridge, Walker, Dilworth*

BELOW: *Munich, 9/10 March, 1943 (last trip)*

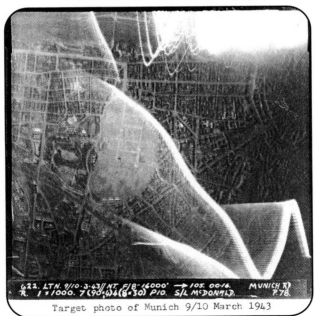

Target photo of Munich 9/10 March 1943

Chapter 4

▣ 1942—1943 ▣

Pershore was a Wellington OTU, I was there a month, put in eighty-five hours, and was privileged to fly with three Canadians who stayed with me for the next seven months: Clare Dilworth, navigator—calm, imperturbable, wry humour, professional; Doc Reynolds, wireless operator/air gunner—quiet, solid, painstaking; and, bringing up the rear, Tim McCoy— small, wrinkled face, not much to say, brave as be damned. At Marston Moor, we were joined by two Englishmen and a Scot: Peter Walker, flight engineer—slight, serious, questioning; Wilf Cambridge, mid-upper gunner—tall, fair, open face, friendly; and Jock Stewart, bomb-aimer—also slight, and a cheerful extrovert.

With Jellings as bomb-aimer (who left us after Pershore), the first three and I flew to Bremen on September 13 and to Essen on the 16th, each flight just under six hours and carrying six 500-lb. bombs. Of the 446 aircraft dispatched to Bremen, twenty-one were lost, fifteen of them Wellingtons, and of the 369 dispatched to Essen, thirty-nine were lost, twenty-one of them Wellingtons (figures from *The Bomber Command War Diaries*).

The consensus among instructors at the time was that, once you were past the enemy coast, you should "weave"—fly in undulations, as if describing a spiral—in order to prevent the flak gunners from predicting precisely where you would be when their shells detonated.

Willie Tait demolished the idea when we got to Linton by explaining that the best use of your time was to fly straight and level, with occasional jigs to see underneath. Then, not only was your time over enemy territory as short as possible, but you also made the navigator's job a bit easier, provided your bomb-aimer with a stable platform, and thus were more likely both to find and then hit the target, which after all was the object of the exercise.

Willie, who ended the war with four DSOs and two DFCs, commanded 78 squadron for the first two months I was at Linton. A friend who was in 617 (the Dambuster) Squadron when Willie Tait commanded it told me, "Willie seemed to have a charmed life. On one trip I saw him fly in low, straight and level through the flak in a Mustang and the aircraft wasn't scratched." Leonard Cheshire did the same, going in low down to mark special targets, and it occurs to me that those two examples, involving not only brilliant pilots but exceptionally brave men, give us a clue not just to wartime exploits, but to life in general. It is the risk-takers who succeed.

In Wellington VS 542, however, on the night of Sunday, September 13, I wove as instructed from the Dutch coast to just before the target, when I flew straight and level until the bombs had been released and the photo-flash had gone off for the target photograph. From Spanner Spence to Pershore's instructors, I had a variety of descriptions of what to expect, but the only way was to go, and if my recollection is true to the experience, I would say I was nervous from the moment we were told, on the day of the 13th, that we would be operating.

Until then, we had carried out night exercises—Bull's Eye was the code word—designed to simulate operations in flights around the British Isles and doing bombing runs over infra-red targets en route. Even these were serious enough: weather was always a threat, the black-out robbed us of pinpoints, and on one flight I had to shut down an engine. But no one was shooting at us, and unless there was enemy activity over England, there were no searchlights.

Searchlights were not so much threats in themselves as in what you associated with them: becoming the focus of flak batteries, and being suddenly illuminated for the benefit of German night fighters. It's hard to estimate distance at night. We flew at 16,000 feet and saw searchlights while we were still over the

North Sea—Bremen is a point or two north of due east from Pershore—and that was really the time when the war started for me. I could see flak bursting among the searchlights ahead, which was where we were going, and it wouldn't be long before we were fired at.

People in other respects much like me would be doing their best to kill me, just as the bombs we were carrying would kill people on the ground; the war was no longer an idea, it had become personal. Yet I wasn't conscious of animosity toward the Germans as a people. They had certainly supported Hitler's revolting regime, but it might have appealed to them for other reasons at first. Once it was in place, they were stuck with it.

A regime that throve on envy and hatred was bound to generate the hatred that is war's most frightening characteristic. That was why, for me and many others, the targets we prized were in the cities we associated with the Nazi movement: Berlin, Essen, Munich and Nuremberg. The Germans might be stuck with the regime, but they couldn't stop it even if they wanted to. It was up to us to do that, and the only way we could stop it from spreading was to defeat it by the same force of arms the Nazis had launched against peaceful neighbours. It was a foul and monstrous tyranny, and neither then did I feel, nor since have I felt, the slightest doubt of the justice of our cause.

Just as imagination plays so significant a role in instrument flying, so did it bear down as you drew near the target. You could see the bursts as flak shells detonated either on contact or at their preset height, and you could see the tracer shells winding their way up. What you couldn't see, but were conscious of all the time, was the shells that weren't tracers but were seven or eight times as numerous.

Yet it was the bomb-aimer who must have felt it most. The pilot saw the scene ahead, but he was also busy handling the controls and checking the instruments. The bomb-aimer lay prone at his station, beneath the guns in his perspex cone, with only the bombsight interrupting his view of the scene 16,000 feet below. Any reader who has experienced vertigo will understand the sensations of those young men, suspended in the machine it was now their duty to guide into the inferno ahead.

For pilots, a lot was happening at once. You saw the puffs of smoke from the shells, smelled the cordite, heard the *crump* of explosions and felt the aircraft shake. You wallowed in the wake of other aircraft and remembered the hundreds of them converging on this one place. Yet if you were "coned" (that is, if you became the focus of a master searchlight which was then joined by others, with you at the intersection of their beams), you dived and climbed to get out of it, regardless of the risk of collision.

You saw other aircraft sustain direct hits from flak and erupt in orange balls of exploding bombs which shed trails of flaming gasoline, and you saw other aircraft, hit by a night fighter's cannon shells, catching fire and falling down.

As time went on during the winter of 1942/43, although target areas were the most visually exciting, it was during the rest of the flights, both inward and outward, that you had to be vigilant. If a lone searchlight or flak battery opened up along the route, there wasn't much to do except try to dodge them after the event, but to avoid the night fighters, you had to watch all the time. "You," in this case, meant the pilot, the front, rear, and mid-upper gunners, and—when he wasn't needed at his set—the wireless operator/air gunner in the astrodome. Those four or five pairs of eyes were busy all the time, searching the darkness for the anomaly, the shape that moved against the gleam of a lake, or the lighter dark of the sky, or near a cloud, gunners and pilot nerved for the instant response to a sighting and the command from the gunner who saw the enemy: "Break right [or left], go."

This applied even more during the flight home, after you had dropped the bombs, the aircraft was lighter, and you were looking forward to bacon and eggs and bed. Then the temptation to relax was very strong, and you had to remind everyone that fighters were still about.

The Halifax's vulnerable area was underneath, where a fighter could stalk it from below, unseen by the gunners, until the bomber's shape was within range, when the German pilot would haul back on his stick and rake the bomber's fuselage with cannon shells before falling away from the subsequent explosions.

About that time, too, the Luftwaffe introduced *Schräge Musik*: fighters equipped with upward-firing cannons which enabled them to fly in formation with their prey, out of sight below. To guard against this, every few minutes you would tilt the wings to give the gunners, and yourself, a look underneath.

However, the blind spot was there. Leonard Cheshire, who commanded 76 Squadron at Linton-on-Ouse when I was a flight commander in 78 on the same station, had all our Halifaxes modified. (Willie Tait, who commanded 78 when I first went there, had left Linton by then, and Chesh was the dominant figure on the station.)

Since the mid-upper turret was of little use in the fighter-sighting game, he reasoned that by taking it out, fairing off the resulting gap in the upper fuselage, and installing a perspex blister in the underside of the fuselage aft of the bomb-bay—by doing this, the mid-upper gunner could be turned into a mid-under sighter to cover the aircraft's blind spot. Moreover, taking out the turret would streamline the upper surface, reduce weight, and thereby add a knot or two to performance.

The first time we flew with that modification was to Essen, where we were coned on the way in. I flung the aircraft about to dodge the flak, and Wilf, scrabbling for a hold above the blister, deposited his operational breakfast in it. (The flak damage was mostly in the wings; the holes allowed the last of the fuel to drain out on dispersal when we got back.)

A word here for the gunners, three at that time, plus the Wireless Operator/Air Gunner, who could take over one of the turrets in emergency. They operated eight guns in all: two in the front turret, two in the mid-upper, and four in the tail; all Browning .303 inch machine guns (.303 inches equals 7.696 mm).

Put yourself in the front turret of a Halifax. You have checked its operation that afternoon in daylight. Now it is dark, you have checked it again, it is time to start engines, and you leave the turret for the cockpit to stand by the pilot as he taxies the aircraft toward the end of the runway. When the takeoff roll starts, your job is to follow the pilot's movement of the four throttles and, when he tells you, to tighten the throttle clamp so that he can use both hands on the stick.

Now the aircraft is into the climb, and you return to the turret. You can rotate it to give yourself an arc of vision about sixty degrees ahead of the aircraft and you can see straight down: there is nothing in front of you except the gunsights, the guns, and the clear perspex of the turret that you cleaned and re-cleaned this afternoon. Over the North Sea or the English Channel, you test your guns with short bursts. En route to the target, you have a grandstand view of searchlights and flak bursts ahead or on either side, until the time comes for you to crawl down below your turret in your role of bomb-aimer.

Now, lying prone, your attention is divided between the target map and the sight you are approaching. It is a mixture of searchlight beams, flak bursts and tracer shells, and, on the ground, fires that have been started by other bombers. You call for bomb doors open, align the aiming point with the grid wires of the bombsight, and call "Left, left," or "Ri-i-i-ght" to the pilot until the aiming point is tracking the wires, when you call "Steady, steady, steady," and operate the release switches. You time the bombs' descent, set off the photo-flash for the target photograph, call for bomb doors closed, and climb back into your turret for the ride home.   In the mid-upper turret, the gunner there has been watching, watching, all the time as he does now, watching the sky, not the fires or the searchlights, because he must keep his night vision intact as he searches the sky for the shape of a Ju-88 or an Me-110 or an FW-190.

Those two have lonely jobs, but at least they are near other crew members. It is the rear gunner who is alone, aft of the tail surfaces, in the slipstream of the four Merlins from the takeoff, when he is first off the ground as the tail lifts with the Halifax's gathering speed, until six or seven or eight hours later, he sees the ground coming closer, the approach lights flash by, and the tail wheel hits the runway.

All that time—the equivalent of a normal day's work that he has put in at the end of a normal day—he has been on his own in the dark; cold, poised at the levered end of a seventy-one-foot fuselage, his head never still, searching, searching, for the moment when one of the shapes he has learned to recognize appears below, or above, or to one side, and he alone must decide whether its pilot has seen the glow of the Halifax's eight stub exhausts, or is tracking another Halifax or a Lancaster that the gunner can't see.

He has already alerted the pilot. If the shape turns, or climbs, or noses down toward his own aircraft, he does two things at once: he calls "Break left [or right], go!" the moment he fires his four Brownings at the shape, and keeps firing as the turret is dragged down and twisted and pulled up in the stomach-wrenching attitudes of the corkscrew.

It took a special kind of courage to fly as a rear gunner, the "two o'clock in the morning courage" that Napoleon said he had very rarely met. When I wrote that Tim McCoy was brave as be damned, that's what I meant. He didn't say much—no-one spoke except for a message (change of course, wireless transmission from base, bomb-aimer's instructions, or a sighting). He never complained.

On the Turin trip, when he was in cloud most of the way, bumped about and half-frozen, I doubt it occurred to him that he might have left his turret for the less cold fuselage while we were in cloud; the cloud might have broken, or a fighter might have found its way to us by radar, so he kept his post.

At Christmas 1942, he and I went to Driffield—he for a gunnery course, I for a Blind Approach Training course on Oxfords. We went by train. I had saved a bottle of rye for an undefined special occasion, and that seemed to be as good as any. We finished it between us en route, went off at Driffield to our respective messes, and had pretty fair evenings by all accounts. The next time we saw each other after Linton was in 1947, when I drove up to the gate at Trenton and there was Tim, raising the barrier. He had left at the end of the war, didn't care for civilian life, and re-enlisted as the Leading Aircraftman he then was, grinning at me, with his air gunner's brevet and his DFM. We lost touch after that, but I still feel closer to him than even the others.

On many of those trips, we saw fighters but were never attacked—a tribute to the gunners' alertness, recognition, and judgment. There were four close calls.

The first was Hamburg, November 9/10, 1942. In putrid weather, we bombed in rough cloud from a dead reckoning position that was confirmed by flak, but the 500-lb. bomb (the load was two 1,000 lb., one 500, and four canisters of incendiaries) hung up, and we had to do three more runs over the target before Jock was able to release it. On the trip back, mostly in cloud, our navigation was thrown out by a faulty P4 compass (sheared pivot, it turned out), and we crept into Acklington on the last cupful of fuel.

The second one was Turin, December 11/12. When we were into cloud soon after takeoff, a faulty Pitot head heater caused the

Pitot head to freeze and, in cloud most of the time except for a brief period over the target, I had to fly there and back with no air speed indicator, directional gyro or artificial horizon. (The *Diaries* noted that "more than half of the force turned back before attempting to cross the Alps, because of severe icing conditions.") An extra incentive to reach the Italian targets from October to December was to disrupt supplies destined for Rommel after El Alamein.

The third was Essen, March 5/6, 1943, mentioned before, when we were coned on the way in. The holes were mostly in the wings; the last of the fuel dripped out on the dispersal bay after we got back.

The fourth was Munich, March 9/10, when we were briefed to go in low over the French coast, beneath the view of German radar, and then climb up to cruising height around Amiens. We knew the location of the German fighter controllers' boxes, and the idea was to plan our routes so that we crossed them where boxes intersected, and so present the controllers with a problem of allocating targets.

Going in low over the French coast might have foxed the radar, but it stirred a whole lot of light flak batteries into action, and I put my pre-war low-flying practice to good use, hugging the contours by the light of the moon, with the Halifax's four throttles through the gate, and flak rattling against the sides of the fuselage. Varying the heights en route seemed to work: the only fighters we saw were in the Munich area. (Munich was the last trip—Clare Dilworth had just been "screened," and we flew with a different navigator.)

At the end of the tour I was awarded the DFC, as was Clare, and Tim McCoy the DFM.

In a summary of bomber groups' operational performance at the end of the book, the *Diaries* record the number of aircraft destroyed in crashes. For example, 1 Group lost 1,016 Lancasters due to enemy action (2.3 percent of sorties flown), and another 199 Lancasters in crashes; 3 Group lost 577 Stirlings due to enemy action (3.6 percent of sorties flown), and another 227 Stirlings in crashes; and 8 (Pathfinder) Group lost 444 Lancasters to enemy action (2.7 percent) and 72 Lancasters in crashes. Germans may have been the prime enemy, but running them pretty close was the weather.

Not that the weather was always bad. For example, our first Italian trip, to Genoa, was on a clear night. (It was also—October 23, 1942—the start of the battle of El Alamein.) The sky was clear, the land blacked out. We climbed in clear air to the cruising altitude of 16,000 feet, but all we saw below over England was the occasional glow of a blast furnace in the Midlands, and all we saw over France was the occasional opened door of a French farmer's house to signal encouragement. The sight I remember best, after the long haul from Yorkshire down over France, was the lights of neutral Switzerland, and the Alps in moonlight.

At other times, mostly in cloud, the Alps were a threat. That night, however, they were a reminder that one day the war would end, and the lights would come on again—in the words of a popular song—"all over the world."

By the time we flew our first op, from Pershore to Bremen, I had six years service and 1,350 hours as pilot of a variety of aircraft in all kinds of weather. In short, I was lucky that the testing time came when I was a product not only of the RAF's superb training methods, but also of enough experience to recognize the cause of sudden changes and to do what was needed in response.

When we took off from Linton for Turin on December 11, 1942, the bombload was reduced to a single 1,000-lb. bomb and nine cans of incendiaries so as to make room for an overload fuel tank in the bomb-bay to get us through the nine-hour flight. But the aircraft's flying characteristics were the same as with a full load of bombs, and as we went into the climb, it was in a by-then familiar attitude that resulted from the throttle settings, the pitch controls of the propellers, and the fore and aft trim settings on the control surfaces. We were in cloud soon after takeoff, but soon after that, the needle of the air speed indicator turned back to zero, signalling that the Pitot head heater wasn't working and the Pitot head had iced up.

The Pitot head, named after the eighteenth-century French hydraulic engineer, is an open-ended circular tube projecting forward from beneath the nose of the fuselage. The air rushes into the tube's open end and supplies dynamic pressure to the air speed indicator which translates it into knots or mph. The same dynamic air drove the gyroscopes of the direction indicator and the artificial horizon. Small holes in a parallel, but closed-end, tube let in static air from the surrounding atmosphere, and this was fed to the altimeter in the cockpit.

Thus, on December 11th, when the Pitot head's electric heater failed, a number of things happened: the air speed indicator ceased to register, the altimeter became dependent on the air in the cockpit, unpressurized, but still warmer than outside and therefore distorting the reading on the altimeter; and, deprived of the air pressure that drove their gyroscopes, the directional gyro stopped functioning and the artificial horizon toppled.

But the engines were working, the aircraft was trimmed for the climb, the grid ring of the magnetic P.4 compass was aligned to the climb heading, and the turn and bank indicator, which functioned independently of the gyros, was there to keep us straight and level in the attitude of the climb. When we reached the cruise altitude, I knew from experience the throttle and pitch settings that would give us the cruise airspeed; also, at the top of the climb, we were in and out of broken cloud which gave us a horizon.

That sequence of events was disturbing at the time. You have only to picture yourself in cloud, with a load of bombs and fuel, and seeing the air speed indicator that is your chief guide to staying aloft suddenly flipping back to zero, at the same time realising that ice is forming in the cloud, to understand the shock to your senses. But the reason I mention it is to make the comparison between my good luck (from the accumulated experience), and the effect on a pilot straight from the conversion unit at being confronted with the same conditions.

To this day, I marvel at the courage of those young pilots, trained in the friendly skies and good flying weather of Canada, or Australia, or South Africa, and thrust into command of five or six crew members and a Whitley, or a Wellington, and flying from an Operational Training Unit to the Ruhr as we did to Essen from Pershore. Those same pilots, after their two weeks at a Halifax, Stirling, or Lancaster Heavy Conversion Unit, would be taking off for Germany over blacked-out England in charge of a four-engined aircraft and facing not only night fighters and flak, but also the assaults of the weather.

Put yourself in the cockpit of a four-engined bomber. You are twenty years of age and you have 250 hours of flying experience, of which the first 180 were in Canada, or Australia, or the United

States, South Africa or Rhodesia, mostly in clear skies and where, when you flew at night, you could see the lights of the towns and villages below. Now, you are on your way back to England after having been shot at, and your wireless operator tells you that base is socked in; you have been diverted to another airfield. It is a few minutes after midnight, and you have been awake for eighteen hours. The navigator gives you a new course, you turn to it, wait for the compass needle to settle down, and reset the directional gyro.

Automatically, you are still watching the sky and the instruments, up left and down, across right, and back to the instruments. The navigator tells you that Gee (for "grid," the navigational aid that used a cathode-ray tube and cross-bearings from ground transmitters to fix position within about six miles) is back in operation (it has been out of service over Germany because of enemy jamming), and that you have crossed the English coast (you are in cloud now, and letting down to 4,000 feet, clear of balloons). The wireless operator tells you the barometric pressure to set on the altimeter so that it will register the height above the diversion airfield, and says that the weather there is broken cloud down to 500 feet, visibility one mile.

You take another gulp of oxygen through your face mask, rub the back of your neck, and straighten up in the seat against the shoulder straps. The navigator tells you the airfield is twenty-five miles away, the highest ground is 800 feet, and you can let down to 2,000. You look out to your left and think you can see breaks in the cloud. From the front turret, the bomb aimer says he can see the Drem lights (dimmed lights surrounding an airfield area that were switched on to guide returning aircraft) and the field's identifying letters on the ground.

You call for landing permission and are told you are Number Three to land. You join the circuit and look for the other aircraft through the broken cloud. Now you are at 500 feet and you can see the blue lights of the runway. You are cleared to land, turn on to final approach, wrestle the aircraft into the correct glide path by keeping it in line with the green light of the glide path indicator, put on full flap, adjust the fore and aft trim, throttle back over the boundary, and hold off, hold off, until the wheels touch, you let it roll, then brake and start looking for the intersection where you can turn off to make room for the next man and find your way to a dispersal.

Now, put yourself in the same cockpit at 2,000 feet, when you find that the undercarriage mechanism has been damaged by flak and the undercart won't come down, or the flaps have been hit and will only come down on one side, or you've lost one engine, have been flying on three since you left the target area, and now see the oil temperature rising in one of those, or part of the tail surface has been shot away and you aren't sure how much control you will have on the final approach.

Or put yourself in another cockpit seven hours earlier. You have just seen the Verey light fired from the control tower that signals start-up time, and you start the four engines in turn. You wave away the chocks, push the throttles forward to break the inertia and get the loaded aircraft moving, and start taxying along between the dimmed blue lights that line the perimeter track. Other aircraft are taxying, ahead and behind.

You get a green from the controller, turn on to the runway, line up, brakes on to stop the wheels, throttles fully forward, brakes off and, as you start to roll, the bomb-aimer standing beside you to follow the throttles and lock them shouts through his mike that there is fire in the starboard outer. You are now halfway along the 2,000 yards of runway with the tail up, and all your instincts are to get the thing into the air, but you force yourself to throttle back while trying to remember the proper action in the event of fire.

The aircraft starts to swing and you realize that the starboard outer's prop is overspeeding. Everything is happening at once: you are off the runway, heading for the ditch, you hope the flight engineer has shut off the fuel, you can't control the swing, you know the undercart will collapse, remember the 8,000 lbs of high explosive and incendiaries in the bomb-bay underneath your seat, and you call through the mike for everyone to get out.

Or put yourself in a cockpit when you are over England on the way home and the weather at base deteriorates much sooner than forecast. Cloud base is low, visibility poor, and there are no better conditions within reach of your fuel state. You reach base and try your hand at an approach, only to misjudge it and have to overshoot. You try again. You're tired and edgy—your attention is split between the instruments, the windshield through which you peer hoping to see the blue lights, and your assessment of where you are in relation to the approach path and the other aircraft you know are somewhere in the circuit. It was on a night like that, December 16/17, 1943, that a force of 483 Lancasters and ten Mosquitoes attacked Berlin. Twenty-five Lancasters were shot down by fighters, and, as the *Diaries* report:

> On their return to England, many of the bombers encountered very low cloud at their bases. The squadrons of 1, 6 and 8 Groups were particularly badly affected. 29 Lancasters (and a Stirling from the minelaying operation) either crashed or were abandoned when their crews parachuted. The group with heaviest losses was 1 Group with 13 aircraft lost; the squadron with heaviest losses was 97 Squadron, 8 Group, with 7 aircraft lost. There is a little confusion in Bomber Command records over aircrew casualties but it is probable that 148 men were killed in the crashes, 39 were injured and 6 presumed lost in the sea.

I wrote the serial numbers of aircraft in my log book, so was able, when *The Halifax File* was published in 1982, to trace the fate of twenty-one different Halifaxes I flew during the period that began with a flight to Cologne on October 15, 1942, ended with one to Munich on March 9, 1943, and included (with the two Wellington trips from Pershore) twenty-eight operations. DT 554, in which we flew four ops, was transferred to a conversion unit and lasted until June 7, 1944; W7928, also transferred, until Feb. 22, 1945. Of the remaining nineteen, twelve failed to return from operations, one ditched, one burned, one crashed on takeoff, one crashed overshooting, one crashed when the undercarriage collapsed, and one was shot down by flak over Essen. Most of the nineteen went down within weeks of our flights in them. DT 780, in which we flew eight ops including Cologne, Nuremberg, Berlin, and Essen, and which was badly damaged on the Essen trip, was fixed up just in time to be lost on a trip to Essen after we left the squadron.

Casualty rates—measured by the number of aircraft missing as percentages of aircraft dispatched—on the trips we flew, ranged from two zeroes in November 1942, when small forces of less than 100 went to Genoa and Turin, to a high of 11.8, when 187 went to Berlin on January 17, 1943, and 22 failed to return. Berlin (the Big City, codename Whitebait), Hamburg, and the Ruhr (Happy Valley) attracted heavy casualties—average 6.1 percent on the trips we made there—yet minelaying (codename Gardening), which we did only once and looked on as almost a night off, could be dicey too: of the eighty aircraft out that night, five were lost for a rate of 6.2 percent.

Behind the percentages were young men in their late teens or early twenties (our second trip to Berlin was on my twenty-ninth birthday), of whom the great majority had not flown until they joined the service (RAF, RAAF, RCAF, RNZAF, Royal Rhodesian AF, Royal South African AF, Royal Norwegian AF, plus expatriate Belgians, Czechs, Dutch, French and Poles), who had been taught to ply unfamiliar trades in an alien element, who knew how slender were the chances of surviving a tour of operations, and who were all volunteers.

One of our Aircrew Association members, Nick Carter, who had been a regular airman (a "fitter" or engine mechanic) before the war, remustered to flight engineer when the four-engined bombers entered the service. I asked him how many hours he had flown by the time he went on his first op. He thought for a minute, remembered having flown first on an air test before going to the conversion unit, and then said "About eight hours." Eight hours' air experience, and off he went to Germany as flight engineer of a Stirling on 7 Squadron.

Pilots with perhaps 250 hours of flying experience found themselves in charge of a four-engined aircraft, climbing sluggishly through bumpy cloud, alert for ice on the wings or in the carburetors, and fighting the battle of the senses that contradicted what the instruments were telling them. If the weather was clear, all the land below was blacked out, making them all the more conscious, when they saw another aircraft, of the red glow from their own stub exhausts in the darkness.

Some years ago, I summed up my recollections:

The first sight of the stars as you broke clear of cloud after a slow, bumpy climb; the lights of Switzerland, and the Alps in moonlight; the sudden blaze of an exploding bomber; tracer weaving lazily upwards; high cloud in the distance against

the moon; the sharp crack of ice particles flung from the propellers into the side of the fuselage; St. Elmo's fire ringing the
propeller tips; the Halifax's buoyant leap as the bombs were
released; the smell of the microphone mask and the magni-
fied hiss of oxygen drawn into your mouth; the brief companionship of the navigator appearing beside you from his
screened compartment below; the sweep of your eyes to left
and right, down and up and across and then back to the
instruments; the red glow of another Halifax's eight stub
exhausts; the two moments of commitment, first at takeoff
when you pushed all four forward and clambered into the
sky, and second when someone said "Crossing the coast;" the
forced banter in the aircrew bus riding to dispersal before the
flight and the moment afterwards when you dropped from the
hatch to Yorkshire soil again; the silence in the mess the next
day for the BBC broadcast and the furtive glances when it
gave the number of aircraft missing; being diverted by
weather to another station and trying to sleep in one of those
wooden-framed green armchairs with the adjustable backs;
the endless repetition of some favourite record on the mess
gramophone (at Linton it was "Java Jive," revived in the 1980s
by the Manhattan Transfer); piling into B Flight's Standard van
on a night off for beer at the Alice Hawthorn; cashing
cheques at the Half Moon in York; standing by for days in the
mess for the "special effort" that grew more dangerous the
longer it was imagined; the fascination of the "Nazi" targets—
Munich, Nuremberg and Berlin—and the long dog leg down
from the Baltic coast to the arching defences of the capital;
the repeated runs over a target while the bomb-aimer fought
to release a hang-up; the crump of heavy flak exploding
nearby and the puffs of smoke from the shells; wallowing in
the wake of unseen aircraft and remembering the three or
four hundred others not far away in the dark.

Chapter 5
▓ 1943—1944 ▓

When we were "screened" we were sent as a crew on a morale-raising round of aircraft factories in the London area. Mid-morning we would be picked up in company cars and taken to a factory where Halifaxes were being built. After lunch in the executive dining room, we were guided to a stage in the manufacturing area where the workers were assembled.

My job was to introduce the crew members, describe their duties, and then describe a typical raid on Germany, from the time of the briefing through the experiences of the flight to the return and debriefing afterwards. Every time I mentioned that Tim McCoy could see the fires from fifty miles away on the flight home, the audience broke into spontaneous cheering.

These men and women had lived through the London Blitz, had lost homes and close relatives, were still at risk from German bombs, and felt, I'm sure, that here in front of them was living proof not only that their work was worthwhile, but that there was hope for an end to the war and their privations.

They, too, had lived through the thirties when Hitler and his brownshirts took power, had witnessed on film and in newspapers the transformation of a country not unlike their own into an armed camp that threatened its neighbours—while bullying or murdering any of its own citizens who dared to protest, or who were judged to be racially or otherwise impure.

Fifty years later, Canadian and other revisionists of history were quick to condemn the bomber offensive against the German heartland. A CBC "docudrama" broadcast in 1992, *The Valour and the Horror*, portrayed Air Marshal Harris as a sadistic monster intent on attacking women and children—"targeting civilians," in a phrase that was copied faithfully by a largely sympathetic media. Yet the program missed entirely the prevailing atmosphere of the period it set out to dramatize.

When the RAF made its first raid, German "civilians" had been terrorized by their own government agencies for more than six years. By the time RAF raids reached damaging proportions (mid-1942), German "civilians" were accustomed to crowding in shelters, losing friends, relatives and houses and so on, as had the British before them. But there was nothing personal about it; it was a condition of war.

Very few warriors are immune to the experience of fear in the face of enemy fire, but a merciful God comforts each of them with the belief that he will escape death in battle until the last moments, when there is no escape. In much the same way, German "civilians" who heard the roar of engines in the night sky were relieved when the roar faded into the distance— "their" city had been spared again. But there was no relief, day in, day out, from the fear of being "betrayed" by a neighbour for a thoughtless word or expression, or simply being picked up by the Gestapo in a random check.

Attributing "terror tactics" to Allied airmen and their weapons has been used, purposely or not, to distract attention from the state-induced terrorism we set out to fight—and which, in the end, we helped to rescue the German people from in the only way it could have been done: by force of arms.

At the end of our tour, we thought we were pretty good and volunteered for the Pathfinder Force being formed from experienced crews who would then do another fifteen or twenty trips and be tour-expired for the duration. Nothing came of the application, and we went our separate ways into the training units that fed the front-line squadrons. I was promoted to wing commander and posted as OC 1652 Heavy Conversion Unit at Marston Moor, the site of the 1644 Civil War battle, and where Leonard Cheshire had just gone as station commander, one of the youngest group captains at his then-age of twenty-five.

Volunteering for Pathfinders was at odds with my inclination, exemplified at Camp Borden, to leave such matters to the air force. From then until the end of the war, I did exactly that—ready and willing if called upon, but content to wait for the call and conscious of the wind on the heath. No one wished to die, yet death was all around. In the seven months I was with 1652 HCU, there were twenty-seven accidents, ten of them fatal crashes due to engine fires or failures, and three fatal for other reasons. Contributing factors were rudder stall and propellers overspeeding.

By a curious twist, those fatal crashes were harder to bear than losses on the squadron. War is by nature brutalizing, and although casualties and the chances of being killed were made light of by euphemisms (aircrew weren't killed, they "went for a Burton," or "didn't make it," or "bought it"), a crew that failed to return from an operation was still "missing" and there was always a chance they might have been able to bail out. Even when deaths were confirmed afterwards, it *was* afterwards, and there had been others in between.

But local crashes were both personal and immediate. You knew the "screened" instructors. As you drove to the scenes, you could picture the pilots in the final moments, struggling to keep the things in the air. When you got there, you saw what was left of them and the other crew members. One of our better instructors had just turned onto final approach at about 700 feet when (we found out later) a bolt in the control rods to the elevators sheared, and the aircraft dived straight in. One night, even closer to home, a Halifax suffered propeller overspeeding just after take-off, crashed and burned in the wood across the field from where Ruth and I were living.

We knew what the chances were from personal experience on squadrons, from the numbers missing reported each day by the BBC, from word-of-mouth accounts of casualties elsewhere within 4 Group, and from passage through the unit of course after course of aircrew to squadrons.

What we knew instinctively was confirmed many years afterwards when the *Diaries* published the mathematical chances of a bomber crew surviving fifty operational flights at various rates of loss. At the highest rate shown—4.0 percent—out of 100 crews, thirteen would survive. Also cited is that "The casualty rate during the coming period, that of the opening operations of the Pathfinder Force [which was when we started operating], would be 4.6 per cent!" We didn't know this at the time, but the average loss rate on the trips we did in that same period was 5.7 percent, and since the average loss rate on our whole twenty-eight trips was 3.7 percent, the chances of surviving another fifteen or twenty weren't very good.

Luck in the flying business is the subject of a book, *Out of the Blue*, by Laddie Lucas, and he mentions my bits: the navigation course, not going to Pathfinders and, in between, an incident at Dorval, when a call came through for a squadron leader specialist navigator to fly with a B-24 to the Middle East. Two of us qualified: John Archer and me. I was stuck in Pennfield Ridge at the time, and John, who was on the ground at Dorval, went with the B-24, which wasn't heard from again.

Not that it was all luck. As I mentioned before, by the time we flew our first op to Bremen, I had 1,350 hours in my log book, made up of single- and multi-engined flying under all conditions—formation, low flying, instrument flying, navigating myself, in all kinds of weather, day and night—and there's no doubt this had a lot to do with survival. I was a squadron leader with six years' service, used to command, used to the need to practice drills so that we all knew what we had to do, individually and as a crew. So you could say that the men I flew with were lucky, as I was, that the testing time came, as I wrote before, just when the Royal Air Force's superb pilot training bore fruit in my accumulated experience.

And yet... it was still luck. At the end of March 1943, I handed over B Flight to another squadron leader, J.H.D. (Jamie) Chapple, who had been in my senior term at Netheravon and was thus six months senior to me, with similar experience and training. Jamie (I found out from microfilm of 78 Sqn.'s operational record) did his first two trips that month on successive nights to rough targets (Duisberg and Berlin), followed by six more to the Ruhr and Stettin in April, only to be shot down on the night of May 4/5 in an attack on Dortmund when twelve Halifaxes were lost out of 141 dispatched, three of them from 78 Sqn. The average of the loss rates on his nine trips was 4.7 percent.

The whole business of courage and leadership was front and centre for six years. I was fortunate, at Linton, to see it practiced at first hand by three outstanding officers.

The station commander was John Whitley, then thirty-seven

years old, with sixteen years' service and a bar to his Air Force Cross as testament to his proficiency in the air. He had more flying time than anyone else on the station and was not supposed to fly on operations. Yet, everyone knew that from time to time, a second pilot would turn up at dispersal, usually with one of the newer crews, who looked remarkably like the station commander, and would sit there throughout the trip simply exuding confidence.

For those trips he made his own preparations, and when later in 1943 the aircraft he was in was shot down, he shaved off his moustache, donned his beret, extended his fishing rod, and made his way down French rivers to Spain. He was back in Yorkshire three weeks later.

Air Marshal Sir John Whitley, KBE, CB, DSO, AFC*, retired in 1962. In the handwritten letter I have, dated May 16, 1990 from Lymington in Hampshire, he told me:

> I go cruising in my boat to the west coast of France every year for the past 20 years. This year wasn't so successful as I went over a rock. Luckily it was a small one and didn't do much damage. Shortly afterwards I got pneumonia of all things. I thought my time was up—85 next month—but was mistaken and have been out sailing several times so there's life in the old dog yet!

78 Sqn. was commanded by James B. Tait, known at that time as Willie, winner of the Sword of Honour on graduation from Cranwell six years before, and a consummate professional who had already completed two tours of operations. In his world there was no such thing as "the CO's aircraft." Every squadron had what was called a hangar queen—an aircraft seemingly beset by minor faults that kept it unserviceable and hence to be avoided by the crews.

When Willie chose to fly on ops, the current hangar queen would be his for the night; moreover, he took care to see for himself how the raid was progressing. When one of the flight commanders was detailed to carry out a special reconnaissance, after we had bombed, we would stay in the target area for long enough to make some assessment of where the bombs seemed to be falling in relation to the aiming point. We did this at about the bombing height, which in the Halifax II was 16,000–18,000 feet. This was far too casual for Willie, whose method was to drop down to 2,000 feet or below and roar across the target, map-reading by the light of the fires.

When I inspected B Flight's aircraft in company with the flight's senior NCO, I would take his word for what was wrong, but when Willie went around the squadron, he would climb up on the servicing platforms, see for himself, and tell the squadron engineering officer when the aircraft should be serviceable. Afterwards, Willie went on to command 617 squadron (the Dambusters), among other feats sank the *Tirpitz*, and ended the war with four DSOs and two DFCs.

In my brief experience of him, he was not an easy man to talk to, preferring when he was in the mess to stand before the fire, pipe in mouth (one thing we had in common) and tankard in hand, and listen with twinkling eye to whoever was talking. From time to time, he would cock the handle of the tankard's lid with his thumb and raise it slowly to take a swallow, then let the lid drop back with a slap and replace his pipe.

He had two other mannerisms. Every now and then, with shoulders braced back, he would stretch his neck from side to side as if waiting for something to click into place. Quite often, the last twist would merge into a sideways glance at the watch facing inwards on his left wrist, upturned as it held the tankard, the elbow close to his chest.

I mentioned the trait of being hard to talk to in a letter to Murray Peden, but Murray, who got to know him many years after the war, wrote back to say,

> I can readily imagine that Willie is not a man with a lot of patience for making small talk; but whenever I have been with him, particularly in his own house or here in ours, the conversation has flowed very smoothly indeed. One reason may have been that I always had a thousand questions to ask, and they were on topics about which Willie was very well informed... I quickly discovered that with Willie you aren't talking on the surface of some question; the conversation quickly takes the shape of a university seminar on the nub of the issue. Your description of him standing in the mess with a tankard in one hand, and giving evidence of his inner tension in half a dozen different body signals, was

absolutely dead on. I can recall, long before I got to know him, seeing him in the mess at Oulton a couple of times and thinking that he was the most intense character I'd ever laid eyes on in that setting. He looked like a hawk that had touched down for a drink, beside a pool somewhere, his head and eyes suddenly swivelling to lock onto someone talking to him.

Leonard Cheshire, who commanded the other squadron at Linton (76), and was nine months younger than Willie, was a natural leader. Innovative and gregarious, he had that special quality that lifts people and makes them think that in a crowd he is talking to them individually; the quality that makes you aware he has entered the room. Nevertheless I felt he forced himself into the role and really was a private person, with strong convictions that drove him to play whatever part was most likely to bring them to life.

His younger brother was shot down early in the war and taken prisoner. This was rumoured to be the reason behind Chesh's ambition to kill Germans, which he spoke about in a businesslike way that surprised me. One incident impressed me particularly. It was a day when bad weather had grounded everyone and a few of us were in the Ops Room to see if there was any chance of flying that night. Chesh was standing in front of the wall map of northwest Europe, the mileage radii centred on the worn spot marking Linton, where a ribbon was anchored with distances inked on it like a measuring tape. He put his finger on a little town not far from the German-Dutch border, between Emden and Wilhelmshaven, and said: "You know, twelve of us in formation could destroy that place. We could go in low in daylight and just destroy it. Kill everyone. Nothing left." He had a dramatic way of saying things, and he meant it.

At Marston Moor, I was privileged to spend quite a lot of time with him. It was his first command other than a squadron. He delighted in familiarizing himself with, and seeking ways to improve, the infrastructure that keeps flying stations going. After about six months, however, he tired of it and took a reduction in rank to return for his third tour of operations. Later he also commanded 617 Sqn., and after completing his 100th operation, was awarded the VC to add to his three DSOs and DFC.

Chapter 6

▣ 1944—1952 ▣

For Ruth, the four years from July 1942 to May 1946 were a blend of loneliness and frustration while she was waiting in Canada, and then in England of trying to cope with rationing and shortages in accommodation that was usually cold, isolated, and uncomfortable. As the wife of an RAF officer, she was entitled to passage at any time after I left in July. Between us—I through RAF channels and she through her Father's political connections in Ontario—we kept up the pressure for a berth in one of the ships being convoyed through the continuing battles between our air and naval forces and the U-boats.

The waiting period lasted until the following April, but we wrote to each other at least once a week and preserved security by arranging that, when Ruth got word, she would cable that she was going to stay with Treca. Dick Waterhouse, whose wife, Noni, was waiting too, was also stationed in Yorkshire. We kept in touch. Ruth and Noni sailed from Halifax on the same ship, the *Baltrover*, 8,000 tons, and with a list while still in port.

The crossing took twenty-one days, during which the two women were battered and bruised from being thrown against the sides of passages and companionways, were not once out of their clothes, and saw three ships of the convoy go down. (Ruth had been seasick crossing Lake Superior en route to Rivers in 1940, and was sick again when we crossed the Atlantic on Cunarders in 1948 and 1957, yet that time, when the little *Baltrover* was tossed about by the storms, she had no qualms.)

Neither she nor Noni had any way of knowing whether their husbands, who they knew were operating, were still alive. Even when they docked in Cardiff, an air raid was in progress and they were kept on board another night. Only then were we told of their arrival and Dick and I met them the next day at Paddington.

Ruth and I stayed overnight in the Waldorf, and the following day we took the train to York. I had saved enough petrol coupons to take us on a few days' leave in the Lake District before settling into the rooms I had rented for us in Mrs. Taylor's house in Boston Spa, about four miles from Marston Moor.

By English standards, it was a pleasant enough house, but all we had was two rooms, a shared bathroom, and worse, a shared kitchen, complete with stone-flagged floor and, another first for Ruth, a gas stove. Mrs. Taylor was separated from her husband, and her mother lived there too, an Army widow, veteran of many years in India, but a cheerier soul than her daughter, and who passed on to Ruth a curry recipe that became an enduring favourite over the years.

Now it was my turn to see the familiar scene through Ruth's eyes. To her, everything seemed small—the fields, the cars, the shops, the narrow roads and twisting lanes, while lack of a car in daytime confined her radius to the village street and an occasional bus ride into Wetherby. By the end of the year, Mrs. Taylor could scarcely help noticing that Ruth was pregnant. We, naturally, were excited about this, but Mrs. Taylor wasn't, and made it quite clear we would have to leave. However, this was also the time when Chesh decided to drop a rank and return to operations.

After the Japanese attack on Pearl Harbor brought the United States into the war, he had been sent there on a publicity tour. When he was in New York, he met Constance Binney, the actress, whom he married. She came to England not long before Ruth, and stayed at the Station Hotel in York while Chesh was setting up suitable accommodation at Marston Moor.

Marston was a wartime station of hangars, Nissen huts, and, except for the control tower, single-storey buildings. All the living quarters, including the station commander's, were heated after a fashion by coke-burning stoves. To improve on this, Chesh acquired a railway carriage from the London & North Eastern

Railway, had it shipped on an RAF low-loader from the nearest branch line, and installed it on concrete blocks in a field of Dawson's Farm some distance behind the officers' mess. The partitions of what had been passenger compartments were taken out and replaced with others, so that the interior comprised a bedroom, sitting room, kitchen and bathroom.

In the kitchen were a two-burner electric stove and a boiler that supplied hot water, not only for cooking and washing (there was a tiny bathroom off the kitchen), but also to radiators in the sitting room and bedroom. The entrance doors to kitchen and sitting room were standard LNER, complete with strap to lower or raise the window. Built on to one side of the carriage, parallel with the end of the sitting room, was a small wooden structure consisting of steps leading to the entrance door and, through another door, to a chemical toilet—an Elsan. Water was piped in from the mess, and Chesh bought a double bed to supplement the RAF furniture shipped over from his quarter.

Constance was a good sort, but quite out of her element, and since she was to return to the States when Chesh left Marston, he offered us tenancy.

The railway carriage was certainly an improvement on Mrs. Taylor's rooms, but hardly the place Ruth would have chosen to live, let alone care for her first baby. We inherited Chesh's arrangement for one of the waiters to bring groceries from the mess (which we paid for). There was a telephone, running hot and cold water and, except in very cold weather, relative warmth inside. We were also free of landladies.

We were also just to one side of the line of takeoff from the short runway, which was used when the prevailing wind shifted, as happened when the Halifax with the overspeeding prop crashed and burned in the wood on the other side of the field. Coke for the boiler was kept in a heap at one end of the carriage, with barbed wire surrounding it to keep the cows and sheep away, but we would often hear and feel cows bumping against the walls at night.

Proc came to see us, flying a Warwick, as did Desmond, flying from Norfolk in a B-17, and two or three Canadian friends from stations in 6 Group—but apart from the occasional mess function at Marston or a neighbouring station, and a few trips into

York for shopping, Ruth and Peter were very much alone in Farmer Dawson's field.

When 7 Group was formed to administer all Bomber Command's Heavy Conversion Units, I was posted to the head-quarters in Grantham as the group's training inspector. With my now proven capacity for finding duff lodgings, I had contracted with Mrs. Edwards, who had made over her large house into a species of flats. Ours consisted of a sitting/dining room on the ground floor, overlooking not a bad garden, and a large bedroom on the third floor, complete with concave double bed, a huge wardrobe that Ruth and I, lying in the bed, decided must have been lifted in by crane while the house was being built, and plenty of room for Peter's cot. "Our" bathroom was on the second floor, shared with whoever the people were who slept on that floor, and Ruth shared the kitchen with a pleasant childless woman whose husband I never met.

In 1944, the domestic side of things was overshadowed by rationing and the attendant bureaucracy, so that Ruth spent days after we got there registering for Peter's concentrated orange juice and powdered milk, for our scraps of meat, and for groceries (cloth-ing coupons were in a separate book). Scarce items like toilet paper were jealously guarded: when Ruth's brother, Bill, came to stay, he was given our roll with strict orders to bring it back again every time. It's quite possible that Margaret Thatcher formed her antipathy to socialism as a result of watching her father wrestling with the coupon-clipping business that beset grocers' lives in those days.

By the time I was posted to 90 Sqn. at Tuddenham (October, 1945), Ruth was pregnant with John, accommodation in and around Bury St. Edmunds was almost non-existent, and after a series of one-night stands in bloody awful pubs, we moved into Lane End Cottage, Fornham All Saints, about eight miles from Bury.

It turned up after a series of evenings touring the Suffolk coun-tryside and knocking at the doors of any house that looked big enough to have the odd spare room; this time, though, at a vicarage. The vicar and his wife entertained us in their spacious, stone-flagged kitchen, lighted by an acetylene lamp on the wooden table. "The local council offered us a choice," the vicar explained, "either the electricity or the water, and [pointing to the sink] we chose the water."

134

Lane End Cottage, his wife confided, was the property of a colonel in the army nursing service who was in Germany and had left care of the cottage in their hands. It was a modern cottage with electricity—looking doubtfully at us, she asked if Ruth knew anything about electric stoves. We drove away hardly daring to believe our luck, but when an approving wire from Germany gave us tenancy and we went to see the place, we found that "modern" had been used somewhat loosely.

The name was dead on: at the end of the lane leading from the village green on which a goat was tethered near the telephone box. Beyond the cottage was a camp for Italian POWs, while on the village side, our nearest neighbours were quite possibly the oldest inhabitants. Entry was through a glassed-in vestibule to a square—and freezing cold—hall. Doors led to a sitting room and a breakfast room (locked, and used by the owner for storage), and a passage at the far side led to the inevitable stone-flagged kitchen and scullery. Upstairs were four bedrooms, one serving as a library that included the complete *Forsyte Saga*.

The "modern" tag derived from an electric stove in the scullery, and alongside it over the sink was a pump that raised water to a cistern in the bathroom upstairs: 200 pumps to a bath, we were told, rather like winding up the undercarriage in the Anson. The kitchen had a coal-fired range that the electric stove saved us from battling with, and although one day I surprised a rat on its way out of it, I didn't tell Ruth until long afterwards; the set-up was grim enough without that.

There were two small anthracite stoves, one in the hall and one on the upstairs landing, that I managed to keep alight from time to time to "take the chill off," in the customary phrase, but all the time we were there, we were very cold indeed. Ruth's brother, Bill, came to stay at Christmas. When we showed him to the spare bedroom, he looked at the rather lumpy bed and said, "There's someone in it already!"

At the station, the squadron commander's quarter was a converted picket post, damp and colder even than the room I had suffered in at Manston in 1937 when, swotting for exams on the sn course, I wore greatcoat and flying boots. Whenever I stayed overnight at the airfield, I woke tired from shifting under the weight of blankets and greatcoat. Years later, when I was at Air

Ministry, I saw a report by Air Chief Marshal Sir John Slessor on wartime airfields—which ones should be kept or scrapped—and wasn't surprised to read his note on Tuddenham: "A bloody awful place which should be returned to pasture."

I had been told I would be going to the Staff College in January (1946), and arranged to take over a friend's flat in Gerrard's Cross, where the college was. Instead, I was posted to the RCAF Staff College at Armour Heights in Toronto, quite devastating news not only because it meant leaving Ruth at the very worst time, but even more because of my going to the place where she would much rather be herself. Worse, a bachelor commanding a squadron at a nearby station, who was going to Gerrard's Cross and was more than willing to swap places with me, was told no dice and I had to go.

Our plan had been for me to look after Peter until Ruth was fit enough to bring the baby home, but in fact she was still in the Bury hospital, both she and baby John with colds, when I left. With the help of the vicar's wife, we arranged for a super woman, a semi-retired Nanny Hunt, to look after Peter in her own house and to lend Ruth a hand when she left the hospital, a grim place with temporary wards and drafts everywhere. Lane End on her own, however, didn't bear thinking about, and I phoned Aunt Treca to ask if she could take Ruth and the babies until Ruth could get passage to Canada.

By that time, Treca had been widowed for some years, her only son Alan was married and living in Devonshire, and although she had generously made a home for my brother Tom after Mother died, she was naturally used to doing things her own way. She agreed at once, but I can understand how hard it was for her to adjust to having a much younger woman and two very young children turning up at short notice.

For Ruth, the next three months were a nightmare. Treca was a kind-hearted woman, but one accustomed to speak her mind. Consequently, Ruth was hypersensitive about keeping the babies quiet and trying to stifle her own coughing at night from the persistent cold she had acquired in the Bury hospital. Shopping, rationing, struggling with pounds, shillings and pence in the household accounts, walking the babies and caring for them— despite all this, she arranged for two maiden ladies who lived next door to look after Peter and John while she took trams into Southampton to pester shipping offices for a passage to Canada.

So soon after the war, priority went naturally to returning US and Canadian forces. Because I was merely attached to the college for a six-month course, the Air Ministry had no interest in us; we were on our own. But Ruth was determined, and we had left some money in Canada that enabled us to pay in dollars, which gave us a little leverage. Her mother died while we were at Lane End, and Mr. Craig lived in the family home with the aid of a housekeeper.

He and I went to see Ontario's lieutenant governor, who put in a word for us to Ontario's agent general in London. Once again, the maiden ladies were called into play while Ruth took train to London, didn't get much joy from the agent general, but struck up a friendship with his secretary, another Ruth (Jennings), and took her to lunch at Fortnum's. Could Ruth travel at short notice if there was a last-minute cancellation? Not long afterwards, there was a phone call from London while Ruth was walking the babies. When she called back, the other Ruth said a man who worked for Heinz had just cancelled his single cabin on the luxury liner *Stella Polaris*.

The only thing was it would be sailing from Bergen—could Ruth make it across London to Newcastle for the ferry service to Norway? One of the maiden ladies agreed to travel with Ruth to Newcastle, and the four of them fought their way across London on the first anniversary of VE Day. Peter was two, John not quite four months, so that trying to feed them both and change John in the succession of trains and then the ferry across the North Sea was something Ruth still doesn't want to talk about. Two days later, she was sailing along the English Channel and passing not far south of Southampton en route to New York.

That passage, although a big improvement on the *Baltrover*, was almost too sudden a contrast with rationed England. The rich food caused her discomfort (Peter saw his first banana), and she had to find ways to wash and dry napkins. By the time we met in New York, she had lost a lot of weight, had not completely shaken off the cough, and was emotionally drained, but manifestly relieved to be home in the land of relative plenty. We stayed overnight at The Bristol and flew the next day to Toronto.

To that extent, things were looking up. Ruth and the children moved into the family home, passing the housekeeper, who had heard that the married daughter was coming, on her way out in the hall. I made my way to Barrie at weekends until the course was over, and in the meantime began to agitate for an exchange posting in Canada.

This wasn't easy. The Forces were winding down, it was hard to get answers from anyone, and we spent two frustrating months, when we might have been trying to get accommodation at the next place, not knowing where it was or even in which country. The resolution was to attach me to the UK Air Liaison Staff in Ottawa to interview Canadians who had applied for short-service commissions in the RAF, a temporary job until Air Ministry posted me as an exchange officer and the RCAF put me in charge of flying training at Headquarters in Ottawa.

That was in September 1946, when accommodation in Ottawa was not to be had, and we spent the winter in a summer cottage in Kars, 20 miles south of the city.

Kars was a village about the size of Rivers, without the glamour of the railway. Running through it is a branch of the Rideau River, and at the end of the village street was the cottage we lived in for the winter and early spring of 1946-47. It was heated by a coal-burning stove in the sitting room, from which the stovepipe rose through the ceiling to the main bedroom above. There, it emerged to the left of the foot of our bed and passed just below the ceiling across our room, through one of the two smaller bedrooms, to the outer wall. The effect, as Ruth and I lay in bed, was rather as if we were spectators at a fantastic game of football.

In one corner of the room, just like Rivers, though private this time, was the Elsan, whose bucket I would carry very gingerly down the stairs at weekends to deposit the contents downstream at the foot of the garden. The kitchen had a coal-burning stove and a two-burner. We fetched our drinking water in pails from a neighbour across the street, but the washing water was drawn by a pump at the side of the sink from a walled tank in the half-basement that led off the kitchen. Rainwater from the roof fed into the tank until freeze-up, when the supply stopped. Toward the end of the winter, the tank ran dry.

This was inconvenient, because Ruth had no source of running—well, pumped—water at the sink, so I hit on the idea of part-filling the tank from the river. It took a while, because I had to break a hole in the ice and cart it a pail at a time through the kitchen, down the narrow stairway, and then hoist it over the wall into the tank. This turned out to be just before the spring thaw, and within it seemed days of that exercise, the river flooded—we were actually disturbed, seated in the sitting room, by the sound of a boat bumping against the wall (the tank was full by then, like the basement).

That was after the incident when, for some reason, I chased Peter up the stairs to his bedroom (at the far side of the goal), forgetting that I had placed a mat over a gap in the floorboards of his room, and stuck my pyjama-clad leg through the ceiling of the sitting-room below, where Ruth was, and laughing.

We drove through Kars in 1989 and it had grown quite a bit in forty years, but the cottage was still there, looking pretty good really, as you can see from the picture. Wouldn't have minded spending a summer there.

However, we spent the summer of 1947 in a house on Fentiman Avenue in South Ottawa while the owners were at their cottage, and, with days to spare before they were due back, were lucky to find 459 Broadview Avenue in Westboro, where we lived for the second year of the posting. That house, too, still looks pretty good.

Where and how we lived for the first dozen years of our married life is a testament to the fact that whatever talent I had was totally unsuited to the elementary duty of finding us places to lay our heads; at that, I was a washout. Even during the war, when accommodation of any kind was at a premium, we might have fared a good deal better if Ruth had been doing the searching. As it was, she was the one who had to suffer the consequences of my conflicting traits. I was too ready to sign for places which, given the chance, she would have passed by; too lazy to keep looking once a Mrs. Edwards or a summer cottage had turned up.

It's no accident that most of the things I remember as part of my life are what I did, what my jobs were, and how I felt about the different circumstances. That Ruth was capable and a good wife and mother is no justification for my being not merely content to leave most of the parenting to her, but being also too selfish to realize the hardships she had to contend with. I assumed that she would adapt to English conditions as different from what she was used to as her condition was from that of English wives. Unlike Ruth, they were in their own country, had parents or other relatives to support them, and had grown used to whatever privations they suffered because they had happened gradually. They were used to cold houses, and rain, and open fires, and waiting for buses, and queueing.

Thus, while Ruth was battling conditions in Kars, I had an interesting job at the headquarters on Elgin Street, where I came to meet a lot of new people as well as some survivors from the early days of the war. In April 1948, when seven of us took a Dakota on a liaison tour of USAF training establishments at Barksdale Field, Louisiana, Gordie Wellstead and I rode in a Mitchell (B-25) while the USAF pilot demonstrated a hands-off blind approach by automatic pilot right down and onto the deck—but on a clear day.

The celebrated size of Texas was brought home to me (it was my turn to fly the Dakota) when we left Randolph (near San Antonio), landed at Biggs Field, El Paso, three and a half hours later, and were still in Texas, on the States' side of the Rio Grande.

While we were there, we drove across the river from El Paso to Juarez (like going from Ottawa to Hull, someone said), and later flew to three different fields in California that allowed us to make the routine tour of a Hollywood studio and have our picture taken with Loretta Young and Robert Cummings on a set which included a swimming pool ($5 a day dry, $10 wet, one of the extras told me). Throughout we were shepherded by a cheery and gregarious USAF major who also arranged a trip to Sutter's Dam, where gold was first discovered in California.

Our route back passed through Albuquerque, where I bought Ruth a turquoise bracelet, and then north to Lowry Field (Denver), before which there was some discussion as to whether we should make a dog-leg into Salt Lake City, Utah, before going on to Lowry. We had been away sixteen days, a vote was taken and the majority was for going straight to Lowry and riding the tail wind the next day to Detroit and Trenton. I remember Tommy Thompson saying: "We'll never remember what we did on the extra day at home; we would never have forgotten a day in Salt Lake City."

At the end of the two-year exchange, my posting was to the Joint Services Staff College at Latimer, near Amersham in Buckinghamshire, for the six-month course there. We drove through the States to Halifax, watched our 1938 Pontiac coupe (bought two years before, quite a prize in the post-war car shortage) being hoisted on to the *Aquitania*, and sailed on that famous ship's last voyage before she was broken up.

Dad's sister, Rose (Auntie Mac), by then Mrs. Paul and living in Harrow, had booked us into the Kensworth residential hotel in Chesham Bois, and we set about the inevitable search for quarters. If you saw the play/film *Separate Tables*, you have the picture of the dining room at the Kensworth. We had "our" table, on which at mealtimes the staff placed "our" preserves and condiments, each bottle or jar bearing its pencil mark at the last level of the contents to guard against pilfering of those treasures. Peter and John were the only children, and of course, they ate with us— both, I'm happy to say well-behaved—but naturally making a bit more noise than the elderly people around us. I remember one occasion when Ruth and I looked at each other, and I couldn't resist saying out loud, "Why are we whispering?'

Our search ended at Manor Barn, of Elizabethan date, on the green in Chesham Bois. This after being interviewed by the owners (he a solicitor in whose rooms in the Temple I signed the lease) to see if we were suitable tenants for their freezing cold upstairs/downstairs flat. We saw it on a sunny, warm September day, when the ancient rose trees trailed their blooms up the walls of faded Tudor brick and, inside, we saw *hot-water radiators*.

The owners occupied most of the barn's ground floor, while our entrance gave onto a small dining/room kitchen from which stairs led to three bedrooms and a large sitting room the width of the barn. Leading off the kitchen was a tiny furnace room, which we were required to service and which devoured a good deal of my pay as the winter advanced.

That was when we discovered that the radiators, in that ancient, uninsulated barn, were adequate for what they might have been designed for, such as airing socks, but of no use at all in a large sitting room with no fireplace. We put our bed in it, used the smallest bedroom to sit in, but were often forced to huddle in the kitchen within at least striking distance of the ghastly furnace.

England in 1948-49 wasn't the cheeriest place, especially after Ottawa. Rationing was still in full force, and the services were dealt a reduction in pay by the Labour government. The pluses were getting to know some fine soldiers, sailors, and airmen, and learning quite a bit about how things were done in the other services. Some had already done great things or went on to them afterwards. John Searby was Master Bomber on the Peenemünde raid in August 1943 that delayed the Germans' V2 rocket programme and scuppered the work on an atomic bomb. Robert Thompson, a foreign office civilian on the course who had emerged from the war as a wing commander with a DSO and DFC, was expert in guerrilla warfare and became an adviser to the White House in the later stages of the Vietnam War, when he finally persuaded the Pentagon to adopt the fortified village technique that worked for us in Malaya.

Field Marshal Slim came to talk about leadership on a morning when the pay cut had been announced. It was pouring outside the Nissen hut-type lecture hall, and many of us had shared petrol-short cars from diggings our wives cordially disliked. He spoke for about twenty-five minutes, and I forget what he said, but when he had finished, we strode out of that room with our chests sticking out, ready to take on the world.

On another occasion, a rather pompous naval commander on the directing staff was describing the role of batsman on an aircraft carrier. He said, "If an aircraft is approaching with only one undercarriage leg extended, the batsman will warn the pilot by standing on one leg and raising the other, like this." As he showed us the movement, buffoon McDonald couldn't resist the question: "Sir, how does he signal if both legs are up?"

Another naval member of the DS had been captain of *Diamond* when she collided with *Swiftsure* during a NATO exercise. He told us, "I got a signal from C-in-C Rosyth asking me what I intended to do, and I made a signal back that I was going to buy a farm."

We were also talked to by Admiral Sir Philip Vian, a brave and stern-looking sailor, who finished his talk and waited for questions, first of which was drawled by a portly RAF member of the DS who stood up at the back of the hall and said, "I hope you won't think me impertinent, sir," at which Philip Vian banged the lectern and said fiercely, "I hope I won't, sir."

Hanging over us as always was the business of postings at the end of the course: where would we go? This brings us back to Croydon and the two houses Mother left, one each to Tom and me. They were rented, and my idea was to get a posting to Air Ministry so that we could give the tenants six months' notice and live at 1 Duppas Road. However, when I wrote to them, I was reminded that they had tenancy under the relevant Act and they were staying.

It transpired that I would have to go to court and try to prove that our family, with two young children, would suffer "greater hardship" by not living there than the tenants with two grown children who were working. I duly went to court in Croydon, won the case, and we moved into the house, which seemed to have shrunk a good deal.

The posting was to O. Est.8 at Air Ministry, in charge of overseas establishments and sundry odd units, and located in Bush House. This was almost back to square one at the Sun Insurance Office. The job was more interesting—if you want to learn how an air force is put together and what the various functions are, get a job in the establishments branch—but once again I was commuting from Croydon to London and working in an office.

Still, Bush House was a walk away from the National Gallery, the Wallace Collection was within reach at lunchtime, and so was the Tate. There were pleasant pubs nearby for a bite at noon, and Ruth soon lined up sitters for the odd dinner and theatre. After trying out 1 Duppas for a few months, we decided to move. Ruth had to drive Peter to and fetch him from his school, taking John with her. She was pregnant with Martha, and we wanted to find somewhere that had a garage and was within walking distance of a school for the boys.

First we had to sell 1 Duppas—soon after we advertised it, we got a nasty letter from the tenants' lawyer alleging that we had never intended to live there and wanted only to get the money for it. I sent it on to Auntie Kit's solicitor in Southampton and heard no more.

Seven Mount Park Avenue suited us very well: double-fronted; garage big enough to squeeze the Pontiac into; two or three minutes' walk from Cumnor House School, and five minutes from some stores and Purley Oaks Station; long garden looking across the valley to Sanderstead.

Unlike standard English kitchens of the period, ours had no boiler, hot water being supplied by an electrically heated tank in the bathroom upstairs. But the kitchen was narrow—too narrow for the washing machine. We put it in the dining room next to the wall it shared with the kitchen, and passed the hoses through two holes bored in the wall to the kitchen where, when in use, they could be lifted to the sink. This made a conversation piece when we were entertaining friends, but it was only one of the innovations we embarked on in the running battle to fit an English house with something like the conveniences that were commonplace in Canada.

Haunting the English was the myth spread by school geography books that the climate was "equable" due to the warming influence of the Gulf Stream toward the end of its 6,000 mile journey from the Gulf of Mexico. Buttressing the myth, and its principal manifestation in a near-total dependence upon open fireplaces for indoor heating, was the assertion that central heating, for a people exposed to propaganda about the virtues of taking cold baths, was unhealthy. Thus, the only built-in means of heating our three bedroom house were fireplaces.

We put gas fires in the dining room and two bedrooms (the smaller third had no fireplace), and decided to insulate the sitting room. It ran the depth and half the width of the house, with tiled windowsills and French doors opening on to a sheltered and tiled patio; a very pleasant room in spring and summer, but when we moved in late November, it was all the colder for its greater volume. We had phosphor bronze stripping installed around the doors leading to the hall and the kitchen, the wooden floorboards that rested a few inches above Surrey soil were tongued and grooved, and we had the gas company fit a burner in the fireplace that would keep its load of coke glowing red. This worked reasonably well until we found ourselves becoming drowsier than usual and traced it to fumes from the burning gas and coke—we were forced to open a window.

As with most English houses, the only things built-in were the kitchen sink (from which the departing owners had removed the draining board), the fixture in the lavatory, and the bath and hand-basin in the bathroom, which in our case also boasted a metal towel rail heated from the hot water system. Since the fireplace in our bedroom stood out a few inches into the room from the centre of the outside wall, we decided to have built-out cupboards fitted on either side of it. Fifty years on, I like to think they're serving the present owners as well as they did us in our two.

One thing you don't get much of in a staff job is flying practice. At first, I drove with Ruth and the boys to Redhill. That was in the summer of 1949. We would take a picnic, and she and they would sit on the edge of the grass airfield while I tottered around in a Tiger Moth. Afterwards, I went to Hendon, where the Air Ministry Communications Flight had some Proctors, and managed to put in about three flights a month—mostly on longish cross-countries to places, I see from my log book, as far as the Welsh border and Anglesey.

But the longest trip was by civil airline to Stockholm, and it lasted from March 27 to April 13, 1951. The visit was prompted by an article in *The Daily Telegraph* alleging that the Royal Swedish Air Force had, in proportion to its front-line aircraft establishment, a very much shorter administrative tail than the RAF. The task was "to discover how this apparent economy in manpower was achieved, and to consider whether any aspects of the RSAF organizational methods might be adapted to RAF needs."

The problem was how to draw a comparison that would not only be demonstrable from the facts, but would also form a basis that the RAF might be able to learn from. Fortunately, the RSAF were exceedingly helpful. The C-in-C was General Nordenskjold, and he set a pattern from the first day's briefing that was followed faithfully by all the officers we met afterwards. They were open and friendly and did everything to make what was a daunting job as painless as they could. The RAF air commodore and senior civil servant who headed our group of three returned to England at the end of the formal meetings, leaving me to write the report. At the end of the stay, I felt I knew more about the RSAF than many of its own staff officers.

I also became victim to an insomnia that plagued me the whole time. Whether as a result of the strain in preparing for the trip, or the high latitude and short nights, or a combination of those, I was quite unable to sleep. The first night I put aside as being overtired, but the next night was the same, and the next, in a ghastly sequence of dreading to get up and face more briefings, more tours of facilities, more socializing, and more sleepless nights.

Too proud to tell anyone, the idea of seeking medical help simply didn't occur to me. The only time I had asked a doctor for pills of any kind was on March 1, 1943, when I had a heavy cold, Berlin came up for the second time, and I got the MO to give me something to dry it up.

The thing became more bearable after the other two left and I was able to get down to writing the report on my own. After trying a number of approaches, I hit on the idea of taking the role of the RSAF's order of battle as a base and constructing on it an air force established to RAF manning scales. This entailed a fair amount of work under pressure, because I needed to know exactly how many people, and of what categories—service, service retired and re-employed, and civilian, ranks or equivalent, trades and job descriptions—the RSAF had, before I could draw any conclusions; and this had to be got before I went back to England.

Major Hansen was a tower of strength (so was Pat Burnett, the RAF's Air Attaché, whose wife, Mary, set a fine example in Stockholm's stratified and ultra-formal social circuit) and by the time I crawled on to the BEA airplane, I had most of the report done. When manning experts in Air Ministry had put the finishing touches to it, the upshot was that if the RAF were to do the same job as the RSAF, to RAF scales, we would have used 19 percent more people (not six times, as the newspaper article had alleged). Most of the difference lay in the staff: we established many more people in headquarters formations than the Swedes did, and the reason was cultural/historical.

Culturally, the Swedes, with about eight million people running a modern industrialized society, were instinctively cost-conscious. Neutrality imposed on them, as it does on the Swiss, a large degree of self-sufficiency, especially in armaments for defence, and if they were to achieve some sort of balance they had to be competitive enough in price and quality to sell the stuff abroad.

So that was one thing: they couldn't afford to waste resources, whether material or human, and they went to great lengths to husband them. Then again, they hadn't been at war for almost 150 years, so that none of their three services had experienced the wartime expansions and subsequent contractions that tended to leave war-inflated staffs in place afterwards. For example, an RSAF Group HQ, with six fighter stations under command, each of them housing three squadrons, consisted of seven officers and two airmen/civilians. For the same task, an RAF group HQ would have employed 18 officers and 106 airmen/civilians.

The RSAF group did its job by personal supervision, by delegating considerable responsibility to station commanders (who were given money and manpower budgets within which to hire and fire people and run the station), and by keeping paperwork to a minimum. One group commander said that he had no wish for his HQ to become a post office, and that he wrote very few letters to his stations. On inquiry, I found that "very few" was less than ten a year; he did his job by flying to the stations—in all weathers in a front-line aircraft—and seeing for himself.

The report made a number of recommendations, each of which was supported by argument that got in some worthwhile digs at wasteful practices. Because of its origins in criticism from the press, the report was circulated to everyone from the Minister down, and it's interesting to look back from now these many years at the way much of what we recommended has come about. No doubt circumstances played a big part, such as diminishing commitments overseas as the Empire shrivelled, and the UK's deteriorating economic condition at the hands of successive Labour governments. Still, what we recommended was rooted in common sense, which tends to work its magic in the end on any system— even, after seventy years, on Communism.

When we were at 7 Mount Park Avenue, Auntie Mac died. I went to see her once or twice while she was in hospital, and though she must have known she was dying, she was as cheerful as ever. She left me fifty pounds in her will, and it seemed absolutely right to spend it on a weekend in Paris, of which I was sure she would have approved.

That was in 1950, when there were limits to the amount of money you could take out of England, but the airfare didn't count, so we had fifty pounds to spend on three nights in Paris. I booked us on BEA, Ruth organized a sitter, and after the usual fight with a Paris cab-driver, we were in a small hotel counting out our French money on the bed to see how much we could spend.

We didn't waste much time in the hotel. The weather was good, we rode the Metro and autobuses, and sat outside cafés, and walked and walked. The photo of Ruth was taken on the paved area outside the Palais de Chaillot. At one in the morning, we were sitting at *un zinc* sipping cognac and arguing about where the children should be educated—a perennial problem for people in the British services, and which we were obliged to face on our next move to the RAF Staff College.

With Treca Maxwell, Southampton, 1943

The Railway Carriage, Marston Moor, 1943–44

Inside the railway carriage

Marston Moor, 1943

Lane End, Fornham all Saints, with Peter and Bill Craig (Ruth's brother, RCAF), 1945

Leaving Marston Moor

Peter at Kars

Halifax, NS, 1948

Peter and John, Manor Barn, Chesham Bois, 1948

Bournemouth, 1949

Bournemouth, 1949

*Ruth with Florrie and Ted
Careless, 1949*

7, Mount Park Avenue, S. Croydon, 1950

7, Mount Park Avenue

RIGHT: *Paris, 1950*

Sweden, 1951, with the Royal Swedish Air Force

Fosca, Costa Brava, Spain, 1953

Bracknell, 1954

Scotland, 1954

*Ruth with Peter, Buckingham Palace,
1953, for Ken's Investiture - OBE*

Chapter 7

▣ 1952—1954 ▣

When the Air Ministry tour was ending I was given the choice of joining the directing staff at either Latimer or the RAF Staff College at Bracknell, and we chose Bracknell. I was a senior wing commander with sixteen years service and getting about two thousand pounds a year. We had sold 7 Mount Park Avenue for 3,450 pounds, and in Canada Ruth had the $10,000 her father left her when he died.

While at Air Ministry I had looked into the possibility of leaving in order to join the RCAF, but it wasn't on. The Korean War was in progress, which was given as one reason, and the Latimer course represented a considerable investment, which was given as the other. We still intended to go to Canada but it seemed only sensible to serve the four more years that would qualify me for a minimum pension. What we hoped for was to round off our service with an overseas posting, almost anywhere except the Canal Zone.

That was where Desmond McGlinn, who had married Irene Coulson in Ottawa during his Canadian tour, was in 1949. I still have his letter, in which he wrote:

> The Middle East Air Force is a snare and a delusion, in a big way, and if you take my advice you will never come within spitting distance of the place. It's a corner of Egypt which should have remained flooded after the deluge. We should certainly never have argued about it with Egypt. A

tour here is nothing more than a prison sentence, and what is worse it's hard work.

Firstly, the whole place is nothing more than occupied desert, occupied in two senses, the first being that if it was unoccupied for 24 hours there would be nothing of value left by the defty wallahs. Secondly, everything is surrounded by barbed wire and needs to be. When the Israel war was on, the Gyppos stole quite a large percentage of their ammo stocks from our dumps. Running battles would take place in the night as they lifted the 500 pounders etc.

From the married families aspect, I feel the place stinks, but generally Irene likes it. This schism is caused mainly by the working hours, which are in accordance with the spokesmen for the trade unions—the Government. Work starts on summer routine at 06.45 and finishes at 13.30, six days a week. Now that wouldn't be too bad if one stepped leisurely out of one's quarter and ambled gently down to the office. I live 25 miles from my office, in a flat in town. Of course I found the flat, it costs 30 pounds a month rent without a stick in it. We had to furnish from scratch again, including buying a cooker, water heater etc. That set us back at least 225 pounds.

I rise at 05.30 and catch a bus at 06.15 which gets me to the office at 06.55. If I miss that bus, it's merry hell to hitch a ride—none of this "send me a car" business. Actually because of the travel distance we leave the office at 13.10, getting home at 14.00, so at lunch time one has completed an eight hour working day, and I can assure you normally one feels it too. So when the work day ends the home day begins. The kids want to go out; being cooped up in a flat is no life for them, and mother wants to get rid of the kids, and father is torn between a sleep and some exercise. And then there's the business of catching ruddy bus etc. The cook is backsliding or the dhobi hasn't come etc., etc. Mother in the evening wants to go out, father wants to go to bed early so he won't be too handicapped at the office. And so it goes on...

Irene normally likes it here because she has no difficulty in catering, she has a cook and good laundry facilities, the weather is warm, and the social opportunities for amusement are many and lively. She never liked UK, particularly London. It's a great problem, that, one that causes me considerable disquiet. At this moment Irene is on a ship bound for Cyprus, with the kids. They have been away from school for about six weeks now and have nearly driven Irene completely round the bend. Poor kid, what a battle. The hot weather tends to make the kids pretty wild and restless, and of course they don't go to sleep until about 8, after rising at 05.30 or 6. It's a long day.

After some solid discussion of what the RAF was doing, what he was flying and so on, Desmond came back to the moving business, and ended with: "What a misery all the moving is, packing and unpacking; what a lot of things fall by the wayside in the process too."

The Communications Flight at White Waltham was equipped with Ansons and a Balliol, which we flew to keep our hands in, and on two occasions three of us flew to RAF stations in Germany to find out what was happening at the sharp end. I flew also to Acklington, where a friend offered to check me out on the Meteor, the first jet I had flown. Its only vice was a tendency to stall if you left the speed brakes out on the approach; otherwise it was a very pleasant aircraft, and of course, very quiet in the cockpit—you leave all that noise behind.

In the second year at Bracknell, two of us were given the job of writing a new War Manual for the RAF: A.P. 1300, *The Principles of Air Warfare*. This was in 1953, when many airmen were convinced that the bomber plus the nuclear weapon had made aircraft carriers obsolete and that the infantry's job would be to mop up and re-establish civil order after the air force had won the (very short) war.

We had a lot of fun writing all this down, egged on by the Assistant Commandant who had a DSO from his bomber ops, and I remember especially the demonstrations we laid on for visitors from Camberley and Greenwich. Soldiers and sailors didn't quite see eye to eye with us. (Looking back to 1991, when the American, British, Canadian, French and Italian air forces won the Gulf War in a few days, our proposition of 1953 wasn't too far off the mark, at that.)

Staff colleges are peculiar institutions. The object is to train officers to think and write clearly, and to study the various roles of the service as well as the elements of strategy and logistics, so that those who later prove suitable for higher command will be prepared to exercise it. In practice, this means that the Directing Staff are engaged in a sort of prolonged examination, not only of the six students in their current syndicates but also of as many of the remaining ninety as they can become acquainted with, so that a body of opinion is formed and prejudices get ironed out.

Since most of us are psychologists under the skin, the business is agreeable enough, flavoured as it is with the knowledge that you in turn are being studied by the senior DS and the Commandant and Assistant Commandant. This served to bolster my tendency to show off in public. I managed to make an ass of myself once or twice, but the two and a half years passed off reasonably well and I got to know many more officers—both of my own vintage and younger—than I could have at a flying station.

On the domestic side, we were faced with two problems: finding somewhere to live and a school for the children. To take schooling first, some people solved it by sending the children to boarding schools, others by wives staying put while the children were of school age. Neither alternative appealed to us. We felt that the most important part of education was in the home, and that although it was hard on the children to be moved about, that too was educational.

At Bracknell, the choice was between sending them as weekly boarders to Papplewick, in Ascot, or carting them back and forth to Holme Grange, near Wokingham, or letting them cycle to the local school not far from the Staff College—Bullbrook. We went to see the Head, were impressed with him and his wife, and decided to send the boys there (Martha was too young for school). It was what we would have done in Canada, and we thought we should support the system.

In the glasshouse atmosphere of the Staff College, I can see in retrospect that this must have set a lot of tongues wagging. We did get into a few arguments at the time, but it wasn't peer pressure that influenced us, nor the quality of instruction, which was quite good, so much as John's susceptibility to the local Berkshire dialect. This was unfair to him, we were conscious of it too, and

156

we moved the boys to Holme Grange.

It was run in a casual way by a brother of the poet Robert Graves, and it was a barn of a place. The assembly hall was heated by one Valor stove the same size as the five we later installed in our quarter, and Ruth has never forgotten the dormitories upstairs: bare floors, rock-hard beds, and no heat at all. When we got our posting to Singapore in December 1954, Mr. and Mrs. Graves pressed us to leave the boys with them (not only the Graves, but most of the wives of the DS were adamant that "you can't take the children to Singapore") but we didn't even consider it.

The move to Bracknell should have been easy. The theory was that we would sell 7 Mount Park Avenue and move straight into a married quarter at the Staff College. New married quarters were being built to replace the temporary ones—prefabs—that had been there since the war, and we had enough points to qualify for the second of the new ones. In good faith, therefore, we sold the house to another wing commander with occupancy in September, which was the month the new OMQs were to be ready, but they weren't, and we were once again without a roof.

Bracknell was still a village then, and since apart from the staff there were ninety-six officers on the course, every possible dwelling had been snapped up by the time I realized the college administrative officer's enthusiastic forecasts of completion dates were unreliable. A friend who had been on the staff for a year and was about to move into one of the pre-fabs offered to rent us the place they had been living in, and I took it.

It consisted of three units: a converted bus (single-decker) that he and his family had driven in around England and Wales on vacations; a caravan they had occasionally towed behind it; and a covered, raised passage between the two that allowed you to walk from the right-hand door of the caravan to the entrance door of the bus.

The passenger compartment of the bus was fitted with bunks for the children, there was a coke-burning stove in it, and the caravan had a Pither stove which heated water for cooking and the tiny bath. For the fourth time, we were back to an Elsan—Rivers, Marston Moor, Kars, and now Bracknell.

This menage was located in the paddock of The Bull, at one end of Bracknell's main street, and when I saw it on a warm

September day not unlike the day we first saw Manor Barn, it rather appealed to me. Blackberries were growing in the hedges, there was a pony in the next field, and although the infrastructure was less than perfect—water was laid on from The Bull courtesy of about a hundred feet of garden hose—you could see that for the week or two we expected to be there, it might be quite a bit of fun.

When I drove Ruth and the children from Croydon to inspect, I'll have to admit she wasn't really taken with it. It was a dull day and no doubt she was tired from all the packing, but I saw her point at once, about its being cramped and there not being any place to put things (most of my stuff was at the mess, where I'd kept a room). Still, the movers had set up the fridge and washing machine in the raised passageway, we did have electric light, and in a week or so we would be in the new quarter.

In fact, we were there for two months. Ruth and I lived and slept in the caravan, which was smaller than the bus and certainly smaller than the railway carriage, and if you haven't had that experience, apart from being lucky you may not appreciate how tidy we had to be. Everything was designed to fold away, so that before you did something else, you had to fold away whatever you were working on first.

Then the roof was just above your head, so that when it rained, as it often does in England, it was quite noisy inside, especially if the rain was heavy, or hail.

Ruth and I get along remarkably well, all things considered, but there were times in that caravan when our customary equanimity was put to the test; for example, when the hose sprang a leak, as it did from time to time, and I—or Ruth, if I was away— had to pull on rubber boots and fumble for the leak in the rain with a flashlight, knife and screwdriver to fix another clamp; or when we had put away the table on which I'd been commenting on syndicate papers so that we could get the bed things out from wherever they were hidden and set the bed up, only to hear one of the children and have to crawl over it to get slippers and dressing gown from wherever they were; or simply lugging stuff in from where the Pontiac was parked in the muddy lane. Most of the time we were able to laugh, at any rate after a while, partly because there was no point in losing one's temper and stamping out of the place. If you did, where were you? In a field in the rain.

Not long after we moved into the new quarter—No. 22 OMQ—the Commandant's wife came to call (there were no telephones; we all had to use the public box located approximately in the centre of the married patch). Ruth was bathing the children, and here I should explain for the benefit of readers unfamiliar with English houses that the overflow pipe from the bath was poked through the wall, on the theory that if it froze, the plumber would be able to get at it, and since the bathroom was immediately above the entrance hall, when the children splashed away and water gushed through the overflow pipe, it cascaded down right in front of where our visitor was standing.

The English building code is designed to prevent people from suffocating in their drafty houses: each room of the quarter, including the bathroom, had a ventilation brick set into an outside wall—that is, a brick with holes in for which the treatment that worked for us was to stuff the holes with wads of newspaper.

We moved in November, and the house was wet. Water literally trickled down the walls of the fourth bedroom, and we had to move the boys into a smaller one. We did our best to heat the place by blocking up the fireplace in the sitting room and installing a slow combustion stove, putting Valor paraffin stoves in the children's bedrooms, the bathroom and halls, and trying to keep the hot water boiler alight in the kitchen (the hot water pipe from it was the only pipe the builders were allowed to insulate, presumably to prevent the kitchen from getting stuffy). Although I seemed to spend a lot of time trimming wicks and topping up tanks with paraffin, there was no doubt that ours was the least cold house on the patch: when the snow came, ours was the only bare roof.

The Staff College tour was educational for me, and when people have been kind enough to say that some article or other explained what they had thought was a complex topic, I am reminded of the debt I owe to the two and a half years I spent encouraging a lot of other officers to think clearly. If they couldn't get it right in the head first, they couldn't put it on paper.

This was at the root of the Staff College method—the vehicle for inculcating it was the Appreciation. Review of the situation; selection and maintenance of the aim; factors affecting attainment of the aim; possible enemy courses of action; courses open to us;

conclusion and recommendations. For a wing commander on the DS, the prize was to be chosen to give the lecture on Appreciations. A friend from Harwell days gave it the first year I was there, and I can't remember whether he wrote the script himself or whether it was inherited from DS in the past. At any rate, when I was given the job the next year, I didn't see how I could improve either on the script or on the supporting charts and diagrams, so I set about learning it.

It was a two-hour lecture, two solid goes of fifty minutes each with questions after the second go, and it seemed far too important a topic to be tackled from notes (reading it was unthinkable). I memorized the whole thing in front of a mirror in the dining room of the quarter, worked in a couple of jokes I thought were funny (one of them got a very good laugh), and felt I had done at least as well as my predecessor.

It was generally assumed that being selected for the Directing Staff was the entrée to high rank, and that wasn't too far off the mark. Most of the DS who were there in my time retired as air commodores, four as air vice-marshals (two of them knights), Chris Foxley-Norris became Sir Christopher and an air chief marshal, and I was told by a former assistant commandant after we had both left the service that my assessment at Bracknell had put me at AVM or above.

Apart from the odd discomfort and one or two dicey incidents in the air, I enjoyed the RAF. The reason I left wasn't only because of wanting to live in Canada; it was a mixture, as most decisions are. The children were high on the list. By the end of the Far East tour, Peter would be thirteen, John eleven, and Martha seven. If we stayed in the RAF, they would grow up English, and at least for the formative years either Ruth would have to stay in one place or we'd be forced to send them to boarding school.

If we went to Canada, they would grow up Canadian and we would be able (here we assumed I would be earning enough) to send them all to university. In England, where going to university was still comparatively rare, we'd have been pressed to afford it on RAF pay. Then again, if we stayed in the RAF, my likely future jobs would have been mostly to do with supervision of or planning changes to activities I had been involved in during the past twenty years. In short, I'd already done the good parts. From there on, the jobs would be less interesting and more and more remote from the flying business.

Not that I wasn't ambitious. I wanted to be a group captain, but that was enough. I knew that, barring accidents, I would reach air rank, but that wasn't nearly enough to compensate for being moved about right up to eventual retirement. We saw this happening in Singapore. An air vice-marshal who was the Senior Air Staff Officer at Far East Air Force HQ, didn't know, when his tour was up, where he was going to be posted, and still didn't know when he and his wife boarded the ship for England. So, when once or twice Ruth remarked that if we'd stayed in we might have been Sir Kenneth and Lady McDonald, it was with a smile that bore no trace of regret. We might not, and where would we have been when we were tossed out at 55? Looking for a job in England.

A favourite, and natural, method among the more ambitious officers was to attach oneself to an acknowledged star. Not only would some of the glory rub off, but as he rose in rank and fame, so would he be inclined to take with him the people he had come to know and trust. Nor should I leave the impression that my passive attitude at Camp Borden in 1939—leaving career matters to fate and the moguls of P staff—was one I adhered to afterwards.

Once the war was over, I used whatever means I could to turn postings to my advantage. Of necessity, life in military service is more structured than elsewhere. Assessments are made at regular intervals, and progress is measured in the eyes of contemporaries by advances in rank and the acquisition of honours and awards. Nevertheless, justice is not always seen to be done.

Willie Tait, whose fourth DSO many of us think should have been the VC, was promoted in 1953 to the rank of group captain that he served in until his retirement after more than thirty years' service in 1966. How could an officer of such outstanding merit be passed over again and again for promotion to air rank? In my opinion, it was due to the quality Murray Peden noted, and that I sensed during my short acquaintance with him: a consummate professionalism that shut off trivial concerns which are the small change of social intercourse, shut off, in fact, everything that might detract from the best possible performance of the job at hand.

When Murray met him socially, he was long retired and settled in marriage, parenthood and civilian life, mellowed no doubt, but still imbued with the professional approach. ("...with Willie, you aren't talking on the surface of some question; the conversation quickly takes the shape of a university seminar on the nub of the issue.") How many of us indulged the prejudices of senior officers, were quick to agree with their opinions, and confused loyalty with subservience? I can see Willie giving a reasoned opinion, regardless of who asked for it, and sticking to it unless or until he could be shown by equally reasoned argument that he might be mistaken. His loyalty was always to the Royal Air Force, and I am sure he never wavered. If he had a passing doubt of the kind most of us felt as we watched the advancing careers of contemporaries, it would be quickly squelched. Whatever his job was at the time, he knew he was doing it to the best of his ability and was content. Very brave men survive more than danger.

Leonard Cheshire's subsequent career was a projection of the qualities he displayed in wartime. After the emotional high that had sustained him for six years, followed by the unique experience as observer of the atomic bomb dropped on Nagasaki, he said that he felt "lost and empty." For a time he worked as a logger in British Columbia, seeking not so much peace with himself as a cause to devote himself to. Many years later, he told a reporter:

> The realization that I had come through the war while everybody else I started with hadn't, made me feel I had to do something to help towards a better world. I went through very difficult stages searching for a big crusade but I never found it.

He contracted tuberculosis, lost one lung and sections of five ribs, and while still recuperating, came across an old man with terminal cancer who had fallen between gaps in the welfare state's manifold agencies and had nowhere to go. Cheshire was then living in "a huge house with no electricity—just three oil lamps." Convinced that the dying man was one of many abandoned by the State, he decided this was the cause he had been seeking. "Suddenly, everything fell into place." He took the man in, cared for him alone, and went on from there. In his autobiography (*The Hidden World*, published in 1981), he wrote:

> I was being given a most valuable lesson in the fundamental human needs and desires of the disabled person... They

162

wanted to feel useful and needed, to find a purpose and a challenge to their lives, to have sufficient independence and opportunity to lead a life of their own choosing. Above all, I found they wanted to be givers to society, not just receivers....

In the Epilogue, he wrote:

I believe that a charitable organization, like a religious one, gains a great advantage when it has slightly less money than it would like to have, and is at a disadvantage when it has more than it really needs. To be short of money, not quite able to see how you are going to make ends meet at the end of the month, is undoubtedly a source of considerable worry for those involved. At the same time, it is healthy. It means that you have to stop and think whether what you are planning to do is really necessary.... History shows how even the religious orders, indeed the Church herself, have lost something of their essential spirit and drive when they have become wealthy....

It is possible to be so obsessed by what is wrong in society as to overlook what is right, and to think that the Golden Age is just around the corner if only we can turn the world upside down, and make others see things as we do.... Man does not become good merely because the society in which he lives has been improved.... I know of no substitute in any field of human endeavour for hard work, for clear and realistic thinking and planning, and, most important of all, for perseverance. The person who ferrets away, who never lets go, who, when faced with an impasse or just cannot see what he should do next, is content to wait and relax until something happens to give him an opening, is the one who usually achieves the most.... It is the multiplication of many people, each working in their own chosen field and in their own individual way that brings about genuine change.

The house where he took the man in was the first of 270 Cheshire Homes that, by the time he died in 1992, he had founded in forty-nine different countries for the care of the sick and disabled. To the Victoria Cross had been added the singular distinction of the Order of Merit, while not long before he died, he was made Baron Cheshire of Woodhall.

In 1959, Cheshire married Sue Ryder (later Baroness Ryder of Warsaw and founder of The Sue Ryder Homes for the sick and disabled—the two foundations remained separate legal entities, complementing each other), and they had two children. When he died, I wrote to her. In her reply she told me:

> Leonard was ill for about a year and he had never experienced really good health. He bore his suffering courageously and with fortitude. Nursing him was a great privilege... Alas, the last months of his life proved really hard for him, especially as he had no saliva for a long time. Normally patients with Motor Neurone Disease [known in North America as Lou Gehrig's Disease] have excess saliva. No pharmacist or hospital could locate the ingredients needed to make up the liquid I used in Relief Teams after the war in improvised "hospitals" amidst the ruins of Poland and elsewhere, and which I knew would relieve his discomfort. For some unknown reason the ingredients were withdrawn from the pharmaceutical firms later.
>
> Leonard told me he was ready to die but added "I am offering up my suffering and small discomforts so that your work should consolidate and grow with more funds and people to help you." The nights were the worst, and when we prayed together we remembered the example of faith and courage of those who had endured indescribable horrors during the years of both world wars and those who continue to suffer today.

On a different plane, and returning now to the matter of postings and careers, officers who were content to leave their future to the moguls of P Staff would have been disconcerted to see at first hand, as I did when I was in Air Ministry, how the business worked.

Not long before, the staff had installed the Hollerith card index system, on which officers' qualifications were recorded in such a way that when jobs became vacant, all that was needed was to plug in the appropriate code and out would come the names of the people who were qualified. No doubt there were also attempts to adapt the system to some form of career planning.

Dennis Rogers was in Adastral House, across the Aldwych from Bush House, where I worked. We'd known each other since he turned up at Portage la Prairie to take over from George Newsome as Chief Supervisory Officer of the EFTS, and he was looking after postings for wing commanders and below. I dropped in to see him once or twice after he told me about the Hollerith system, and saw at first hand why it didn't work the way it was supposed to.

Let's say a vacancy was coming up at a flying station for a Wing Commander A (for Administration)—that is, the wing commander who was responsible to the station commander for all the housekeeping aspects except the technical ones connected with servicing the aircraft. Servicing was the responsibility of the Senior Technical Officer who, together with the Wing Commander Flying, constituted the third wing commander of the "three-prong" system then in vogue.

Dennis would plug in the requirement, and out would come the names of the men who were qualified. He would pick a name and "offer" it to P Staff at the relevant Command HQ. That was when the phone calls would start, and since I was in Dennis's office when some of them came in, I'll describe the scene.

Even then, Adastral House was quite an old building. The lifts had steel-webbed gates that the operators clanged open and shut before manhandling a brass-topped lever not unlike the stop-and-go control of a tram-driver. In the basement was a cafeteria I went to sometimes when funds were low, from which the smell of cooking reached the second and third floors and made me think of Coleridge's line about caverns measureless to man. The offices were of a pattern: dark cubby-holes with desks and telephones and wooden chairs, in-trays and out-trays bulging with files that were carted back and forth by messengers wearing the same uniforms as the lift operators, navy-blue serge with gilt crowns on the lapels. Batmen wore them, too.

The phone rings and I hear Dennis's end of the conversation. It's from a more senior officer at Command, and Dennis says, "Good morning, sir." Pause. "He has all the right qualifications, sir." Another pause, while Dennis looks at me, eyebrows raised, and says, "Well, sir, there's so-and-so," and he offers another name. Evidently, the man at the other end says, "Not *him.*"

Dennis, admitting defeat, forgets about Mr. Hollerith and reaches for the box of dog-eared cards on his desk, flips through them as he calls out the names, and arrives at one that passes muster.

Dennis was good at that job, and before the Bracknell vacancy came up, he not only gave me the chance to go to Karachi as the air attaché, with the acting rank of group captain, but was also good enough not to mind when I turned it down.

However, the posting to Singapore was sheer luck. We had told ourselves that the next posting would be our last, and first prize would be overseas, but I didn't push for it. When it came through at the end of 1954, we were as excited as you might expect. Our reservations on the score of tropical climate, malaria, and so on were dismissed by the report of a journalist—Vernon Bartlett—who had served there not long before, and we set about the business of getting ourselves prepared for the trip.

This involved a number of steps, starting with the obvious ones of getting inoculated and kitted out—there was one store in London where Ruth was able to get summer clothes in December. It was on the domestic side that things were more complicated. We decided to take the washing machine (a mistake), but not the fridge. Then we had some furniture to sell and some to put in storage, in case we decided to take it to Canada with us. We sold our bed and a beautiful bow-fronted highboy of mine to a USAF lieutenant colonel, sold the Valor stoves to a Canadian officer, and were quite ruthless with odds and ends of ours and the children's, which we turned into a splendid bonfire across the road in front of the rhododendron bushes.

Our faithful 1938 Pontiac coupe, FTR 668, was left with Bob Humphries's local garage to sell for us. We heard afterwards it was bought by an Australian officer on the next course. Driving it in England had been a mixed blessing—it was high enough that you could see over the English cars ahead of you, but without traffic indicators and of course with a left-hand drive, you couldn't signal except by waving your hand inside the car in the hope that the driver behind would see and understand.

Once when we were driving around St. James's Square, looking for a vacant spot to park against the railings, I saw one, pulled in quickly, and was berated by a taxi-driver from behind: "Miracle-man; droives wiv no 'ands." The only accident we had

166

in eight years of driving was in South Croydon, when Ruth was struck from behind by, of all things, a London County Council tram. Not only that, but she had the presence of mind to take its number and we got the LCC to pay for the damage.

For all this, Her Majesty's Government compensated us with Disturbance Allowance, which I was entitled to claim after we got to Singapore—twenty pounds in those days, raised later to thirty. Auntie Kit came to see us off at the dockside, and we boarded the *Empire Orwell* of the Bibby Steamship Line for the mysterious East.

Chapter 8

▣ 1954—1957 ▣

Enshrined in song, troopships were part of RAF lore. Older types would reminisce about Habbaniyah and The Gulf, Peshawar and Mauripur, pith helmets and spine pads, dengue fever and malaria, mosquito nets and dhobi-wallahs—and troopships, of which the one celebrated in song was said to be "leaving Bombay/ bound for old Blighty shore/ full of flight sergeants and W.O.1s/ bound for the land they adore/ from the side of the ocean where you got no promotion," and enjoined the listeners to cheer up and fuck them all.

The *Empire Orwell* was a pleasant surprise. We had a spacious cabin on the port side—Port Out, Starboard Home was a sound rule, keeping the sun on the other side of the ship both ways (however, the acronym POSH is disavowed by the P & O company which operated troopships for almost a century until air trooping took over). Jumbo Preston of the Lancers was an amiable Ship's Commandant, and the Bibby Line set an excellent table. School and games were organized for the children, and we amused ourselves by getting to know the other officers and their wives, most of whom were army people en route to the Malayan "emergency" which had been in progress against the Communists since 1948.

Shipborne service, unhurried days during which betting on the logged mileage was a major event, the changing blues and greens racing aft from the bow wave, the diminishing furrows of the wake—all this was relieved from monotony by the ports of call.

We stopped at Port Said, where bumboats with names like *Gordon McGregor* pulled alongside, laden with merchandise which the Arab skippers offered for sale to passengers leaning over the rails. When transactions were completed, ropes would be thrown up, caught by passengers, threaded over the rails, and passed down again with the agreed price to the boats, where the packages would be tied to the rope-ends for recovery.

Progress through the Canal was up to expectations. To the east, the ship's shadow moved silently along the endless sand; to the west, men and veiled women, mules and camels made their way along the banks of the palm-lined Sweetwater Canal. The Red Sea in January was cooler than advertised, and after passing through the Strait of Bab-el-Mandeb, we reached the forbidding shore of Aden.

At Steamer Point (Aden), David Dixon from Bracknell days was commanding, waiting for his wife and young children to arrive, and he showed us around that parched, scorched settlement: the water storage vats originated by the Queen of Sheba and restored by Turkish army engineers during the Great War; and the so-called yards, where dhows were built to pretty much the same design as in the Queen's time.

The yards turned out to be a stretch of beach. The ships' skeletons were assembled in wooden jigs, and as soon as the ribs were boarded over, the insides were waterproofed with shark oil, which you could smell a fair way off. David had plans to install a shark net across an inlet of the point, and until that was done, he was properly strict in forbidding the troops to swim in the sea. It was especially tragic, therefore, that when his wife arrived some weeks later, she should have been standing in shallow water, facing the shore and playing with the baby, when a shark took her in the back and killed her. David was posted home on compassionate grounds—we heard afterwards that he married again.

At Colombo, we went ashore and saw something of the city, with its London-style double-decker buses; drove along the south coast to the Galle Face, and spent an afternoon in the grounds of the hotel at Mount Lavinia, where a gulli-gulli man performed his repertoire for us, including the removal of an egg from a pocket of John's shorts. On the way back to the city, we saw our first banyan tree and watched a crowd walking from the racetrack, the women colourful in their saris.

This was the East, and we were suitably impressed. In the passage across the Bay of Bengal, we spent a lot of time leaning on the rail to watch the flying fish, the changing shades of green, and the wake stretching behind, until, stifling at reduced speed, we sailed down the Strait of Malacca between Sumatra and Malaya.

Singapore is one degree of latitude north of the Equator, and we drew near to it in the early morning: red laterite soil showing through the green foliage overhanging the water's edge; gardens of spacious bungalows, bright with bougainvillaea and hibiscus, oleander and frangi-pani. Going there was the fulfilment of dreams when I worked at the Sun in London, especially during the restless period before I left.

Joan Foxley-Norris was at the dockside to meet us, a number of people we knew from other postings were round and about, and these formed the nuclei for friendships in the manner of service life everywhere.

The headquarters was at Changi, some eighteen miles along the East Coast Road from the city of Singapore. For the first few weeks, we stayed at the Grand Hotel, in the suburb of Katong, which served as the gathering place for officers and their families until they could find more permanent accommodation. This eased us into the heat and the surroundings while we shopped for tropical clothing and began the search for somewhere to live.

Not far away was the Singapore Swimming Club, complete with tennis courts and an Olympic-size pool where Martha soon learned to swim and the boys practiced their diving. But the ritual that amused us was our joint appearance before two of the club's board members to ratify our own membership. It was to make sure we were white.

This was our first experience of a truly multiracial society, and although we were somewhat insulated from it because of the job, we were able to see at first hand how well people of different races get along given half a chance, and given particularly an underpinning of order in the streets and access to properly constituted courts. Given also, I might add in retrospect, freedom from the interference of busybodies who want to run other people's lives by splitting them up into state-subsidized racial groups, as Canada has done through its divisive policy of "official multiculturalism."

We bought a second-hand Studebaker, a good-looking car with leather seats, and drove it up the west coast of Malaya to Butterworth, where we took the ferry to Penang and spent several days on that beautiful island, mostly at the Penang Swimming Club but also taking in the usual sights: Victoria Peak; the snake temple; one or two kampongs; the Pagoda of a Thousand Buddhas; and of course George Town, the capital, which contrived in spite of the heat to remind me of an English cathedral town.

Because of the Emergency, I kept my service revolver under the front seat for moral support and we stayed one night at the rest house in a fortified village. We negotiated the river at Seremban via a ferry that consisted of a wooden platform on a powered barge, and absorbed not only the heat but also the sights and sounds of Malaya. Along the hills' lower slopes, roads wound through the edges of the jungle. Clear streams from the hills fed irrigation ditches on the coastal plain, where Straits Chinese women wearing wide-brimmed hats worked in the fields, farmers guided water buffaloes, and the landscape was dotted with the now-familiar assortment of trees and flowering shrubs: palms and casuarinas and frangi-pani, hibiscus and oleander and bougainvil-laea. When we stopped, we might hear the screech of a parrot or a monkey, occasionally a temple's bell.

I won't say we were used to the heat by then, because that didn't happen: all the time we were there, it was a constant companion. You sought shade and even at night, when Ruth and I would walk a little after dinner, we longed for a breath of air that would register on the nostrils going in. The only times when there was some relief were in the rainy season, after showers.

After five months at the Headquarters, I was promoted to group captain and posted to command RAF Changi. This brought a considerable change in our circumstances. We moved from the house we were renting in the Singapore suburb of Katong to the station commander's quarter, 12 Fairy Point. The house rested on pillars, high up, so that the sitting room, sixty feet long, jutted out to form a wide porch over the entrance which provided shelter from sun or rain when boarding a car.

As you walked in, the black-and-white tiled floor and the comparative gloom after the sun's glare gave an illusion of coolness and, to the dining room on your left, an air of formality. On your right was a washroom and shower and, facing, wide stairs leading first to a landing and then to the sitting room, where you arrived facing the opposite direction from the one you started on in the hall.

The part that projected over the entrance was about eighteen feet square with a white rug over the tiled floor, and from there, the room ran to the back of the house, flanked on either side by three bedrooms, three more bathrooms, and a butler's pantry, from which stairs descended to the servants' quarters.

Jao, the cook, and his wife, Amah—who kept the house shining as she padded quietly about, slap, slap of her thongs on the floors—lived with their three children in the house immediately adjoining, but Jao's own house was in Pasir Ris village, about ten miles away, where his mother lived. (He took Ruth and me and the children there once to meet his mother, and cut us a pineapple from his flourishing garden.)

12 Fairy Point was open to the air. Shutters were there to be pulled in case of heavy rain, and wire screens were installed across the bedroom windows to keep bats out at night. The natural ventilation was assisted by ceiling fans. Ruth had her desk in an alcove near the head of the stairs, where she worked at organizing the various committees that came with the job. Her diary was also the record of invitations accepted or refused and of our own entertainments.

Outside, she could see through the giant casuarinas to the waters of the Johore Strait, see in our garden the reds and pinks of hibiscus and the purple bougainvillaea, smell the scent of frangipani, and hear the fluted call of golden orioles. My desk was at the far end, beyond the pantry and facing the playing fields—the padang—but what I remember best is sitting in the part over the entrance with my legs along one of the window ledges, at about 5.30 with a glass in my hand, just before the sun began its final dive, looking across the water to the blue haze of Johore and listening to the record player—Benny Goodman, Nat King Cole, Doris Day. From time to time we put those records on, and it all comes back, the scents and the colours and the heat.

The station covered an area three miles square, had a service population of about 5,000, and included the village of Changi.

There were about 850 married quarters for officers and airmen, so that except for the Commander-in-Chief, who lived at Air House in Singapore, most of the Command staff's senior officers—some seventy wing commanders and above—lived on the station. Consequently, the station equipment officer—one of six wing commanders on the station staff—was the focus of endless demands for furniture, curtains, decorating, and repairs, from which I shielded him as best I could.

In Malaya, the British strategy was to treat the Emergency as a police action and always to confine the armed forces' role to the normal one in a democratic country: aid to the civil power. It was the prototype of wars that were said to be fought "for the hearts and minds of the people," and it was founded on securing the public peace. The promise of self-government, which was the British government's declared intention, would build confidence and encourage the people to support the police and the armed forces.

The tactical battle was won by denying the communists their hoped-for recruiting base in the rural areas. This was done by resettling about half a million Chinese squatters in fortified villages where they could be protected. At the same time, they were given title to the land they farmed, and Malayan-born Chinese and Indians were granted citizenship.

The army's job was twofold: to seek and destroy communist terrorists in the jungle, and to protect the civil population. Foot patrols in the jungle were supplied by helicopter, and heavier materiel was dropped in cleared dropping zones (DZs) by RAF Valettas and RNZAF Bristol Freighters. Air strikes were provided by RAF and RAAF squadrons in Singapore and Malaya.

The communists' strength was most visible in the cities, where they organized and led "spontaneous" demonstrations with the object of turning them into riots under banners proclaiming *Merdeka* (Freedom)—the last thing they had in mind for the people they were inciting.

On the service side, the British organization consisted of air, land and sea headquarters in Singapore, below which were the forward formations, located in Malaya, to direct and control operations against the terrorists. Thus, the air element consisted of Far East Air Force HQ, whose territory stretched from Ceylon to Hong Kong, with local air headquarters in Ceylon, Singapore, Kuala

Lumpur and Hong Kong. Air HQ Malaya in Kuala Lumpur was the directing formation for the Emergency.

Changi, at the east end of Singapore island, was the RAF's main base, the site of FEAF HQ, the staging post for traffic to and from Australasia, the Far East and the UK, and the base for the five transport squadrons which did double duty in dropping supplies to the land forces in Malaya and keeping a regular supply chain going to the staging posts. These were located at Negombo (Ceylon), Car Nicobar in the Indian Ocean, Labuan off the coast of Borneo, the detachment at Clark Field, USAF, in the Philippines, and Kai Tak (Hong Kong).

Tengah, at the west end of Singapore island, housed fighter/ground attack squadrons and a RAAF bomber squadron, while the Fleet Air Arm's naval air operated from Sembawang, on the north side, facing the Johore Strait. Seletar, in the middle, was the main RAF equipment depot which also housed a flying boat squadron, a flight of helicopters, and AHQ Singapore.

As well as its five transport squadrons, Changi supported a variety of units connected directly or indirectly with the strategic effort. An offshoot of the Royal Corps of Signals, the Air Formation Signals Regiment, was responsible for the communications network that was a key factor in the CTs' eventual defeat. Soldiers in the RAF were trained for the defence of airfields at the RAF Regiment (Malaya) Depot. Jungle Survival School; Parachute School; the FEAF Band; Joint Air Traffic Control Centre; Crippled Children's Home; European schools; Malay school; golf club; swimming pools; yacht club; cinema; churches; clubs and messes; transit hotel; hospital—there weren't many dull moments.

Since I was responsible for the care and feeding of these units in addition to those directly associated with the flying job, and since I had nearly 300 officers under direct command, many of them aircrew upon whom I must write confidential reports every six months, I devised a roster of short visits, published beforehand in station routine orders, which took me to every section on the station once a month. As these included all the barrack blocks and the bigger buildings, such as hangars and the hospital, I did quite a lot of walking and climbing stairs—all of which, no doubt, contributed to the fact that I didn't have a day's sickness all the time we were there.

Ruth, too, escaped the ailments associated with the tropics, as did Peter, but Martha contracted measles soon after we arrived and spent a miserable two weeks isolated from us in the Army hospital in Singapore. John's sinus trouble—residual, we thought, from the ghastly hospital in Bury St. Edmund's—was aggravated by the heat and humidity, and although the RAF surgeon tried to ease the passage with an operation, John had to stay out of the sea and swimming pools for long periods (he also put the time to good use by building two pedal-operated wooden cars).

The staging posts at Labuan and Car Nicobar were also under command, and I combined business with pleasure by flying a Valetta to one or the other on alternate months. Most of the time the weather was good, but I remember one flight to Labuan when the Inter-Tropical Front lay along the route and we were in cloud from a few hundred feet off the runway until just before landing at Labuan—four and half hours of fighting the battle of the instruments, bounced all over the place by embedded cumulus, and with rain leaking through the windshield into my left boot. That was when I sang to myself verses one and three of what I think of as the airman's hymn, No. 373, "In Times of Trouble":

God moves in a mysterious way
His wonders to perform;
He plants His footsteps in the sea,
And rides upon the storm.

Ye fearful saints, fresh courage take;
The clouds ye so much dread
Are big with mercy, and shall break
In blessings on your head.

Labuan was a port, with a sizeable population, but Car Nicobar was isolated except for when aircraft arrived and when the ship brought supplies in exchange for copra, standing off beyond the reef while the Nicobarese paddled their boats back and forth. Those voyages were arranged by the Indian trader who lived on the island: R. Akoojee Jadwet. He came to Singapore from time to time to see about the cargoes, and would usually call at 12 Fairy Point for a cup of tea and an exchange of news. He looked after the natives' temporal needs; their spiritual needs were under the care of Bishop John.

The Nicobarese are a sturdy people, with round faces and very dark skins. They were then about ninety-nine percent Christian—the balance in those days being accounted for by Mr. Jadwet and his family. Bishop John was taller than the average and his hair was grey, so that in his cassock, he cut a handsome figure. The last time I was there, he and his flock were putting the finishing touches to the cathedral they had built from brick and tile brought in by ship.

Copra was the cash crop, and it was a fine sight to watch the young men race up the tall palms, with their arms around the trunk, gripping the blunt edge of the parang to press the blade in for a hold, bringing up their legs at each new position, and taking the weight on the soles of their feet, pressed inwards on the trunk. At the top they would slice the stems of the ripe pods and race down again to gather them. One man opened a coconut for me to drink by holding it in his left hand and slicing off the top with a flashing cut of the parang.

For fishing they used circular nets, weighted at the circumference, which they flung with a graceful sweep of the arms so that the net spread over the surface and sank like a parachute, trapping the fish in the canopy.

At feast times, the men staged canoe races and afterwards the women danced for them on the local version of a village green—the flat, tramped-down space in the circle formed by the thatched beehive houses that stood on stilts. The high point of the feast was the ritual killing of the pig, a wiry animal with tusks and a wicked eye, that was released from a bamboo cage, chased and caught. Then its throat was cut and the body was carried on a bamboo pole at the head of the procession to the fire.

My last visit was in September 1956, for the purpose of handing over the airfield and associated facilities to the Indian Air Force. An IAF squadron leader and his staff flew in the next day, and we worked out a simple ceremony that ended with the hauling down of the RAF ensign and its replacement by the IAF's.

Though not so numerous as Canadians, Australians had made up sizeable contingents of every RAF unit I served with. When the air staff authorized a training flight to Australia, I jumped at the chance to see some of the country. Our route lay south to Djakarta and then a few points south of east along the line of islands through Surabaya to Darwin, so that sitting in our unpressurized Valetta at 8,000 feet, and in clear weather, I enjoyed exceptional views of Bali and Lombok, Sumbawa, Flores and Timor, as they sailed past our port side under their mantles of cumulus.

At Darwin, the RAAF people were obviously glad to see almost any visitors to that isolated spot and we spent the night there. The CO told me that attempts to employ local aborigines on the station were frustrated by the abos' ingrained habit of going walkabout without warning for weeks at a time into the depths of the surrounding bush.

Its vastness was brought home to us the next day as we flew across the Northern Territory and Queensland to the east coast. At intervals we passed the stations—cattle or sheep ranches—that epitomize mankind's ingenuity and resourcefulness, homesteads where the farmer and his wife perform the whole range not only of husbandry but of the civil arts: engineer, veterinarian, nurse, plumber, electrician, teacher.

In its essential features, the country's geography is similar to Canada's. Superimpose a map of one on that of the other and see the major cities. In the southeast corners, the Sydney-Canberra-Melbourne line parallels Montreal-Ottawa-Toronto. To the midwest lie Adelaide and Winnipeg; on the southwest coast, Perth matches Vancouver. To the north lies desert, hot in Australia, cold in Canada.

Regardless of their countries of origin, air force people have much in common, but national characteristics inevitably show through. In their own country, the RAAF officers I met were more surely Australian than the generality spread more thinly through the RAF. Polite, yes, but not habitually so in the manner of Canadians. Outspoken, but challenging rather than fearless, as if to guard against an expected slur, even to hide a contradictory lack of confidence.

From the ritual of the five o'clock swill, when bartenders hosed beer into rows of glasses before the six o'clock closing time, to the rigours of surfing and Australian rules football, to the saturnalia of Anzac Day, it was unquestionably a man's country. The geographic similarities to Canada extended to both countries' abundance of natural resources. Just as Canadians' standard of living was boosted by its export of minerals and foodstuffs, so did Australians speak of living off the sheep's back.

However, Canada's climate imposed demands of self-reliance upon Canadians which were reflected in the national character, whereas even though the sub-tropical equivalent might impose similar demands upon the pioneers of Australian homesteads, your city-bred Australian of the mid-century was content to make enough for his three squares (meals) and head for the beach.

One of Changi's responsibilities was to monitor and periodically calibrate the radio/navigation facilities for the airfield in the Cocos Keeling Islands that served as a refuelling stop for Qantas and South African Airways. When one of the regular checks was due, I was invited to spend a long weekend there by John Clunies-Ross, whose islands they were.

They lie in the Indian Ocean some 900 nautical miles south of Singapore and 1,500 north-northwest of Fremantle, or about 12 degrees S by 99 E, as they would have been reported in the 1820s when first sighted by a Royal Navy navigator sailing to Fremantle. On that vessel was John Clunies-Ross, Lieutenant RN, who on his return to England claimed and was granted the islands in 1827, where he founded a dynasty whose sixth member was my host.

Three main islands form the group: West Island, where the airfield was built during the Second World War, Direction Island, and Home Island. Direction Island got its name from the wireless station established there in the early 1900s, and it was off Direction Island in 1914 that the German light cruiser *Emden* was sunk by HMAS *Sydney*. The subsequent escape by survivors of *Emden*—who navigated a long boat across the Indian Ocean to the Arabian Peninsula, and thence made their way to Turkey and Berlin—is a classic of navigational skill and human endurance.

The Clunies-Ross's lived on Home Island in a fine stone house with thick walls and wide windows open to the South-East Trades, which supply a cooling eight-knot breeze throughout the year. The house and its predecessor had been there long enough for topsoil to accumulate, and the grass that surrounded it under the palms was lush and springy. My visit coincided with a Qantas pilots' strike which grounded a Super-Constellation and produced another houseguest, a psychology professor named Osler from the University of Melbourne.

John's wife was away in England, so the three of us spent three evenings together, dining superbly from dishes borne by graceful Malay girls, and then continuing the talk in the big airy room while the breeze rustled the rattan blinds and, in the background, we heard the muffled roar of the surf. I remember standing alone one morning under the palms by the shore, gazing south towards distant Australia with the South-East Trades in my face, and being moved by the immensity of the globe.

A Malay took me fishing in a sloop, of which a replica sits with its jib and mainsail still intact on a bookcase behind me as I write. We, or rather he, caught a sand shark, the species that lives on shellfish and is a harmless member of its revolting family. But the Clunies-Ross's family business was coconuts, and whenever John went to Singapore, the orchestra at Raffles would salute his entrance to the room with a rendering of "I've got a luvverly bunch of coconuts."

He gave me a conducted tour of the coconut plantations, where land crabs scuttled out of our way with a dry crackling sound, and the copra lay on trays in the sun. The work of planting, cutting, drying and collecting was done by Malays, Javanese, East Africans, and Chinese, who with their families made up a population of about 450. They lived in stone houses equipped with electricity and appliances, and were a good deal more comfortably off than most islanders of the period. John dispensed justice, and taught their children in his own school. Much later I was sorry to learn that the Australian Government, after a long battle with John inspired by busybodies in Canberra, had taken over the administration of his workers.

One of the more engaging characters at Changi was Ramsan, tailor and barber—a stockily built Indian of medium height, with luxuriant black hair, and limpid brown eyes shining through steel-rimmed glasses. He had a knack of appearing at the right time, so that it seemed you had only to think that perhaps you needed a haircut in order to see his eager face at the door of office or house.

When I moved into the job, he presented himself to measure me for flying overalls, and soon afterwards he brought them—one pair so long in the legs that they dragged behind me, covering my feet, and the others so short that I felt I was already off the ground. Beaming earnestly at me, he explained not only that the first pair would shrink but that the second pair would undoubtedly stretch, and the funny thing was that standing there in the heat, looking into those brown eyes, you could almost believe him.

His franchise as tailor and barber made him a target for intrigue among the large civilian staff, and from time to time he would appeal to me for protection against the "bad mans" conspiring against him.

Station Headquarters was a two-storey building overlooking the airfield, and from my office on the second floor, I could see airplanes taking off and landing and, beyond them, the Singapore Strait. The apertures for windows and door were open to the air, so that it was quite noisy and you acquired the habit of not speaking while an airplane took off, until the noise faded and you continued the sentence.

On the plus side, you could smell frangi-pani and see the flame trees, scarlet against the white walls of the squadron offices across the road. In that office I would hear charges and dispense punishment, if not justice, to the variety of miscreants paraded before me with a clatter of boots ("lef' ri', lef' ri', halt, lef' turn, cap off") by the Station Warrant Officer.

At the far end of the building was the parade ground, the scene of many colourful ceremonies. Parades were held soon after sunrise because of the heat, and music was supplied by the band of RAF (Malaya) in dress uniform: white tunic and slacks with a blue belt worn Sam Browne fashion and a blue pill-box cap—the songkhu. As the band played, the different units marched on to the parade ground: Malays and Chinese of the RAF Regiment (Malaya) in dark khaki; red-faced Englishmen of the Air Formation Signals Regiment in jungle green; Royal New Zealand Air Force in light khaki and pale blue caps; RAF officers in bush jackets; WAAFs in crisp khaki dresses. On special occasions, the march past the saluting base would be synchronized with a fly past of aircraft in formation, dipping in salute over the parade ground.

In England, the RAF custom when prayers were said at morning parades was to preface them with the order: "Fall out the Roman Catholics and Jews," whereupon any of those persuasions would march to the edge of the parade ground and stand with backs to it while prayers were said. Since large numbers of the air-men at Changi were Muslims—there was a mosque off to one side of the square—the idea of ordering them to fall out seemed ludicrous to me, so I invited the local Imam to attend, together with the C. of E. and Presbyterian chaplains, and at the appointed time each in turn would say his piece while we all inclined heads out of respect, it was obvious I thought in the circumstances, to one God.

To complete the team, I invited the Roman Catholic chaplain to attend, too, but this innocent suggestion drew a censorious letter from the Command Chaplain (RC) requesting that any of his flock be permitted to fall out in the customary fashion. So much for ecumenism in the Far East.

Ruth and I made a determined effort to learn enough Malay to carry on limited conversations, but without much success. Nevertheless, we were privileged to attend a number of social events to do with the Malay school and the Malay community in and around the station. Mr. Wan Chik, JP, tall, round-faced, smiling, who had tried valiantly to teach us Malay, was our host on these occasions, introducing us to the brightly clad women, the always-smiling men and the shy children, after which we would sip tea or soft drinks and perform as best we could the roles that were expected of us.

We were entertained in Malay homes at the time of the Hari Rayah festival, and in Chinese homes at the Chinese New Year. We were in Malay villages and, in Johore Bharu, in the quiet beauty of a mosque, tiles cool under our stockinged feet, where also we watched the Sultan's Diamond Jubilee parade and counted thirteen Straits Chinese getting out of a Morris Minor. We experienced a sumatra, when the sky was dark brown and the rain beat horizontally through the shutters of the big living room until the white rug was awash and our dinner guests took off their shoes and pitched in to clear the furniture back into the room.

All the time, we were amongst the Asian people, Chinese, Malay, Indian, Sinhalese, Tamil, Ghurka—lawyers, merchants, farmers, storekeepers, street cleaners, labourers, policemen, soldiers—living on the whole in civil harmony and founding what has since become the most prosperous state in Asia.

In my mind are three snapshots from the air. One is of the Malay peninsula on a clear morning from 40,000 feet in a Meteor, silent in the cabin, and with the sense, familiar to jet fighter pilots, of being suspended, nothing in front of you except that immensity of space. Another is of the same peninsula from the east, flying back from Labuan in the late afternoon, when you saw the lightning flashes lighting up the clouds over the highlands, just as the bomb bursts did through the clouds over Germany. Another is flying low off the east coast of Malaya and seeing, close to the surface in the clear water, three manta rays in perfect vic formation.

The communists' organization of riots to undermine the civil power were regular occurrences. The leaders were "students" in their late twenties, and we would be called upon to back up the police with shows of force. The jeep that I used to get about the station was then fitted with wire screens, as were any vehicles that went into Singapore, and in order to discourage malcontents in our own thriving Changi village, we had companies of the RAF Regiment Depot march along the main street in full kit.

When we went as a family to visit a planter friend in Johore State, we were met at the landing stage by an armoured car which took us to the house past places where ambushes had taken place only days before, all to the delight of the children.

The station crest was a starfish, and the motto—"*Kami Melindongi Semua*"—means "We gather them all in." Since Changi was the crossing point for military and other government traffic to and from the UK and the Pacific in general, there was a constant stream of visitors of varying degrees of importance, and I was surprised to discover that the station commander was expected to greet them on the strip. That seemed to me, as it still does, a great waste of time, and I introduced a system whereby one of the six wing commanders in turn would take on the chore for a week at a time. This fell foul of the C-in-C, Air Marshal Sir Frances Fressanges—a stickler for protocol who even had me drawing up seating plans for spectators at rugby matches—and I was instructed, through channels, to be at the strip, day or night, for all visitors of the rank of group captain or above, or the civilian or military equivalents. If they were accompanied by wife, so should I be.

Even in this there were compensations. We met some interesting, indeed celebrated, people. Most of the ordinary ones were pleasant, and the really important were charming. Ruth, who is not easily impressed, was enchanted by Lady Mountbatten, who was practical, understanding, down to earth, and a great success with the troops in the hospital. (Her hubby came, too, with not a little ceremony, including yours truly wearing a sword.) Lord De L'Isle and Dudley, who won the VC at Anzio and was also Governor General of Australia, had lunch with us in Temple Hill Mess, while Ruth entertained his lady, and he was a simply delightful guest, modest but stimulating and with a terrific sense of humour.

A less welcome visitor, in the sense that the circumstances were sad for him, was Dick Waterhouse, who was then a group captain commanding the RAF's main transport station at Lyneham in Wiltshire. One of Dick's ambitions was to see New Zealand, and when he learned that the Chief of the Air Staff (then Air Chief Marshal Sir Charles Elworthy, himself a New Zealander) was slated to go there for the RNZAF's twenty-fifth anniversary, Dick arranged to get passage on one of the Comet flights in advance of the visit to make sure that all was in order.

Dick was a recognized "character," well known even when, as a flight lieutenant, he came to Canada in 1939. Pluto, the black Labrador, was a prop to round out the character. Dick had played rugby for the RAF, did a tour on Wellingtons after he returned to England from Canada, and was a most amusing companion, with a fund of stories. While we were at Marston, he was CO at Leconfield, also in Yorkshire, and we drove there once (in the black-out, slotted beams of light flickering through the screened headlights of the little Ford 8) for a mess dance, the first time Ruth and Noni had seen each other since their trip on the *Baltrover*.

Afterwards we lost touch, and the first news I had of Dick's impending arrival was a signal from AOC Ceylon (Air Commodore Tubby Mermagen, who also had played rugby for the RAF) to say that the en route Comet had Gp. Capt. R.H. Waterhouse on board and requesting that I make arrangements for him to be hospitalized.

I went to the strip with an ambulance to meet the Comet, climbed aboard, and was greeted by Dick, obviously in an advanced stage of intoxication, rolling down the aisle toward me (he was a portly chap) with glad cries. He had always enjoyed a drink, like the rest of us, and I remembered from Borden days that after a fair amount, he could be pugnacious.

The last thing I wanted was a scene in front of the troops, so I dispatched the ambulance to 12 Fairy Point and drove Dick there myself in the staff car. We sat in the dining room while Ruth, who had been warned by telephone, kept the children upstairs. It was pathetic, sitting there, to see my friend begging for a drink and knowing that he had botched his career. We had a weak whisky together (Jao had been hovering just out of sight, taking it all in) and after a while, I persuaded Dick to go with me in the ambulance.

What had happened, he told us two days later when he was dried out and was once more the Dick we knew, charming and thoughtful, was that he had been on the wagon for at least a year after realizing that he was an alcoholic. The day before the flight was due to leave, he and Noni went to a neighbouring point-to-point and on the way home, when they dropped in on some friends, Dick was offered a glass of sherry. Exhilarated by the prospect of the coming trip, and thinking "What's one glass of sherry?" he took it and was hooked again. By takeoff time the next morning, he was well away, although no doubt apparently under control, and he kept it up during the flight from bottles he had secreted in the Comet's passenger cabin.

He stayed with us for a day or two, until a UK-bound flight came through (his Comet had left for New Zealand as soon as it was refuelled), and told us what a terrible time Noni and the children had because of his weakness. A sad story. Dick retired as a group captain in 1962 and Noni died not long afterwards.

Leonard Cheshire turned up while we were there, well into Cheshire Homes by then and on the prowl for a site in Singapore. Within it seemed hours of landing, that remarkable man had all the local bigwigs scurrying about to help. I drove him around the station and he spotted at least two possible locations along the south side of the airfield, where the land sloped gently to the sea, and I found out after we had left that he got what he wanted.

Earlier I mentioned the social life we were involved in at the house as part of the job. We made a point of entertaining all the station officers and wives, as well as those from Command staff and other formations who lived on the station, and those parties were usually fun. Aside from that, however, we were caught up in the social round not only of the three services but also of the civilian world that radiated from Government House. At one dinner party, for example, Ruth and I were the only un-knighted couple.

Before long we found ourselves dreading one more duty cocktail party, one more duty dinner, seeing the same people, and listening to the same conversations. (An exception was the annual garden party at Government House, which was worth the trip for the sight and sound of the massed bands, in whites, marching in slow time across the manicured lawns and Beating Retreat while the sun sank behind the casuarinas.)

The civilians we met at those affairs were either expatriate Europeans who had been there too long, or Straits Chinese who were doing well from government contracts, or rising politicians preparing themselves for independence. There were also people whose company we really enjoyed, and with all or any of whom we could spend relaxed evenings talking about the things that interested us. In short, we had our fill of a really busy social round, and learned instead to savour the company of a few friends who shared our prejudices and had something to say for themselves.

The flying side of the job was a mix of more-or-less straight-forward route-flying between Ceylon and Hong Kong, with occasional training flights to Japan, Australia, and Nepal (to my lasting chagrin, I missed the trip to Khatmandu), and the more military task of supply-dropping to the troops fighting in the jungles of Malaya and Borneo.

Malaya is about the size of England. The Cameron Highlands and the Fraser Hills reach in places to 7,000 feet and run the length of the peninsula, parallel ranges that descend in altitude to the foothills where crops are grown on the lower slopes. About four-fifths of the country, including all the high ground, is jungle—and it was among the rugged green slopes that many of the Dropping Zones were established. The job called for considerable skill in pilotage and navigation, and although the techniques were practiced diligently, we suffered a number of casualties.

Drops were timed for the early hours of daylight, before cloud formed in the valleys. The terrain imposed its own limitations, and often you would have to come in steeply down a slope, with full flap and throttled back in order to drop at the right speed before easing in the flaps and pulling up again at full power to keep your speed and climb away safely. As in a lot of military flying, you had to be quick.

Accidents were often ascribed to "pilot error," a euphemism familiar to pilots the world over, which does nothing to evoke the final seconds of frenzied activity, usually in bad weather, when disaster stares him in the face and he hauls in vain on the stick or kicks too late at the rudder to avoid the tree or the cliff jutting out of the mist.

One valley looked very much like another and you had only to be in the wrong one, with a wall of rock where you thought the passage was clear, and cloud forming ahead of forecast, to find yourself with very limited alternatives. I was fortunate to have learned that lesson in 1939, flying back to Shawbury from Joan Burpitt's wedding in Cardiff, although the Hart was a good deal more manoeuvrable than a Valetta.

Running that station had a lot of bad moments, but the worst ones came after crashes in the hills. When the crash site was located, the rescue team would be dropped nearby and fight its way in, to report many hours later and then start the job of making a clearing big enough for a helicopter to lift the team out with the remains.

Usually the crash was on a hillside, so that the team would have to get down to some level ground before starting to clear it, and that meant cutting every step ahead with a machete in ninety-five percent humidity and a temperature to match, beset by leeches and mosquitoes. It would be some time before you knew for certain the fate of the crew. If they were married, Ruth would visit the wives, and I would write "next of kin" letters for those who were single, or whose wives were in the home country, to follow the formal telegram.

When the remains were flown back to Changi, we would stage the military funeral. In the early morning the cortege forms and makes its way to the military cemetery. The pallbearers stand in line, the crispness of their khaki drill showing creases from the ride, and shoulder the biers, while the band plays softly and the bugler prepares himself. Beside the graves, the guard of honour is silent and motionless, the firing party stiffly at ease. The chaplains speak their words, the pallbearers lower the coffins into the ground, and the guard commander orders the firing party to present arms. The echo of their salvo fades, the bugler sounds the Last Post, and we stand at the salute looking out over the ranks of stone markers and thinking of the young men who died in the air.

It was at Changi that Josh Braithwaite was killed, an air vice-marshal then and a very nice man. He was the Senior Air Staff Officer at Command HQ and thus felt obliged to keep his hand in, which he could have done by flying one of the communications aircraft. Instead, he chose to fly one of our two Meteors, in 1955 still widely used as an operational trainer with a top speed of Mach 0.8, or 540 mph, and really no vices other than the one I mentioned before—if you left the speed brakes out at too low an airspeed on the approach. At all events it was a jet, which was the mark of distinction between operational types and the rest, and I was down at the strip to make sure he was buttoned up.

Josh had put forty minutes in the Authorization Book, but it was less than that when the controller called me from the tower to say there was no word. At the last contact, Josh had been heading west over the islands which dot the Durian Strait between Singapore and Sumatra, and I didn't like the sound of it because the whole of that part of the sky was dark grey, the horizon was obscured, and it needed little imagination to picture the Meteor reaching the curtains of rain and then, very quickly, the violent clouds that lay behind them.

As I've said before, instrument flying is a psychological business. In rough weather, you have to keep telling yourself that in spite of the mad dance of the indicators, if you keep the right throttle setting and a little flap, the right heading, and more or less the right attitude, you can't go far wrong. The aircraft is stressed for two and a half times the force of gravity, and it will stand the strains if you keep within the speed limits.

Not that anyone flies knowingly into a thunderstorm. If you get into one by mistake, the standard drill is to do a 180 and get out again. Most of the time they are isolated and you can fly around them. For many years, before the jet aircraft raised our ceilings, we thought the tops were around 40,000 feet. However, a Canberra arrived at Changi with dents in the fuselage and wings from hail the crew had met over Ceylon at 50,000 feet, and the tops were higher still.

These thoughts were in our minds while we waited, and as soon as the Meteor's flight duration expired, we took off to look for it; eventually the wreckage was found on one of the islands.

When I came to write my comments on the findings of the Court of Inquiry and looked through Josh's log book, I saw that he had a history of accidents, as if he wasn't really cut out for the business and had forced himself to keep at it just too long. He had taken over from Pete Gillmore, who had been Commandant at Bracknell, and was a great help to me when I was settling into the new job.

My immediate boss was the Air Officer Commanding AHQ Singapore, Air Commodore Clouston—a very forthright New Zealander with a fine war record, who had made a name for himself before the war through a series of solo long-distance flights. On one of them, I learned from his book, *The Dangerous Skies*, he was crossing the Alps in a single-engined monoplane, in cloud, picked up ice on the wing which forced him down, was lucky enough to come out in a valley, climbed through the clag again, was forced down a second time in another valley, climbed a third time, and when the ice forced him down again, he was past the peaks and heading for the lower slopes.

He had commanded stations himself, and I suppose naturally enough found plenty to criticize in the way I did things at the beginning. At any rate, he told me quite often, and since he was a rude man, this was getting me down. It was hard enough trying to cope with Sir Frances Fressanges's petty complaints without having Clou walk all over me, and I went to see Pete, who had the quarter next to ours. He was sympathetic and encouraging, and I think he must have had a quiet word with Clou, because the pressure eased off soon afterwards and although Clou was never much fun to work for—my predecessor couldn't stand him, and told me that when he got back to England if there was one thing he was going to do, it was to make absolutely sure that Clou didn't go any higher than air commodore—in fact, we got along pretty well, all things considered. (He retired as an air commodore.)

Promotion was a constant source of speculation, and every six months, when the lists were published, they would be scanned to the accompaniment of recollected reasons why the people listed shouldn't have been there: "Not *him*," rather like the scenes in Dennis Rogers's office. At my end, every six months I had to write confidential reports on all the officers on the station. Even though the wing commanders they worked for directly had commented first, this was a very demanding job because you wanted to be fair and you knew that liking or not liking people didn't mean they were—or weren't—good at what they were doing. You had to guard against what was called the halo tendency: assessing the people who worked for you as being above average when really they were simply loyal and conscientious, the way officers are supposed to be, and therefore average.

Sometimes, of course, you ran across people who were so outstanding that you couldn't go wrong. The officer who had the key job of Wing Commander Flying was first class: dedicated, thorough, professional, courageous, good sense of humour, in short a natural leader. I remember writing on one of his reports that he could not fail to reach air rank, and sure enough, he retired as Air Marshal Sir Thomas Stack after a distinguished career which included a tour as Captain of the Queen's Flight and another as Air Officer Commanding the highly successful (and, in the British fashion, unpublicized) joint operations against the Indonesia-backed communists in Borneo in the 1960s.

I was not so lucky with the officer who should have relieved me of most of the administrative burden, the Wing Commander A, and this forced me into a decision that still bothers me, even though I think it was right. Unfortunately, he was in the wrong job—a brave pilot who had little aptitude for paperwork. I consulted Clou, who had known him before, because I wanted to use the K.R. paragraph about officers unsuitable for their postings, which obviously applied, but Clou pointed out that wouldn't be fair to the next CO or in fact to the officer himself, so I had to write an adverse report and invite him to sign it. He did, was gentleman enough to say that he agreed with it, and left me with the nagging sense that although we might have arrived at the truth, justice hadn't been done to a good man.

His place was taken by another officer who was actually senior to me, but had been held back by a heart problem—not serious enough to take him off flying, but still a handicap. He did the job well and his wife would have liked Ruth's. When we left, he asked me to check his prospects with P Staff in Air Ministry, which I did—he wasn't going to be promoted—and he retired soon after to stay in Singapore. His wife had been born in Kuala Lumpur, he had served in Malaya before, and he got a good job as manager of Singapore's leading club—the Tanglin.

The other wing commanders were good at their jobs, and one, Tom Pritchard, who was the Chief Technical Officer, was unusual for his interest in philosophical pursuits. He introduced me to Ouspensky, and until he died in 1995, he sent me books on Buddhist meditation, Zen Buddhism and, later, Zen in the Art of Archery, which Tom was then engaged in. Zen left me pretty much unmoved, but Ouspensky, and his mentor Gurdjieff, have things to say that are relevant and timely.

The book he gave me when we left Changi was Ouspensky's *The Fourth Way*, just the thing as it turned out for the long voyage home on the *Oxfordshire*. I was at a change point after two years in an exhausting job that still left time for reflection, especially among people—the Malays—whose association with the world beyond the physical senses was remarked by both Conrad and Tomlinson. Ouspensky got my mental juices stirring and taught me two things: that we pass much of life in a condition of waking sleep; and that negative emotions can be guarded against. Thus, he interprets Jesus's exhortation to watch and pray as a reminder of this tendency, and to be conscious and alert: Give us *this* day our daily bread. Also to be on guard against negative emotions, anger, remorse, bitterness, envy—the if-onlys of the night; to train ourselves to recognize their approach, and to stop them entering the mind.

However, the prospect of leaving the RAF and of finding a job in Canada before our savings had run out was of more immediate concern, and as soon as we docked at Liverpool, we started on the chain of events that led us to Montreal.

ABOVE: *Parade Gound and Airfield, Changi, March 1956*

BELOW: *Morning Parade, RAF Regiment (Malaya).*

Raising the Flag

Taking the Salute

193

The Malayan 'Emergency.' Killed on Active Service.

LEFT: *The Imam, Rev. Sims, Rev. Galbraith*

RIGHT: *Beehive hut, Car Nicobar, 1956*

Tea at Mr. Wan Chik's, 1957 (back row, left)

Tea at Mrs. Wan Chik's, (on Ruth's right)

Supper Party

Dinner Party at Sqn. Ldr. and Mrs. Jacobs', 1956

Chapter 9
▨ 1957—1969 ▨

Sir Frances Fressanges, who left just before we did, knew that I was going to retire. He was thoughtful enough, when we went with a host of others to the ship to see him off, to take me aside and tell me about a forthcoming scheme that would encourage people to retire early with substantial bonuses. "Don't put in your application, Mac, until you see the fine print." So when we arrived—Auntie Kit took us all in at Avenue House—I went to Adastral House to see Jimmie Ronald, who was in charge of group captains' postings, and told him of my intention. He showed me the Air Ministry Order and explained that the purpose of what came to be called "the golden bowler scheme" was to get rid of people who had reached their promotion ceilings, so as to clear a path for others coming along and to combine this with a reduction of the total manpower. He said it didn't apply to me, but since I was going to apply for retirement "at own request" anyway, it was worth a try. Meanwhile (he said), I was posted to a policy job on the Air Staff in Air Ministry. We had to live somewhere, so why not fix us up with a married quarter in the Air Ministry "patch" at Bushey Heath while the paperwork got itself sorted out?

This was the first in a series of events that caused us to leave the Royal Air Force with a very good taste in the mouth. I did as Jimmie suggested by putting my all into an application to retire early under the terms of the AMO, we moved into No. 3 Finucane Rise, Jimmie further suggested I take some leave, we bought a sec-

197

ond-hand Vauxhall Velox from Bob Humphries's garage in Bracknell, and set off for a three-week tour of Europe: Dover-Ostend; Bruges; Cologne; Pforzheim; Innsbruck; Padua; Venice; Florence; Bolsena; Rome; Viareggio; Cannes; Grenoble; Geneva; Auxerre; Paris; Ostend; Dover.

When we got back, there was no word on my application, it was already September (1957), and we were starting to twitch about being in time for the last boat before freeze-up—the *Sylvania*, sailing in November. We booked passage, and Jimmie and one or two of his chums hand-carried the papers from office to office to meet our deadline. My retirement was approved with days to spare (no golden bowler, though), and here again the RAF came through. The local CO, who was responsible for the Air Ministry's married quarters, instead of doing the requisite "marching out," which would have meant checking everything in the quarter the day before we left and taking all the linen and blankets back into store, sent a warrant officer over to do the bookwork with instructions to leave everything in place until we had gone.

Then both at King's Cross and at Liverpool, RAF Movements officers sought us out to make sure we and our luggage were taken care of and saw us to our cabins. We kept the car until the last morning, when one of Bob Humphries's people met us at King's Cross and drove it back to Bracknell to be sold on our behalf.

In Montreal we were met by Ruth's brother, Jack, and his wife, Sylvia, from Barrie; Ruth's sister, Hazel, and husband, George Rogan, from Ottawa; booked into the Laurentian Hotel, bought a new 1958 Chevrolet sedan, and a few days later drove to Barrie. We had enough money to last for six months, and I was confident of finding a job well before they were up.

While we were in Montreal I went to see two people whose names I had from friends in England. One was a stockbroker, and the other the V-P Sales for Seagram's. I didn't have much idea of what to do, and while still in England had written to a number of Canadian companies to describe what I thought I had to offer them. There were no replies, and I concluded the only way to find out was to be there. However, I wrote to a Canadian in the RAF who had taken early retirement as a group captain the year before and was then working for MacMillan Bloedel, the lumber people, in Vancouver. His advice was to stay with big organizations: they worked much the same way as the air force. So when the Seagram's man asked me why I was going to see brokers and distillers, when all my experience was with aircraft, and why didn't I go to see people in the flying business, I saw his point.

I called Al Lilly, whom I'd met briefly at Borden in 1939 and who, after being Canadair's chief test pilot, was then director of sales, and went to see him. George Keefer was there, too—one of the RCAF's leading fighter pilots in the war, whom I'd met at Armour Heights in 1946, and who was then in charge of contract administration. While operating in the Western Desert, one of the pilots in George's squadron had to forced land behind German lines. George landed nearby, threw out his parachute so that the downed pilot could sit in the bucket seat with room for George to sit on his lap, and George flew the Spitfire back to base.

I met Peter Redpath, V-P Sales, a well-known navigator who had flown for many years with SAS, and the atmosphere appealed to me: the hangars smelled the same, aircraft were about on the airfield, and the offices in mahogany row were pleasantly appointed.

Nothing was decided, and we went off to Barrie to see the rest of Ruth's family while I did side trips to de Havilland, A.V. Roe, Field Aviation, and Hunting in the Toronto area. I knew people at both de Havilland and A.V. Roe, and was encouraged by being offered a job at the latter. It was now December, and we were in a somewhat similar situation to the one we'd been in eleven years earlier after the Armour Heights course—except that I wasn't being paid, we were living in Mayor's Motel on Dunlop Street, Barrie, and I needed a job. I phoned George Keefer and found out afterwards (not from George) that he had gone straight to Peter Redpath, said nice things about me, and as a result Al Lilly called me and invited me to go there for an interview. I went on the overnight train from Barrie, saw Peter and Al again, was offered a job as Al's assistant, and took it, starting January 2, 1958. So again I was lucky, with a job just three weeks after landing, and we set about looking for somewhere to live in Montreal, which also appealed to us from our having spent the honeymoon there in the Berkeley Hotel in 1940.

After putting in more time in a motel, we rented an upper duplex on Soissons Avenue in Outremont and started house-hunting. The city was in one of its periods of relative calm, and we confined the search to Hampstead and the Town of Mount Royal, where the children would get good schooling in English-speaking surroundings and I would be close to Canadair. We bought 114 Normandy Drive in TMR for $38,500 in February, moved in on April 1, and lived there while the children graduated in turn from Town of Mount Royal High and McGill University, not unlike the scene we had anticipated at Bracknell in 1954.

Ruth credits me with the initiative to leave the RAF; even though her natural instinct was to return to Canada, she felt that the service was looking after us—how would we manage outside it? Yet in their treatment of families, the British services were far behind their Canadian counterparts, whose personnel staffs arranged postings to coincide with school years and recognized that families in transit deserved to be put up in hotels—much the same, as we were to discover, as the way private businesses operated.

Although the British services were becoming more considerate by the time we left—witness Jimmie Ronald's thoughtfulness—the RAF was still shaking off the bonds of its early association with the Royal Naval Air Service, which denied recognition in the form of allowances to officers who were foolish enough to wed before they had reached either the rank of lieutenant or the age of thirty. Right up to the outbreak of the Second World War, younger married officers below the rank of flight lieutenant were said to be "living in sin" in the flats or rooms they had been able to find for their wives in neighbouring villages.

My only knowledge of the aircraft industry, other than in the secondhand capacity of end-user, was limited to the wartime morale-raising round of factories in the London area, and visits to de Havilland and the Bristol Aeroplane Company that were part of the Staff College curriculum. On those occasions I could see how material went in at one end and aircraft out at the other, but what I could never find out was how much they cost, in short how it all *worked*. Even after many years at Canadair, and despite quite diligent inquiry, I wasn't much wiser.

Canadair was primarily a government contractor, contracts were cost-plus, and when engineering changes were made to aircraft in production, the costs of incorporating the changes were added on, too. The place was dominated by the engineering department; the sales function consisted chiefly of jollying along the RCAF officers who had to do either with requirements, purchasing, or flying the product, and performing similar duties vis-à-vis officers of other air forces who might conceivably become purchasers.

I swotted up performance details of the aircraft in production or being designed, learned enough about manufacturing processes to answer questions, showed visitors around the plant, and renewed acquaintance with RCAF officers who had survived the war.

I joined a Berlitz course that was laid on at the plant and followed it with lessons from a private tutor to improve my French, but so many of the senior airline and air force people spoke and preferred to practice English that the only times I remember using French were with a government minister in Brazil who was a francophile, with a group of aircraft executives in Belgium, and with two Americans from Northrop who had got hold of a competitor's proposal in French and needed me to translate it for them.

At Canadair, as in other manufacturing plants in the Montreal area, the cut-off point was foreman. Foremen were bilingual. Above that line, the common tongue was English; below it, French.

This educational divide, which local nationalists made a point of blaming on anglo-oppression and "two hundred years of injustice" was the inevitable result of the Roman Catholic Church's domination of the education system: congregations confined themselves to its approved callings, medicine, the law and, of course, the Church. In his book *French Power* (1978), BMG author and historian Sam Allison wrote:

> Despite efforts and complaints by Quebec's [English-speaking] minority, the French majority of Quebec refused to institute compulsory education until 1943—one of the latest dates amongst Western nations... French Quebec failed to finance either French or English education to any degree until the 1960s. In 1960 (as in the rest of North America), 65% of Quebec's school expenditure came from local as opposed to provincial sources—Quebec's English minority had to over-tax itself to spend money on education and it is now experiencing the repercussions of this. In effect, the major culprit in failing to ensure an adequate French-speaking system of education was French-speaking Quebec itself. Surprisingly, French ultranationalists in Government posi-

tions criticize only English Canada's neglect of French-speaking education [outside Quebec].

Ten years after Allison's book was published, McGill University economics professor William Watson wrote in *The Financial Post*, April 8, 1988:

> What is conveniently forgotten—indeed can no longer be spoken of in polite circles in Quebec—is that the crucial event in the economic and social liberation of the French-speaking majority was its decision, in the early 1960s, finally to transport its school system forward from the 17th century. That Quebec's secularization came so late was hardly the fault of the English minority. Guilt that it wasn't no doubt explains much of the majority's current animus.

Tucked away in the sales department was an embryo commercial sales branch in the person of Karl Larsson, a talented design engineer who had been hired by Peter Redpath from SAS to assuage the company's guilty feeling that it ought to diversify into the commercial airline market. With the end of the Korean War, which had been so profitable for Canadair (at the peak of production, it was turning out two F-86 Sabres and one and a half T-33 two-seat trainers *a day* for an eventual total of 1,815 and 656 respectively), the company needed to become less dependent upon a Canadian military budget which was already declining.

I ran into Karl fairly often because the company was redesigning the basic Bristol Britannia fuselage—which had already been redesigned to form the RCAF's CL-28 Argus maritime patrol aircraft—to make it into a military transport for the RCAF, the Yukon. This involved installing a big cargo door on the port side, and Karl's interest naturally was to tell his airline friends about possible commercial applications of the same aircraft. As Al Lilly's assistant, therefore, I often found myself carting civil as well as military visitors around, and must have made a fair enough fist of it, because when the possibility of the company's getting seriously into the commercial business cropped up in 1958 and Karl began hiring people, he asked me to be his manager of commercial aircraft sales. Given my persisting ignorance of what airplanes cost, I wasn't too confident about this.

However, the money was good, and surely I could pick up the new language.

This introduced me to the difference between military and civil life. In the RAF, for the most part you went where you were sent. In the business world, I discovered, it wasn't like that. Companies would hire people they thought were good investments even if there wasn't a job for them—something would turn up. At Canadair, for example, I was intrigued by Ivan Manley, a plain-spoken American (his favourite phrase was "the hard-grilled truth of the matter is...") who occupied one of the offices on mahogany row and who, whenever I happened to pass that way and looked in, would be sitting before a desk empty save for a yellow legal-size writing pad and a cylindrical pencil holder filled with needle-sharp pencils, ready to chat, his telephone as silent as, in the outer office, was the typewriter of his secretary.

The rumour was that Ivan was very knowledgeable about Latin America and about the niceties of administering contracts, yet he seemed to have no connection with George Keefer, who administered contracts for the company, or with Karl or Al, who presumably wanted to get Latin American customers interested in what we were trying to sell. Later on, Ivan became involved in negotiating some of the sub-contracts from major US manufacturers that constituted growing amounts of business, and there's no doubt of his being an experienced and competent chap. Still, there he was, and to me an enigma.

Then again, within two or three months of my joining, we learned that there was not only a Royal Australian Air Force requirement for a new maritime patrol aircraft, but that the RAAF were looking seriously at our CL-28. Presto! the company must have an office in Australia, and since by then it was known that yours truly was personally acquainted with not a few senior RAAF types from Changi days, and Latimer, and Bracknell before that, I was offered the job. Ruth and I considered it for about as long as, in South Croydon, we had considered the proffered move to Karachi. I explained to Al that I had given up a promising career in the Royal Air Force for the express purpose of living the rest of my life in Canada, and that although I liked Australia (my second choice after Canada for a place to live), we had just bought and moved into a new house, the children were settling into school after having been out of it for six months, and Al nodded, smiled, and said that would be fine: they'd get someone else.

The spark that prompted my move to commercial sales was not so much the commercial prospects of the four-turboprop-engined military Yukon (later it was redesigned for the commercial air freight market as the swing-tail CL-44) as the redesign of the Convair 340 and (later) 440 series of twin-piston-engined airliners to a turboprop version that would challenge the Vickers Viscount and Fokker F-27 for re-equipping local airlines in the United States. This was the brainchild of Sammy Sammons, the genial general manager of Napier's, a British engine manufacturer of long standing and some repute in the military field—the Hart variant I mentioned before, the Hector, was fitted with the Napier Dagger engine in 1936.

Napier had designed the Eland engine, a turboprop of 3,500 equivalent shaft horsepower, which they had fitted to a Convair 340, and Sammy's idea was for Canadair to build a fleet of the new combination for the RCAF's Air Transport Command. The RCAF order would kick-start a production line from which a civil version—the Canadair 540—would be offered to airlines.

The first part of the plan was accepted by the Canadian government and work began on ten aircraft for the RCAF. However, the Convair airframe that would be produced for the RCAF was a military modification which Convair had built for the USAF as the C-131F. It had a cargo door on the port side, and the fuselage had been strengthened by increasing the number of under-floor beams. These changes had the effect of reducing the number of floor fittings for seats, increasing the structural weight, and hence reducing the payload. Also, the modified airframe had not been certified by the Federal Aviation Administration (FAA) for the simple reason that it was never intended for commercial use. Nor did the RCAF need any certification other than its own very comprehensive testing and supervision of the aircraft's production. Thus, Canadair and Napier had to get the civilian version (no cargo door, standard 440 fuselage, but with the more powerful Eland engine) certified by the FAA before any US airline could be expected to show interest.

Then again, because the Eland was considerably more powerful than the Pratt and Whitney R 2800 piston engines in the 440, the engine-out performance was affected: with one engine out, more power on the opposite side would impose more pressure both on the rudder and the vertical stabilizer to keep the aircraft straight. Therefore, some people said, the vertical stabilizer should be modified to provide a larger surface that would compensate for the extra power in the engines.

Not included among the "some people" was Canadair's engineering department, which maintained that the existing tail surfaces were adequate and safe. It did include Canadair's potential customers, as I soon discovered when the very knowledgeable ex-pilots who ran the US local airlines lost little time in explaining their doubts to me. They also expressed doubts that the FAA would certify the Eland-powered Canadair 540 unless such modifications were incorporated.

This was at a time when the Canadian dollar was at a premium over the American, Canadair's accountants insisted on quoting the 540's price in Canadian dollars, and consequently our potential customers discovered that by the time taxes and duties were added, the price to them was not the $1,250,000 shown in the literature but US$1,400,000. (Chief reason for the high price was Canadair's setting the break-even point at thirty aircraft, which would have made us a bundle of money if we had sold sixty, but had the prior effect of preventing us from selling any at all.) At a time also when the piston-engined Convair 440 was still in production, with the same number of seats—52—as the Eland version, fully proven and selling for US760,000, while the Fokker F-27, also with 52 seats although not so fast as the Eland version, was being offered at about the same price as the 440, fully certified from a company with a long history of commercial aircraft production, and with Rolls Royce Dart turboprop engines.

Still, Napier's prototype was a very nice aircraft—it leapt off the ground, it was quiet, the performance figures were impressive, and the two companies decided to mount demonstration tours of North and South America.

Arranging the tours fell to me, and the ensuing weeks are a dark period in my life not unlike the time in Sweden. First, I knew not nearly enough about airlines, and much of the patter was Greek to me—seat pitch, balanced field lengths, payload/range curves, break-even load factors, mail pay, direct operating costs, cost per seat mile—so that in talking to airline people I had little to fall back on except flying itself, which to them was almost incidental. Second, I was not convinced that the tail surfaces would do without modification, and however often I listened to the project engineer making his case for not modifying them, I couldn't see how the arguments would hold together in front of customers. (Not long after this, Allison Division of General Motors got into the business of converting 440s to Allison turboprops, and enlarged the tail surfaces as part of the conversion program. The only rejoinder open to us when customers mentioned this was to point out that the Allison engine was more powerful than the Eland!) Third, there was a mountain of administrative work to be done in too short a time: planning the routes; arranging for fuel and accommodation; agreeing times of arrival and departure with potential customers; finding out their peculiar requirements and making appropriate studies of the 540's performance in those circumstances; preparing brochures and other promotional bumf.

For their sales effort in the USA, Napier's had hired Raymond J. Pflum, a US Navy captain who retired retaining the rank of rear admiral and didn't mind mentioning it, an inveterate smoker of cigars, and a very forthright speaker. Years afterwards I was privileged to meet a lot of serving US Navy officers, and one thing I can generalize about, apart from their professionalism, is the modesty of their language. In moments of stress they might be driven to a "Gosh!" or even a "Golly Gee!" while the accolade bestowed on achievement of any kind was "Outstanding!" Not so with Ray, whose use of the "F-word" was indiscriminate and evidently habitual. He and I had service background in common, as we did ignorance of the airline business, but ignorance didn't worry Ray: his approach to that was to raise the voice; his approach to the niceties of persuading our own pilots to perform for the customers was to treat them as no doubt he had treated recalcitrant midshipmen.

Demonstrating an aircraft's performance is an art. It demands skills not only in pilotage, so that the aircraft's good features are given prominence to the exclusion of any that are not so good, but also in appreciating the customer's natural desire to find out all he can about what the aircraft might be able to do for his operations; in short, tact and judgment. Napier's chief test pilot, Mike Randrup, was well suited to that demanding job. He knew the aircraft and engine well, was able to get the best out of the combination, and was the veteran of a lot of demonstration flying in Europe and the UK. If Mike had been in the front office during the tours, my life would have been much easier. Instead, since Canadair was paying most of the shot, its chief test pilot appropriated the job for himself.

Bill Longhurst had succeeded Al Lilly as chief test pilot, and it would be hard to find two men so opposed in everything except the actual business of flying. Al might well have been the best liked man, for his time, in Canadian aviation: friendly, sympathetic, thoughtful, modest about his considerable achievements. Bill was not like that. You might describe his as an ingoing personality: gruff, even surly, and very jealous of the least intrusion on what he regarded as his personal turf. Since this included the left-hand seat in the cockpit, since he would only grudgingly let a customer's chief pilot into the right-hand seat, and since under no circumstances would he allow Mike Randrup any closer to the controls than the jump seat behind the two pilots' seats, you could say that the North American tour faced a pretty stiff built-in headwind.

On the logistics side, there was not only an acute shortage of engines, but the engine itself, which had yet to pass its certification tests, was subject to what are no doubt customary teething troubles with any new design, but which didn't make life any easier for us. The starting system gave endless trouble, the fuel metering system was so sensitive as to cause, if it were not precisely adjusted, the engine revolutions to surge, and the air conditioning system was temperamental. Sweden came back to haunt me when, the night before we left Montreal, I couldn't sleep, then repeated without sleep for the next three nights at Utica and White Plains. There, however, a stone from the runway punctured the de-icer boot on one of the propeller blades, and we were forced to return to Montreal for a replacement—which gave me a night at home and, at Ruth's insistence, a chance to get some sleeping pills.

In the 1950s, air-conditioned and pressurized airplanes were still comparatively rare. (In Colombia, we found that airlines flew their unpressurized DC-3s and DC-4s regularly across the Andes at 20,000 feet, on the assumption that the passengers wouldn't miss what they didn't know about.) However, as we flew south from Montreal, the weather warmed up and air-conditioning became critical for passenger comfort, especially when the passengers were potential customers. Thus, it was embarrassing, when I was describing the aircraft's virtues in the (fairly) quiet cabin, to have the air-conditioning system back up and deliver blasts of scalding air that shot the cabin temperature into the nineties, or, as a variation, to have it shoot puffs of steam, so that in an otherwise clear sky, the only clouds were the little ones inside the cabin.

Despite these shortcomings, we met some very nice people, had some good evenings, and educated ourselves in the workings of the local airlines, many of which have since fulfilled the promises of expansion that were anticipated by the far-sighted entrepreneurs—mostly pilots—who put them together soon after World War II. At Las Vegas, where we went for the 1959 World Congress of Flight after spending two blissful days in Santa Monica while an engine was changed, I met the C-in-C of the Pakistan Air Force, who was interested in the CL-44. When he retired he became president of Pakistan International Airlines, one of the select band of CL-44 customers that got away in the years to follow.

While we were in Las Vegas, Desmond turned up with Irene to see the show. They had lived in Santa Barbara for the two years since he left the RAF (eleven months before me, after suffering a nervous breakdown which, had he stayed in, would have meant a shift out of General Duties to a non-flying branch). It was the first time we had seen each other since 1949, when they came to London and the four of us spent an evening together not long before they went to the Canal Zone. In the intervening years he had put on weight, and Irene seemed just as discontented as she was before. Desmond was trying his hand at something to do with real estate, but I could tell his heart wasn't in it. What he really enjoyed, he told me, was sailing alone—and although he didn't make the comparison at the time, it was of a piece with his enjoyment of flying single-seat fighters, as he had at Biggin Hill before being posted to Flying Training Command, and where again he flew Furies and Gauntlets.

Irene disliked service life, particularly in England's wartime and post-war austerity, not least because of separation from her brother and sisters and the cocktail circuit kind of social life she had been used to before marriage, and still sought, I gathered, in Santa Barbara. Ruth and I thought they were ill-matched from the start, that it was chiefly a physical attraction: slim, handsome young pilot meets vivacious young woman in moneyed surroundings and is carried away. Desmond needed time alone, time to be quiet, while Irene throve on company, the more and livelier the better.

By contrast, the South American tour was quite relaxed. In Miami we laid in a stock of American cigarettes to bribe our way past successive customs officials, the front office was occupied by Scott Maclean and Bud Scouten, both cheerful souls who got on well with Mike Randrup, and everything went swimmingly apart from the usual mechanical snags. These were, first, replacing an oil pipe that had split an hour out of Montreal, causing us to shut down the engine and forced land at Williamsport, New York, where we were lucky to find a welder. His repair got us to Miami, where a replacement was flown in. The new pipe chose to fail halfway between Santiago and Buenos Aires, past the highest peaks of the Andes, but still over inhospitable country, and we were glad to creep into Ezeiza airport on one engine, at dusk, and get the pipe welded in time for the morrow's demonstrations. All this was in the port engine, and nothing untoward happened during the flights in Argentina, although I remember one airline's president, who was resting his chin against his right hand, raising three fingers unobtrusively to signal the personal commission we would have to factor into the quote. In that country, too, flying with a local airline, it was disconcerting to notice not so much how both the pilots crossed themselves before takeoff as the other routine—when the stewardesses served wine, their first call was in the cockpit.

In Rio, the chief pilot of VASP, who naturally didn't know the history of the port engine, took off from Santos Dumont on the 4,200 feet of runway that aimed us at the Sugarloaf mountain overlooking Rio harbour. As soon as the wheels were unstuck, he shut down the starboard engine to test our assurances about the Eland's single-engine performance, and the rest of us had some tense moments visualizing the pressure on the weld in the oilpipe of the engine that was keeping us aloft.

It's easy now to say that those two demonstration tours were a waste of effort—they produced no business—but at the time, it was the right thing to do. We had a product, we needed to get into the commercial market, and we had to try. The market was there, but as a company we weren't ready for it, and the combination of an unproven engine with too expensive an airframe was simply uneconomic. We sold the prototypes to Quebecair, but the operating costs proved too great for them and the three ended up as additions to the RCAF's fleet—all of which were later re-engined with the Allison turboprop.

In the CL-44, on the other hand, we had a good product, and although it came out toward the end of the first turboprop era when the major airlines were enamoured with jets, there were smaller airlines that could take advantage of its low operating costs and make money. In the passenger market, Loftleidir, the Icelandic airline, bought two, we almost captured Trans-Caribbean Airways, and would have sold to Max Ward if Canadair's accounts people had been more enterprising (they were spoiled by years of government contracts and couldn't grasp the fact that Max's expertise was more important than his credit rating).

Flying Tiger and Seaboard World, the two leading US freight carriers, ordered enough aircraft for us to engineer and install the swing-tail modification, and we came within a whisker of selling twenty to Pan American Airways—a breakthrough that would have led to other sales worldwide, had it not been scuppered by the legal counsel from our parent corporation, General Dynamics, wearing both sides down, back and forth, a comma here, a fresh interpretation there, until the whole thing died.

But it was Canadian politics that robbed us of an order from the USAF's Military Air Transport Service for forty under a Canada-US defence arrangement whereby Canada would buy some used McDonnell-Douglas F-101 Voodoo two-seat fighters for Air Defence Command to replace its ageing CF-100s. The Diefenbaker government had just cancelled production of the Avro Arrow and was unable to stomach the prospect of criticism from Toronto if, so soon after that traumatic event, it were to approve a substantial US order in Montreal. This led to a suggested compromise wherein Canada would assume costs of installations on the Distant Early Warning Line, but it was vetoed too. The irony—and agony for us—of that purely political decision was that sub-contractors in the Toronto area would have got about half of the work. (Later, and without a Canadian manufacturing offset, Ottawa bought F-101s anyway.)

From then on, the CL-44 bore the totally unwarranted stigma of having been rejected by Trans Canada Airlines (which chose to be the sole foreign purchaser of the UK's Vickers Vanguard in preference to the passenger version of the 44), Pan Am, and now the USAF. For a few more years we pursued customers, were frustrated on the point of selling five to Pakistan International by Ottawa's refusal to issue an export permit for fear of offending India, saw as a result of that refusal the demise of an order from Saudi Arabian Airlines, and eventually lost heart.

For me, it was a relief to get back into what Al Lilly maintained the company should have stuck to all along: military sales. Under licence from Northrop, we were building F-5s for the Royal Netherlands Air Force and the RCAF, and this gave us a leg into other European air forces. During the mid-1960s, I spent a lot of time in Belgium, Denmark, Norway, and Switzerland promoting the idea of combining the Canadair-designed CL-41 Tutor jet trainer with the CF-5, and offering the CL-41 jigs and tooling for licence production. At the same time, Hedley Everard stationed himself in Kuala Lumpur until his persistence paid off in an order for twenty CL-41s from the Royal Malaysian Air Force.

Northrop had given us tacit agreement to offer CF-5s in South America and we hit all the right notes in Brazil, where the government actually ordered fifteen CF-5s, with an option for fifteen more. I attended the celebratory luncheon with the ministers of defence and finance (the name of one was Diocletio, who claimed descent from Diocletian), only to be frustrated again by Ottawa's reluctance to grant an export licence for fear of starting an arms race in Latin America. My friends in the BAF were obliged to soldier on with their ancient Meteors until the practical French sold them Mirages—far more warlike than our CF-5s.

By definition, military sales are made to governments. You deal in the first instance with the air force, because it has the responsibility to write the requirement that fits the roles assigned to it by the government. But the government has to find the money, and most governments are swayed by the same political considerations as Canada's; you must cater not only to the flying and technical staffs, but also to the civil servants and their political masters. In the long war, you pick up allies where you can, and often they are to be found within the country's own aircraft industry. Thus, in Switzerland I worked with Pilatus, an enterprising company which stood to gain from Swiss procurement of a replacement for its ageing fighters, and was interested in the idea of a CL-41/F-5 combination which would allow Pilatus to build the CL-41 under licence and sell it elsewhere. In Great Britain, when there was the possibility of a joint licence production program of McDonnell-Douglas F-4 Phantoms for the RAF, RN, RCAF and US Marine Corps, we worked with British Aerospace and with Rolls Royce, whose Spey engines would—and subsequently did—improve the aircraft's performance by about fifteen percent over the original version powered by General Electric J-79s. Later, when the RCAF initiated the concept of a Canadian Advanced Multi-Role Aircraft (CAMRA), we worked with British Aerospace and, in Germany, with Messerschmidt.

This may sound like a cameo of a military-industrial complex in Canada, yet it is hard to see, given the need for Canada to defend its sovereignty, how things could have been otherwise. Canada's record of military-industrial endeavour was marked by two conflicting strains: a high degree of professionalism in the military services, supported for the most part by equivalent standards of competence in industry; and a lack of political attention to the country's need for an adequate defence. Under Lester Pearson and Pierre Trudeau, the defence capability was not so much neglected as ignored. Defence spending fell from twenty-five percent of the total to eight percent, with the result that, when the end of the Cold War presented Canada's allies with a so-called "peace dividend" by way of reduced spending on defence, Canada's dividend had long been consumed and its shrunken forces, starved of modern equipment, were inadequate to meet the country's national and international commitments.

Canadair became too dependent, for too long, on government work that was always subject to the whims of politicians and their advisers in the public service. Whatever initiative individual engineers or salespeople might show was subjected to the artificial test of approval by a handful of mandarins in Ottawa; artificial because the ingredient of successful enterprise—risk assessed and taken—was absent: none of the participants had a personal stake, save furtherance of their careers, in the outcome. Senior management was so sensitive to the whims of the mandarinate that when the incumbent of the company's Ottawa office in the mid-1960s lost favour with one particular mandarin, the company's president fired him.

When a military order was coming to an end, the modus operandi for getting another one was to dust off the manpower charts and send the president to Ottawa, where he would display to appropriate ministers the dire effect upon Montreal and Quebec if Canadair were to experience the layoffs that the charts projected. In short, purchasing decisions were made for the wrong reasons, Canada's defence forces were either lumbered with inadequate equipment or denied it altogether, because political leaders were more concerned with their own survival than the country's. Between 1964 and 1992, the decline in defence spending from about twenty-five percent of the total to eight was offset by a doubling of expenditure on health and welfare from about eighteen percent of the total to thirty-six.

Much has been written about the cancellation of the Avro Arrow; nothing at all about the opportunities thrown away afterwards by Pearson and Trudeau and their henchmen in External Affairs. Their attitude was epitomized by the comment of a senior mandarin—the same one who had persuaded John Diefenbaker to cancel the US contract for forty CL-44s—after his department had scuppered the CF-5 sale to Brazil. He said, "Good. Now we can forget about Brazil."

When I wrote just now about a high degree of professionalism in the military services, it was in the past tense. Decline of the Canadian military, in equipment, in capability as a combat force, and in the morale that sustains the whole endeavour, has been a feature of the Canadian scene for forty years. The causes are plain: first is the policy switch from defending Canada to "peacekeeping" abroad; second is the substitution of fluency in French for professional merit as the criterion for advancement; and third is the political obsession with the welfare state's uncontrollable costs. Neglect of the military offends only a small audience. Neglect of "universal" social programs can bring down governments.

The eleven years at Canadair were productive in a number of ways. They allowed us to stay in one place, in comfortable circumstances, while the children completed their education. They taught me a lot about the relations between big business and big government, and how the softening of distinction between the upper levels of both has the deleterious effect of most compromises: in the face of superior power, compromise for the lesser power means surrender. (Contrary to myths of the Left, business, however big, is always subject to the dictates of government, which sets the rules.)

I learned, by going there, about conditions in other countries. However badly they were run, and however unenviable the lot of the masses, there was always some money for the military. In Latin America, bribes were a prerequisite for doing business, as they were in Africa and East of Suez. In Germany, Austria and Italy, they were called commissions, dispensed by intermediaries, and it was par for the course that the company would be expected to pick up the tab for government officials who expressed a desire to visit Canada. In Canada, the bribery was merely political and consisted of Canadair's share of the larger blackmail that Quebec has practiced so successfully upon the rest of the country since Confederation.

All the time, thanks to Ruth's good management of the household, we were saving money steadily and accumulating a respectable balance that was helped in the mid-1960s by a bequest from Auntie Kit's estate. Her husband, a builder, fell victim to rheumatoid arthritis that worsened until he was confined to a wheelchair. He died while I was still at school, Auntie Kit took over the management of the business from her house in The Avenue—Avenue House—and displayed such a talent for buying and selling that she became quite a wealthy woman. A generous one, too, not only in her habit of sending money to nephews and nieces while she was alive but even more so in her adoption of an extended family of friends—and friends of friends—who were down on their luck. She was always cheerful, bursting with a spiritual strength that radiated from her slight, almost boyish frame, and delighted in caring for the assortment of dependents she took under her wing. When my cousin Peggy's parents died, she lived with Auntie Kit until Bill Forsyth came along and married Peggy just after the war.

Looking back over those years in Montreal, I see a mixture of experiences: frustrations that I'm sure weren't half as bad as those

Dad faced in London; rewards derived from new surroundings or new acquaintances or both; and a general sense that most of the time I knew what I was doing, so that however tricky the spot, I would be able to work my (and the company's) way out of it—if not to the customer's entire satisfaction, then at least with the door open for a fresh assault.

It was, after all, not much of a hardship to fly to new places, especially in the early 1960s when you could still get the odd flight in a Super-Constellation and many local airlines in North and South America were flying their Convairs in a companionable sort of way that made you feel part of the operation. When the jets came in, there was the novelty of smoothness and higher altitudes and the luxury of getting to know individual airlines' characteristics, so that you could treat yourself to Air France's meals, or Lufthansa's stern efficiency, or Swissair's clocklike punctuality, or SAS's cabin service, or Qantas's mateyness, or Varig's caviar. Nor do I feel deprived for having eaten quite decent meals while barges chuntered by on the Rhine, or beside the brown Danube, or overlooking Rio's harbour, or Sydney's, or in Beirut the Med. And in Europe, there were galleries to be patrolled as well as other cultural amenities that abound in the various capitals.

But the pleasant memories, like the sunny days of childhood, are foremost; behind them is a host of occasions that were no fun at all. The sudden calls to rush somewhere when you would much rather stay home, dashing to the airport with minutes to spare knowing that it was a forlorn hope but still worth trying, or steaming in the shuttle at La Guardia lined up twelfth for takeoff, or facing strangers in their offices after a sleepless night across time zones, or simply hanging around for days in a foreign country while the officials you needed decisions from argued among themselves. This happened in Canada, too. When Hedley Everard was getting close to his sale of Tutors to the Royal Malaysian Air Force and we needed confirmation of the government credit arrangements quickly, I went with a contract administrator to Ottawa for an emergency meeting on a public holiday, some kind of record on that score alone. The two of us from Canadair were outnumbered about ten to one by the civil servants, and in the midst of the discussions one of them said, "But Ken, you must remember we have to co-ordinate the work of seven different departments."

Long before Saudi Arabia entered the world scene as the sponsor of OPEC, I was minding my own business at Canadair when Security called to say there was someone asking for the sales department. The guard was Scottish and added, "And he seems to have forgotten his camel." Soon appeared a man of about Ramsan's build, but clad in the traditional robes of the desert and claiming direct access to the Saud family on whose behalf he was interested in the prospect of using our CL-44 freighter to carry water to the parched Bedouin. His name was Mahmoud Ibrahim, and his lifeline was the long-distance telephone. During the several weeks that he wove his spell not only over Canadair's senior management but over Canada's then minister of defence, he kept before our minds' eyes a fleet of CL-44s carrying not only water to the desert but also fruit and vegetables from the Ethiopian highlands to Arabian cities and, at the time of the Haj, planeload after planeload of pilgrims from as far as the Philippines and home again. Lest anyone doubt his royal connections, he let slip that the thin gold watch on his wrist was a gift from one of the princes; at lunch in the executive dining room, he shyly took it off to show the Arabic inscription on the back which he translated for us.

In the few moments when he left us alone, this sounded somewhat far-fetched even for the make-believe world of international aircraft sales, so Eric McConachie and I were deputed to go and see. As ever, there was no time to lose—off we went in a nightmare chase from Dorval to Rome, where we switched to MEA for Beirut. At the airport, Ibrahim displayed us briefly to a shadowy figure who he said had arranged our entry to Saudi Arabia, and after an unexplained stop in Abadan, we raced on to Dhahran and reality.

Our accommodation in the annex to the airport hotel was reminiscent of wartime airfields in England, but warmer, and the urgency came to an abrupt halt as we waited, and waited, for Ibrahim to produce someone of substance for us to talk to. After several days of drinking tea and eating unspeakable meals, during which we conducted halting conversations with acquaintances of Ibrahim (their surname was Arab) who appeared to be general traders unfamiliar with aircraft, we were whisked to the Amoco compound and the air-conditioned quarter of Prince Mohammed, the defence minister. He sat in an overstuffed armchair and pretended to listen while Eric and I expatiated on the virtues of the CL-44—and, for good measure, the CL-41—after which we returned to our crummy accommodation and waited.

Eric is a very bright engineer and an entertaining companion, but suffered the disadvantage of being too young to experience English wartime airfields and was in consequence so put off by the appurtenances of the annex that he wore his slippers in the trickling shower, which also enabled him to stamp on the cockroaches.

We got an undertaking that suitably accredited representatives of the government would come before long to Canada, and left via a shaky charter service that lobbed us into Bahrein to make an airline connection home.

In due course, the younger brothers Arab showed up, very well turned out in European dress and tasteful but still-impressive flashes of jewellery. Canadair's management liked the look of them, Ruth and I entertained them at 114 Normandy Drive, and as I said before, they were given a good reception in Ottawa by Douglas Harkness, the defence minister, the reason for that call being to assure him—and through him, the Government of Canada—that under no circumstances would the CL-44s be used for military purposes.

By this time, the fleet had dwindled to a more practical two aircraft, still worth pursuing, but also dependent, as was Saudi Arabian Airlines, on technical support furnished on an agency basis by Pakistan International Airlines, whose president was by now the air marshal I had met in Las Vegas. Since we were already well advanced in negotiation with PIA for five CL-44s, this fitted in nicely and I made two more trips to Saudi Arabia—Jedda those times—for further talks. A few days before Christmas, we got Ottawa's guarantee for the credit arrangements. I flew to Karachi to take the good news to PIA. Earl O'Mara, who had been concentrating on PIA, met me in Karachi, we buttoned everything up with the airline and our agent Hamid Khan, and flew home on Christmas Eve in good spirits with seven aircraft sold bar the shouting and about $40 million worth of export business.

Brigadier Jim Roberts, a fine Canadian soldier with a first-class war record, was the associate minister of defence production, and it was he who called me a few days into the new year to say, "Ken,

I'm sorry, but we've let you down. External won't grant an export permit to Pakistan for fear of offending India."

That scuppered the Saudi Arabian sale, too, and Ibrahim dropped from sight, but I ran across his trail again when I happened to mention his name to Chafic Badre, a friend of ours who lived in Beirut. Yes, he remembered Ibrahim because of the watch. Ibrahim had not only bought it second-hand, complete with Arabic inscription, from a jeweller in Bahrein, but persuaded the jeweller to accept Ibrahim's personal cheque on a Montreal bank; a cheque that eventually found its way back to the jeweller with a different inscription on the back in English.

About four years later, when I was changing currency at the Frankfurt airport, I saw Ibrahim at another wicket, in European dress, showing the cashier a picture of his daughter, not missing even that fleeting opportunity to practice his skill. Long after we had left Montreal, I read in a Toronto paper of an elusive chap who had conned several quite senior airline people into attending what turned out to be a mythical conference in North Africa for which he had pocketed their attendance fees. No name was given, but it had the authentic stamp of Ibrahim.

Canadair suffered a full-blown strike while I was there, and I experienced at first hand the derivation of labour unions' military vocabulary: strike, picket, the strike weapon. When I got to the plant, the entrance was blocked by a mass of people through which security guards were trying to clear a path for the men and women, mostly supervisory staff and clerical workers, on their way to work. As I joined them. I found myself in a free-for-all among knots of burly men hustling anyone, man or woman, who tried to move toward the plant gates. This was the "peaceful picketing" of union legend, performed with the aid of elbows, knees, fists and boots. Thirty years after that experience, the only noticeable difference is that strikers are better organized. As I write in Toronto after a week of the same sort of activity by striking postal workers, Montreal is enjoying a strike by the Canadian Union of Public Employees which is marked by the usual acts of violence to which politicians of all stripes turn blind eyes—for example, four private vehicles belonging to city non-union staff fire-bombed (as were six others mistakenly thought to belong to non-members); dozens of city buildings spray-painted or their windows smashed;

seven greens at the sole city-owned golf course torn up; death threats to city managers and foremen and their homes spray-painted or windows shot out.

By necessity I learned the price structure of the aircraft we were making, but finding out the cost of changes to the basic design was another matter. When we started trying to sell to commercial customers, chiefly airlines but also corporations that operated their own aircraft, our hardest job was to persuade Canadair's engineering department that it had to yield some ground to the customer. This required such a dramatic change of attitude that it's remarkable we were able to sell anything. Accustomed to years of long production runs in which the only variations would be those initiated by the RCAF, or proposed by Canadair, and always paid for as the work progressed, our engineers were simply not prepared for a competitive market in which aircraft on the same production line might need to match different customers' peculiar requirements: in seating and interiors generally; in cockpit layout and instrumentation; in exterior finish; and in performance for the airline's route structure. The finance department was even less prepared for customers who not only were not funded by government but were looking upon the aircraft as the means to make their business profitable, and consequently required extended payment terms, at competitive interest rates, so that projected revenue would offset the payments.

It was hardly surprising that a company grown used to the placid life of government contracts should be peopled with senior staff to match. Thus Ed Higgins, the chief engineer for most of the time I was there, was what you might call a product of cost-plus: dour, enigmatic, taciturn save when in the company of more senior people, when he would suddenly become loquacious and force smiles upon his normally forbidding features. Ed's approach to potential customers who wanted design changes was to tell them very firmly why the changes were not needed.

This trait came to the fore when we tried to sell the CL-41 Tutor—which Ed had designed—to the RAAF. I was still in commercial sales then, but when the prospect arose and the military sales people realized, just before launching a team that Ed was to lead to Australia, that they didn't know nearly enough about the RAAF's requirements, I was corralled to go there first and find out.

Time was limited, and I set some kind of record for hurried journeys by going there and back in five days which included business meetings in Melbourne, Sydney, and Canberra.

The RAAF chief of staff was Air Marshal Sir Frederick Scherger, whom I had met at Changi when he landed there in a Canberra on his way to see the RAAF squadrons at Tengah and Butterworth. He heard me out politely and then said, "Mac, you're wasting your time. We're going to buy the Macchi." This was plain enough, and subsequent chats with RAAF types I knew confirmed that the Italian trainer was the one they wanted. It had a proven engine, the Armstrong-Siddeley Viper, and it had tandem seating, naturally preferred by embryo fighter pilots—whereas the Tutor had side-by-side seating and was powered, not by the proven Pratt and Whitney JT-12 it was designed around, but by the General Electric J-85, which the RAAF didn't like and said so. (The engine change was the result of yet another Ottawa-inspired transaction, whereby the Orenda company in Toronto had been given a contract to produce J-85s under licence for political reasons connected with the manufacture of CF-5s, which the RCAF didn't want either, but weren't able to refuse.)

When I returned to Montreal and reported this, the reaction was predictable. The projected team visit had its own momentum and off they went, to return in due course with the same finding. Nevertheless, rather like the 540 before, the company had to keep trying, and I went back to Australia afterwards to see if there was any chance of influencing the decision. By that time Scherger had retired, and his successor decided to resolve the competitive situation (the Americans, British, French and Swedes were pushing their trainers as well) by launching a small team headed by Air Commodore Brian Eaton on a fact-finding tour of Canada and the other countries.

Their first call was on Canadair, where they asked a number of questions related to changes they would need to meet their requirements, what those changes would cost, and so on. That was when Ed was at his best, explaining, boot-faced, why his aircraft was perfect as it was. When, grudgingly, he undertook to take some of the customer's requests under advisement, it wasn't until after the team had left that estimates as to cost and performance were forthcoming. By then, however, the team had been to Italy, where the Macchi people (I learned from Brian, when I met him in Paris) had taken the RAAF's changes in their stride and produced drawings, performance estimates and firm prices the following morning. In due course, the Macchi was chosen.

I mentioned the company's hiring a man to open an office in Australia. His no doubt many fine qualities were offset by eccentricities, among which the one I remember was a habit of standing on his head. Since he did this once or twice in the presence of potential customers from the RAAF and RNZAF, and since other activities unbecoming a company representative were filtering back to Montreal from our agents in Melbourne and Wellington, the company decided to cut its losses and I was delegated to go to Australia and fire him. He may have been eccentric, but there was nothing wrong with his intelligence, and when I walked through Customs at Sydney's Mascot airport, there he was, all smiles, to meet me. I'll have to say I didn't enjoy that trip, not nearly as gut-wrenching as the episode with my Wing Commander A at Changi, but still troubling. I wasn't surprised when he sued the company for better terms than the ones I was obliged to hand him.

Toward the end of 1968, the fact of a US Navy requirement for a new trainer encouraged us to enter into a joint effort with Convair to sell a carrier-capable version of the CL-41 Tutor. We demonstrated the aircraft to the Marines at Patuxent River and to the Navy at Pensacola, and spent some time at Convair's plant in San Diego preparing the inevitable masses of bumf that accompany formal proposals. For me, the rewarding part of the exercise was the opportunity to meet some fine carrier pilots—a breed unto themselves—and to observe the modest forms of speech I mentioned before. What I didn't enjoy, even though San Diego itself appealed to me as a place to live, was being separated from home once again and, at the end of the week, clambering aboard the red-eye bound for New York, and waiting there, sleepless, for the first flight out to Montreal.

It was from San Diego, therefore, that I phoned Ruth, reminded her that with the children off our hands we would have enough private means to live on, and agreed with her that it was time to quit. I requested early retirement, the president asked me to stay on at half-pay for a year, part-time, to promote the water-bomber with the Ontario government's fire-fighting service, and I left with a small pension to add to that of the RAF, itself reduced by our having commuted half of it into a lump sum to help buy 114 Normandy Drive.

I had always wanted to write, and we had just about acquired the necessary private means for me to practice that particular kind of virtue.

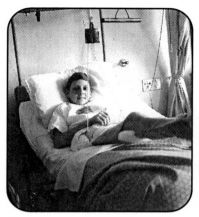

John with broken thigh from skiing
accident, Montreal, 1961

Ruth with John, Montreal, 1967,
in John's new TR4

114 Normandy Drive. McDonalds' home from 1958–1971 (photo taken
in 1992 by Martha)

Cottage Lac Echo (1964–1971)

Lac Echo, 1970

With Collin Brown, 1980

Florida, 1982

123 Burbank, 1985

Lake Louise, 1985. Susan, Duncan, Sarah, Ken and Ruth

Lake Louise, 1988

Barbados, 1986

123 Burbank, February 1987

123 Burbank, April 1987

Canadian National Exhibition, Toronto 1987, with Grandson Eric

123 Burbank, 1988, with Grandson Eric

227

Kars, the cottage, 1988, home from November 1946 - June 1947

with David Somerville, (Colin Brown Award Dinner), 1991

December, 1991

Our fiftieth, Susan, Sarah, Duncan and John at Martha and Gord's, 1990

Peter and Keith's balcony, 1992

at Martha and Gord's, 1996

Our 60th wedding anniversary, May 17, 2000

Peter, Keith, Amy, Scott, Sarah with Erin, Duncan, John, Julie, Peter, Eric, Susan with Lindsay, Martha, Gord, Kristin, Ken and Ruth, May 17,2000

Chapter 10
▦ 1969—1992 ▦

It was in the same year, 1969, that Ruth and I flew to England for what has turned out to be our last visit. Martha was working in London for the summer and she joined us for the trip down memory lane to the places we had lived in during and after the war.

From time to time, friends who go to England for squadron reunions or just plain vacations have asked me why I haven't done the same, and although I have to scramble for an answer, the truth is that in a way I've never left. The feel, the scents, the scenes, the past are tucked away in their various compartments. I read Housman and am back in Shropshire, tramping that border country among its rhododendrons; read Trollope and am in Wiltshire; see flashes in TV programmes of Yorkshire and Oxford, London and Salisbury and Bath.

In the 1930s, when we flew our Harts at 2,000 feet over southern England, we saw the ancient earthworks, the Roman roads (Watling Street, the Fosse Way), the huge figures cut into the chalk, the spire of Salisbury, and recognized the continuity. When I was a boy in Bristol, you could still hear the Saxon in "Wherre bist going tu?" Grandfather McDonald, bearded and retired from the sea, who took me to watch Phil Mead at Southampton's County Ground, was born only forty years after Waterloo. Housman wrote in *Wenlock Edge*: "The tree of man was never quiet: Then 'twas the Roman, now 'tis I."

At Shawbury, The Wrekin was our landmark, and when we flew to armament practice camp at Penrhos, we passed over not only the Welsh Hills but also the places we knew from the ground: Betws-y-coed, Blaenau-Festiniog, Llangollen with its inn where on the tenth of April 1798, William Hazlitt "sat down to a volume of the *New Eloise* over a bottle of sherry and a cold chicken."

Still, this leaves the question unanswered. Those memories are real because they are mine. Llangollen might be the same as it was then, but the London I remember is by all accounts very different. Even in Bristol, only forty-three years after I left, although we found 8 Cornwall Road and took its picture, and although the Cathedral was unchanged, I couldn't find where Brighton House had been.

It's a truism that you can't go back, either to the Bristol of my youth, or even to the Canada that impressed me before and after the war.

Immigration has changed the face of London and the bigger cities to a degree unforeseen when, on one of my last business trips in the late 1960s and sitting on a bench in St. James's Square with my friend Salim of Pakistan International Airlines, it seemed perfectly natural for him to look at the passersby and say, "There are a lot of foreigners in London, Mr. McDonald."

In Canada, the changes, also man-made by professional politicians and their offspring in the immigration industry, have been one more outgrowth of Canada's eternal paradox; namely, that French Canadians commanding the federal government, and bringing to it the centralization of power that marks the French tradition, must always antagonize governments of Quebec that are determined to employ the same top-down system within the province.

Pierre Trudeau, the master strategist who imposed organic change upon our system of government, used the paradox for his own purposes. Unaware or igoring the fact that his centralizing policies were food for Quebec's sovereigntists, he set out to thwart them by making official bilingualism the centrepiece of his Charter of Rights and Freedoms. As he said afterwards: "And we've got the entrenchment of both official languages, which can never be removed." The whole of Canada would be opened up to French Canadians.

At the same time, and in accord with his long-held view that nations belonged "to a transitional period of world history," the traditional Euro-British sources of immigrants were effectively shut off in favour of migrants and their extended families from the Third World. Multicultural Canada was to lead the way to a federation of the world run by a giant bureaucracy for which his "furtive expansion of [Canadian] central agencies" was a model.

Combine this with changes to the structures of the civil and military services, which substituted (French) heritage and language for merit both in recruiting and advancement, and domination of the levers of power by the French Canadian minority was assured.

This was already on the cards at the time I retired. I had seen the changes happening in an Ottawa that was mixed up with so much of Canadair's business, and yet although I wrote a book that described the growth of the State—*The Taxpayers' Revolt*—it didn't fly, and I spent the first two years of the new career struggling with novels.

By then Peter and John had left home, Martha was working in England for the summer, and we began to think about leaving Montreal. Politically inspired hostility between the two language groups was poisoning the atmosphere, and we were becoming less and less inclined to indulge our habit of dining in the old city at restaurants where we were increasingly made to feel unwelcome.

First on the list was selling the cottage. Built of logs, with four bedrooms, central heat, and a dining-living room overlooking Lac Echo near Morin Heights, it had served us well while the children were still at home. Motorboats were prohibited, there was a twenty-foot depth of water off our dock, and many a summer morning I shared the unruffled surface with a solitary heron before diving in. In winter, while the children skied, I snowshoed through the woods or across the lake. For those few years, in a different but still mountainous setting and with smoke rising from logs rather than peat, it fulfilled the dreams of my youth. I saw myself sitting before the desk in the library off the sitting room, year round, conjuring characters and situations into money-earning sequences.

Ruth shot that one down with commendable realism: prettier and more comfortable, but hardly less lonely than Dawson's Farm or Lane End; and where would I find inspiration away from the world? We put it up for sale. The cottage market was as much a victim of the anglo exodus from Montreal as the market in the city and we waited a year for a buyer, then another year to sell the city home.

233

Two years after leaving Canadair we moved to Toronto, where the influx from Montreal had the reverse effect on the market: few houses for sale and at prices about forty percent above the Montreal equivalent. In the areas we chose to look, only four houses were for rent, and we took one on Glencairn Avenue in North Toronto for a year while we renewed acquaintance with the city. I wrote another novel and some short stories, but although an article I sent to *Maclean's* on why we left Montreal came within a whisker of acceptance, nothing was published. A second novel—*Finland Court*—sat with Lester & Orpen Dennys for a year, but was then so nearly accepted (Gena Gorrell wrote "We find the writing, and particularly the use of detail, extremely convincing and well done. The style is most readable and enjoyable, too, and we were most reluctant...") that I took heart; all was not lost. Yet the next, despite a thoughtful and constructive telephone call from the publisher (Anna Porter) to explain what was wrong, didn't fly either, and after two more failures, Ruth suggested I try writing about business and politics instead.

Soon after, the new *Toronto Sun* published an article about the telephone monopoly (paid me ten dollars); *Financial Post* published one on defence, and the *Globe's* Report on Business published one about wage differentials. For a year or so I was appearing regularly in both the *Toronto Star* and the *Globe* (ROB editor Ian Carman asked me once if there wasn't a certain similarity in the material?), as well as running my own version of a syndicated column by mailing copies every other week to dailies in Victoria, Vancouver, Edmonton, Calgary, Lethbridge, Regina, Winnipeg, Hamilton, Kingston, Montreal, and Halifax. Later, the *Toronto Sun* syndicated my column, but I had a poor experience with the *Calgary Sun*—the only time I registered a bad debt—and I ended up sticking to the *Globe*, which published my columns until 1987 when Peter Cook began his regular stint. By mutual agreement, I bowed out.

Not that those shots at fiction were wasted. I learned by writing, and described the fictional experience in a Mermaid Inn column published by the *Globe* on February 2, 1980 (see p. 291).

In the early spring of 1972, we started looking for a house—a very useful exercise, because in the course of finding the right one, we got to know the city. When we moved into this one, in

Bayview Village, I opted for the room I'm in now at the front of the house, where I can see what's happening, still see birds and trees, and have the things around me that are part of our life: wall map of the world from my office at Canadair; silver hawk from the tour on the directing staff at Bracknell; crests from Changi; teak busts of a Malay man and woman; boomerang from Australia; models of a CL-44 and of the CL-41 in US Navy colours; photo of Desmond and me going into Collier Street United Church, Barrie, on May 17, 1940; a favourite photo of Ruth; group photos from Netheravon, Camp Borden, Armour Heights, Latimer, and Bracknell; framed route map of the stages radiating from Changi to Ceylon and Hong Kong; an Eskimo carving for speaking to the Society of Financial Analysts; the sloop from Cocos; the pictures John took from his TV of me on *The National* when the CBC interviewed me in this room about Jock Andrew's best-seller, *Bilingual Today, French Tomorrow*; and books, including Adam Smith's *Wealth of Nations*, in three volumes, leather-bound, the eighth edition, and dated MDCCXCVI—all in a splendid box bearing, on the spine, the title, and "Presented to Kenneth McDonald with Gratitude, the National Citizens Coalition, October 18th 1988." The original price is still visible, pencilled on the flyleaf of Volume 1: 5/-6, 3 vols.

In 1974, I wrote *Red Maple* and showed it to John Bulloch, who was then expanding his Committee for Fair Taxation (in response to Edgar Benson's White Paper on Taxation) into what is now the Canadian Federation of Independent Business. He liked the manuscript and suggested I show it to Winnett Boyd, who was the Canadian authority on Employee Share Ownership Plans (ESOPs). John was in a small office on Eglinton Avenue East with a secretary (Laura Stambler), and Winn ran the Canadian office for the American consulting organization, Arthur D. Little, on the same street. (Both John and Winn lived within two blocks of our new house, another coincidence.)

John was a fascinating man to work with: restless, perfectionist, articulate, determined. When CFIB was properly launched, he and I initiated its weekly syndicated columns and we worked together on them for a year and a half, from 1975 to 1977. Before that, however, Winn and I got ourselves into the publishing business.

When Winn had read *Red Maple*, and briefed me on the principles of ESOPs that are featured in the book, he told me he wanted to write a book, too, and suggested we work together on it. He was chief designer of Canada's first two jet engines, the Chinook and the Orenda, and later chief designer of the Canadian nuclear research reactor, NRU, at Chalk River, which at least until the mid-1970s was still the world's largest research reactor. In the 1972 general election, he ran as a Conservative and, although a political neophyte, and with no help from the party's brass, he cut the Liberal cabinet minister incumbent's majority from about 22,000 in 1968 to a bare 1,847. When I met him, he was still in the process of broadening his knowledge and reading voraciously; almost as an aside, he ran a discussion circle.

We co-authored *The National Dilemma and The Way Out*, with illustrations by Orville Ganes, and began the round of publishers. At Macmillan we met an engaging chap with a gold earring who told us it wouldn't do: too radical (the theme was that all three parties were singing the same socialist song and it was time for one of them to embrace popular capitalism through profit-sharing and employee share ownership).

Next, we tried McClelland & Stewart, and after readers had looked at it, we sat down with Jack McClelland. He was not optimistic. We wanted to get the word out and we thought that in order to sell it widely, the paperback price shouldn't be more than $2.95. Jack said the best M & S could do was $4.95, and although he was polite, we could tell he didn't want to go with it—until Winn offered to guarantee the first 5,000 sales, when he brightened up quite a bit.

When we drove away, however, we looked at each other and wondered why we should subsidize M & S's overhead when we could form a company and put the thing out ourselves. We formed B (for Boyd) M (for McDonald) G (for Ganes) Publishing Limited in November 1974, and published the first printing of *The National Dilemma and The Way Out* in February 1975.

Most of the first printing was pre-sold to business friends and acquaintances who ordered and paid for them by the hundreds for us to distribute to our political mailing list. Copies were sent also to Coles, W.H. Smith and Classic, and I called on every independent bookseller in Toronto. At political meetings, Winn and I would station ourselves near the door, in front of two cartons of the book, and sell copies.

As orders came in, the paperwork of invoicing was handled by Ellen Davies in Winn's office, and the physical work of packing and mailing was done by B, M, and G, with occasional help from their wives. Subsequently it was contracted to a woman who worked in the warehouse of one of Winn's companies. Ruth and I made many trips to bookstores, in the city and at the airport, to the bus station and the post office, where I would unload a trolley from the trunk of the car and manhandle the cartons inside.

It was strictly a sweat equity operation. No one took a salary. Instead, when we had enough in the kitty we bought three company cars, and later were able to declare dividends. In keeping with the idea of employee share ownership, Ellen Davies was made a shareholder and provided with a car.

The business side was handled by Winn as Secretary-Treasurer, and this gave me an insight into how a successful entrepreneur creates wealth. It is a combination of a number of talents: imagination; readiness to take a calculated risk; persistence; patience; close attention to costs; absence of *amour propre* (i.e., rolling up sleeves and getting on with whatever needs to be done); above all, courage and self-confidence.

We ordered a second printing in April 1975, and during the next five years we published seven more books, all of them in paperback, two at $2.95, two at $3.50, two at $3.95 and one at $4.50. All of them sold more than the 10,000 copies generally accepted as best-sellers in Canada, all were controversial, and all the manuscripts had been rejected by the established, and mostly government-subsidized, publishers. There was, in short, a market for reasonably priced books on topics that Canada's emerging New Class and its cultural hangers-on regarded as taboo.

The National Dilemma and The Way Out showed how there was little to choose between the three parties and set out a detailed plan for achieving widespread capital ownership in Canada (the way out). (My) *Red Maple* described the centralization of political power in Ottawa under Trudeau, and forecast, six years ahead of the event, his imposition of a written Constitution to seal the centralizing process. Lieut. Cdr. J. V. Andrew's *Bilingual Today, French Tomorrow* (a runaway success with final sales of

130,000) described the use of political power to colonize English Canada by imposing official bilingualism. (My) *Green Maple* explained the need for changes to Canada's parliamentary system, including the use of referendums, if democracy is to be preserved and strengthened. David Somerville's *Trudeau Revealed* allowed readers to form their own opinions of Pierre Trudeau from that enigmatic politician's actions and words. Sam Allison's *French Power* exposed many myths that have been put about to expand Quebec's influence, and showed how areas outside Quebec that were never French are colonized. Doug Collins's *Immigration— The Destruction of English Canada* documented the astonishing transformation, through policy changes that were never, and still (2001) have not been, put to the people in a general election, of what once was known as English Canada. Finally, Jock Andrew's *Backdoor Bilingualism* described how the Davis government laid the foundations for Ontario to become officially bilingual.

While this was happening, I was going about the daily business of writing, interspersed with occasional guest editorials on CBC radio after the morning news, and it's remarkable, looking back, how things would turn up at the right time. Late in 1975, Winn introduced me to Colin Brown, the outstanding Canadian who founded the National Citizens' Coalition as a private venture in response to his concern at the growth of the State in Canada. Colin began to phone me about things, and the next year, when the NCC started its newsletter *Consensus*, I wrote for and edited it; a job that grew during 1976 and 1977 as its other newsletter, *Overview*, was added on alternate months, so that by the time John Bulloch's CFIB was able to hire a full-time writer, and I stopped doing his columns, that suited me as well.

It was at that time, also, that I ran into another courageous Canadian, Anthony McVeigh, then editor and publisher of *Executive* magazine. I had written a piece called "The Myth of Bilingualism" about the lop-sided influence of Quebec upon federal politics and the divisive effect of imposing official bilingualism upon the whole country. There was no point in sending it to *Maclean's* or *Saturday Night*; I hand-delivered it to *Executive* and was delighted to get a phone call from Tony that afternoon. He wanted to make sure I hadn't offered it to anyone else, and when I invited him to drop by on his way home (he, too, lived a couple of blocks away), it turned out we had a good deal in common. Originally from New Zealand, he had been a carrier pilot in the Korean War, and we saw eye-to-eye on politics: what Friedrich Hayek called a politics "that favours free growth and spontaneous evolution."

He published the piece in the October 1976 issue, knowing it would draw bitter as well as favourable responses, and he was right. In the following March, he published another on the politics of immigration, in September (1977) "Who Guards the Guardians?" which was reprinted in *The Freeman*, and twenty-three more in similar vein until 1983, when Tony left to start another magazine and return to writing himself. *Executive* was put in the hands of an aspiring member of the New Class who was horrified at what I'd been writing, and soon afterwards the magazine folded.

Only half in jest, John Bulloch spoke of me as "that dangerous radical," and that is how I think of people like him, and Colin Brown, and Winnett Boyd, and BMG's authors, and Tony McVeigh, and Peter Worthington, and the handful of journalists and businesspeople—notably William S. Allen of Allenvest Group, and Adam Zimmerman of Noranda Forest—who not only kicked against the pricks but were ready to stand up and take the heat from the wrath of Canada's New Class of Guardians.

It was on October 25, 1976, that I went to see Verne Atrill. There had been a piece about him in the *Toronto Star*, claiming that he had an answer to inflation. I called him and he invited me to his house. This was after dinner and he sat me down with a glass of Armagnac to listen while he expounded his theory of how all economies worked. Verne was a good talker (sad to say, he died just before Christmas, 1989, of a heart attack after having fought and lived with the consequences of a previous one eight years before), not easy to stop once he was in full sail, and I sat there for two hours without saying much and trying to grasp the findings of some thirty years' inquiry by a mind as close to genius as I had run across.

In essence he claimed to have taken up where the eighteenth-century Physiocrats left off, to show that economies are governed by natural laws, and that the fundamental error of modern economists has been to insert decision-making man at the centre of economies whose workings they do not understand. This wasn't clear to me at the time, and after trailing behind a dissertation that ranged from Aristotelian philosophy through Venetian bankers' discovery of double-entry book-keeping to the subjective economics of Lord Lionel Robbins and Frank H. Knight, I eased my way back to the car in somewhat of a fog.

In the course of the next few days, I thought I could see my way through to write an article about it, which I showed to Verne, and which was destined for *Executive*, but I knew there was something missing. To write an article, it's axiomatic that you have to understand what you're writing about, and I hadn't reached that stage with Verne's new science to justify going into print, even though Tony had expressed interest. I explained this to Verne, who took it in good part, and put the article aside.

After more discussions over a period of weeks, I suggested finding a means for Verne to demonstrate that his discoveries about the workings of economies had a practical application. Only then would people start to pay attention and only then would he be able to generate serious responses, not necessarily from his peers in academe but rather from businesspeople, accountants and financial analysts whose livelihoods were bound up with the economy he claimed to understand.

Here I was treated to another of the coincidences I mentioned before. William S. Allen was then president of Housser & Co., one of Toronto's older investment dealers, and he invited me to lunch after one of my regular pieces in *Report on Business* reminded him, he was kind enough to say, that he had been meaning to do that for some time. He was concerned, as I was, about the state of the economy, and after we had run through the usual options, none of which seemed likely to be adopted by Canada's socio-economic elite, I told him about Verne's work, suggested that a practical application for it might be through a study of companies listed on the Toronto Stock Exchange, and arranged for them to meet.

This proved to be a successful association. With Bill's help, Verne was able to apply his principles to the balance sheets of the 100 largest companies in the Composite Index of the exchange. By examining them over a seven-year period, he demonstrated that the economic state of an entity, whether a corporation, an individual or a government, is determined by certain values of the debt structure ratio (the ratio between what is owed to, and owed by, the entity, i.e. between its receivables and payables), and to show how rising and falling values of that ratio reflect the entity's degrees of solvency. In 1981, I edited Verne's book, *The Freedom Manifesto* (in which at my suggestion he inserted a note about Ouspensky, another coincidence) and in my introduction I quoted words from Dr. Warren J. Blackman, Professor of Monetary Theory at the University of Calgary, which are worth repeating here:

> The physical sciences are concerned with the observation of nature and in the discovery of natural laws which govern natural phenomena. It so happens that throughout all these laws there exists one over-riding principle and that is that Nature always directs her affairs with an economy of effort, and it is precisely this economy of effort, which means the attainment of the highest possible level of efficiency, that the businessman shares with Nature in his attempts to remain solvent...
>
> The physicist in the process of arriving at Nature's laws has discovered some mathematical constants which define some important relationships, among these being the speed of light. Incredible as it might seem these same constants are observed in Objective Economics and it is to the credit of Verne Atrill's mathematical genius that he has derived them quite independently of the physical sciences...
>
> Does this mean that men in pursuit of their economic objectives are governed by the same natural laws that exist in the science of physics? The answer is yes, and will continue to be so as long as humans follow the general rule of economy of effort in their economic processes. Dimensionless physics and Objective Economics are in truth sister sciences and the early efforts of the Physiocrats to discover the natural laws governing the economic system of their day are justified....

In the years that have passed, Verne's work has gained increasing acceptance by financial analysts, accountants, and others whose business it is to assist in the wealth-creating process, as distinct from the students and proselytizers of the subjective economics that has made economies hostage to central bankers. By the mid-1980s he was Chairman of The Solvency Analysis Corporation, and its record of forecasting the share price movements of companies regularly outperformed the TSE composite index. Bill Allen's new company, Allenvest Group, published a newsletter, *The Objective Economist*, of which Verne was the editor, a continuation of Bill's role as sponsor for new ideas. Until his death in 1990, what wealthy patrons used to do for the visual arts, Bill Allen did for the art of economic science.

The conjunction of Allen and Atrill was not the last of things turning up at the right time. In March 1987, Colin Brown died, and that was the signal for another chain of events. Colin was a sailor. He joined the Royal Canadian Navy at the outbreak of war in 1939, spent most of it on the North Atlantic and ended up as a lieutenant commander, and every October 21 I used to call and wish him, as a former naval person, a happy and prosperous Trafalgar Day. Not that Nelson's celebrated victory over the French was especially symbolic of anything in modern Canada, except perhaps as a reminder of the way an earlier victory, in 1759, seemed to have dropped out of sight. Colin and I would speak about that occasionally, as we did about so many things in the Pearson/Trudeau years when most of the damage was done, but Colin harboured no animus toward the French in Canada.

In 1968, when French Canadian nationalism was nearing its sometimes violent peak, he organized an exchange of citizens between London, Ontario, and Quebec City. Out of his own pocket he paid $24,000 for air fares to help take 300 adult Quebecers to homes of London residents in an attempt to lessen tensions and promote understanding. Called Lonbec, the operation was repeated with visitors from Trois Rivières, and the exchange was rounded off when a group of Londoners was entertained by civic and provincial officials in Quebec City.

Colin showed what could be done at little cost by individuals using their own initiative and goodwill. Instead, Pierre Trudeau brought in the Official Languages Act, and the money cost of enforcing it has risen annually, to over $4 billion today by the federal government alone (more than it spends on medical research and the environment): an attempt to legislate language that has served to increase rather than reduce the strains between the two language groups.

Colin and Trudeau personified views of Canada that were 180 degrees apart. Trudeau, the supposed intellectual (George Grant, the Canadian philosopher, called him a "show-biz technocrat") believed, as he wrote before he came to power, "in the necessity of state control to maximize the liberty and welfare of all, and to permit everyone to realize himself fully." Brown, the admitted non-scholar, believed that he governs best who governs least, which is why he chose for the NCC's motto "For more freedom through less government."

In the last year of his life, and when he knew he had not long to live, Colin was concerned about finding a successor who would carry on his work, representing the more than 40,000 people who gave money so that the NCC could advance the case for individual freedom, free markets and a strong defence. His method had always been to seek a consensus before committing the NCC to any public activity. Whether it was to expose excesses of government, or unions, or government-funded advocacy groups, or special privileges of any kind that flowed from the misuse of State power, he would call around a wide circle of friends and acquaintances to test the water. If there was a consensus to go ahead, he would test it again by submitting the text of the advertisement (the NCC's usual form of exposure) to experts in the field to make sure the facts were right.

He offered me the job of replacing him and I said no: we were the same age and it needed a younger man. While he continued to canvass potential candidates, we decided to appoint a formal board of directors, with Colin as chairman and chief executive officer, in place of the voluntary advisory council, so that both Colin's successor as chairman and the board itself could see David Somerville, who was then president, through the period that would follow Colin's death.

We had to recognize that Colin was irreplaceable. He had a remarkable faculty of projecting his personality to people who had never met him. NCC supporters felt that they knew him, that he would understand their concerns, and that he would stand up for them. I doubt if he had an enemy, yet he was the reverse of a political compromiser: he was guided by principle, loved his country, had abiding faith in ordinary people, in their decency and goodwill, and was always ready to take on the principalities and powers that oppressed them. His was the inspiration behind the NCC's "cheeky" ads, their seriousness invariably relieved by his puckish sense of humour. David simply wasn't Colin and it's unfair to fault him on that account. He has many fine qualities, and under his presidency the NCC both increased its support and modernized its operations. If, in the process of becoming a substantial corporation, it lost the intimacy that Colin's personality gave it, that was inevitable too. Also lost, however, was the cheekiness, and the *lightness* that made people smile while they were getting the message.

Just before Colin died, he chose William Gairdner to replace him as chairman, on the face of it a good choice given Bill's impressive qualifications and his subsequent career as author and speaker. Unfortunately he and David were unable to agree about the future direction of the NCC, I didn't like the power struggle that ensued and resigned from the board. That was also a good time to find another editor for the newsletters, which we did, and I was able to take a fresh look at what I wanted to do, freed from deadlines.

I wrote *Harry Cross's Revolution* in the style of *Red Maple*, a retrospect from about 2005 that told how a dedicated group of free enterprisers infiltrated the federal and provincial civil services, and turned the emphasis away from collectivism towards classical liberalism; what Friedrich Hayek called free growth and spontaneous evolution. However, after getting comments from people whose opinions I respected I decided to rewrite it as straight non-fiction. As *A Solution To The Problem Of Quebec*, it repeated the Harry Cross solution: an amicable Declaration of Sovereignties in which Canada allowed a sovereign Quebec to keep its part of Rupert's Land in exchange for the whole of the south shore of the St. Lawrence, with the stretch of Highway 15 from Montreal to the US border becoming an international route similar to the Seaway. The rewriting put me in touch again with a lot of people in different parts of Canada, and I came to the conclusion that despite the politically inspired divisions that the media portrayed as wrecking the country, there was a solid majority of Canadians, deeply conscious of the country's true worth, that wanted to keep it together.

On Bill Gairdner's advice I changed the emphasis in a shortened version (*Keeping Canada Together*) that showed how a true federalism with a clear division of powers could both accommodate and satisfy Quebec's aspirations, and began looking for a publisher. A canvass of the leading companies revealed the same reluctance that led us to form BMG in 1974, and a friend, William Bolt, who was also a publisher of business systems, decided to take it on as a first venture.

Thus when Peter Brimelow reviewed the book in *The Financial Post*, after generously describing me as "probably the closest thing the Canadian conservative movement has to a writer-in-residence," he added as an aside:

> Ramsay Business Systems Ltd.? I'd bet that most Financial Post readers have never heard of it. It's an example of the way in which the Canadian conservative movement is gradually developing its own institutions beyond the political establishment's control—exactly the process that in the US culminated in the election of Ronald Reagan in 1980. I estimate the Canadian conservative movement is about where the US movement was in the 1950s. Let's hope that Canada can wait 25 years.

The theme was straightforward. Canada had undergone, or rather had been subjected to, a revolution from above that destroyed the basis of the federation (division of powers between the two senior levels of government) and changed it into a collectivized welfare state without asking the people. The revolution consisted in what former Supreme Court Justice Willard Estey called "an organic change" to our system of government.

Before 1982, we were inherently free to do anything that was not prohibited by the law, the Common Law built of legal precedents over the centuries, the case by case tradition that kept pace with the times and formed an evolving framework of our social order.

In that tradition, government's duty was to protect our inherent freedom so that we could go about our business taking personal responsibility for our actions and our lives. But in the French tradition that was imposed on us (former Clerk of the Privy Council Gordon Robertson's word), there is no inherent freedom. Instead, government confers certain rights upon the people, "guarantees" them in the words of the Charter.

Such conferred rights are immediately vulnerable to whatever meaning the government or its courts decide to give them. The courts define the rights, and by doing so they limit them. Moreover, the written Charter is now "the supreme law of Canada" (Section 52 (1)). Parliament is no longer supreme, supremacy has passed to unelected judges; nine men and women who are as susceptible to differing shades of political opinion as anyone else.

Writing a book, even so slight a paperback as *Keeping Canada Together*, tends to calcify the mind for some time afterwards. What *The New Yorker* once called infatuation with sound of own words is reinforced by the computer's facility to recapture favoured phrases. These are then substituted for the hard work that must accompany writing if it is to achieve its purpose of conveying ideas.

This little-noticed effect of substituting mechanical memory for the human may well be responsible for perpetuating old ideas in the print and electronic press. Even in the 1990s, when the collapse of command economies in thrall to centralized political regimes had shown the abiding need to limit the power of the State, journalism in Canada was bedevilled by name-calling and abdication of responsibility that the perpetrators should have left behind them in the schoolyard.

There was a war of words between those (mostly unpublished and therefore unheard) who recognized government as an essential partner of private enterprise, and those (editorial writers and bureau chiefs) who confused government with the State.

It is government as referee that makes the game worth playing, but the State as player that spoils the game for everyone. Since the mid-1960s the Canadian State's growing interventions in citizens' affairs had reached such proportions as to give government a bad name. "Cut government spending" cried taxpayers loaded with the interest costs of national and provincial government debts, yet it was the State as player that accumulated the debts.

It was the unchecked power of the State that laid waste to the economies of the USSR and its satellites. Laboriously they were trying to construct the foundation—that is, of law, security of contracts and of property—upon which citizens would be free to conduct their affairs; the foundation that our own Canadian governments had steadily eroded for thirty years.

Yet until the Canadian Alliance Party's appearance on the political scene there was no sign that the erosion was even recognized: federal and provincial governments alike had succumbed to the idea that "democratic socialism" was not merely harmless but beneficial, of course to political elites, but even to the citizens as well.

Meanwhile the New Class that comprised the political Left was not content with rewriting the morals of today; those of yesterday that reside in Canadian history must be rewritten too. Particularly offensive to elites of the CBC and the National Film Board was Canada's gallant record in the two World Wars, a record singled out by two accomplished filmmakers, Brian and Terence McKenna, for special treatment.

Historian Desmond Morton called them:

> ...an articulate, mediawise duo with opinions well in the mainstream of the CBC-NFB elite [who] were granted the funds and the time to produce their version of Canada's experience in three brutal episodes of World War II. Part of their claim was based on their interpretation of Canadian experience in World War I in *The Killing Ground*, a mixture of pompous preaching, carefully edited quotations, and unauthentic dramatic turns by actors. It was a fair replica of how the literary crowd saw the war in the 1920s and, for all I know, still do.

The McKenna's version of the "three brutal episodes of World War II" was called *The Valour and the Horror*. The second episode, "Death by Moonlight: Bomber Command" was met by protests so widespread as to cause the whole series to be placed on the agenda of the Senate's Sub-committee on Veterans Affairs. Hearings were held at which historians and other witnesses testified to the defamations and falsehoods perpetrated by the producers.

However, although at first the CBC's chairman undertook to correct the Bomber Command episode's many errors on air, this was not done, and it was not until January, 1993, when the Government of Ontario proclaimed The Class Proceedings Act, that aggrieved veterans of Bomber Command were afforded a means of redress through the Courts. Their Statement of Claim against the CBC *et al.*, together with a thoughtful introduction by the plaintiffs' counsel, Ian W. Outerbridge, and a lengthy Afterword composed of items by journalists and historians, was published in book form as *A Battle for Truth* by the Bomber Harris Trust in January, 1994. (I put the book together and also edited the Trust's newsletter *Flarepath*.)

Veterans and other critics identified specific instances where the filmmakers made false, misleading, incomplete or exaggerated statements. Throughout were attitudes of people apparently driven not by pride in country and its achievements but the reverse, not by a desire to seek the good and give credit, but to seek the faults and magnify them out of proportion. The atmosphere was a composite: condemnation of wartime leaders; breathless revelation of "secrets" that had been in the public domain for decades; selective reporting, from almost six years of war, of incidents or episodes to support the underlying theme of blame and discredit; all the while ignoring the context of Nazi aggression and atrocities that threatened European civilization with a new Dark Age.

Chapter 11

▓ 1992—2000 ▓

The Bomber Harris Trust's action against the CBC took a lot of my time between 1992, when the film was first aired, and 1996, when the Supreme Court refused to hear our appeal against the lower courts' rulings and we published the eighth and last issue of the Trust's newsletter, *Flarepath*.

From start to finish, it was a fight between the left-liberal print and electronic media led by the CBC, and aircrew veterans of Bomber Command. The media's cry for "press freedom" ignored the veterans' powerlessness to compete with the audio-visual effect of a government-sponsored film aired twice in prime time on national television and aimed at the schools.

After trying with little success to get their views published, the veterans' case was championed by Senator Jack Marshall, who held hearings by his Sub-Committee on Veterans' Affairs. This gave voice not only to veterans but also to military historians who roundly condemned the production even though half of them were picked by the film's producer.

In 1994, we published *A Battle for Truth*. Centred on the Trust's Statement of Claim, it examined "forty-one statements, dramatizations, inferences, innuendoes, depictions and distortions that 'are not true.'" A forty-page Afterword was composed of comments by historians and others who had written about the film.

Rebuffed by other publishers, we called again upon Bill Bolt and Lester Machan, whose help in putting out the newsletters had been invaluable, and under the Ramsay banner we printed 4,500 copies. Bob Tracy, publisher of *Airforce* magazine, hit our problem on the nose when he invited us to write an article for his magazine. He said, "We're the only outfit in Canada that will do it."

The article (see Afterword) was truly a corporate effort, the result of many drafts to and by members of the Trust, but although I sent it in with the byline "By the Trust," Vic Johnson, the editor, printed my name as author "with files from members of the Trust."

All this involved a lot of concentrated work that brought on fibrillations, visits to a cardiologist, and fortunately a successful regime of medication which is still doing its stuff.

A personal reward came in the shape of a charming letter of appreciation from Ian Worrall Outerbridge, QC, the gentleman and patriot who served as the Trust's volunteer counsel.

Meanwhile, I was dissatisfied with my memoirs and asked Bill Gairdner to read the current version. He made a number of suggestions, most of which I incorporated. Then I sent it to Anna Porter, who read it herself, said it was an interesting life, but explained that she had just dispatched Ed Mirvish on a cross-Canada tour to sell the book of *his* life, and the results were disappointing. Then she said, "How about doing a political book based on the last two chapters—the Trudeau revolution?" I said, "30,000 words?" She said, "Make it 40,000," and that started me into what became *His Pride, Our Fall.*

This was the first time an established publisher had done a book of mine, but the results were much the same. Key Porter sent a copy of HPOF to every newspaper in Canada—more than 100 copies—and tried hard to get excerpts in *Saturday Night* magazine. In addition, and also at the time of publication, Key Porter sent autographed copies to thirty journalists of my selection, only one of whom even acknowledged receipt. There was a review in *Quill & Quire*; another in the American magazine *Telos*; David Somerville wrote a very favourable review in the NCC's newsletter, and so did Virginia Byfield in *Alberta Report.* Virginia wrote: "Mr. McDonald raises many points which at a minimum deserve answers. This is unlikely to happen, of course. Indeed, even mainstream reviews may be few and unfavourable...."

Back, as you might say, to square one—a phrase, incidentally, which originated in England before the days of television, when the BBC broadcast soccer and rugby matches. The playing field was divided into four squares, enabling the commentator to say where the action was taking place.

Key Porter soon sold out its printing of 5,145 copies, but didn't order a second printing, preferring (I was told) to wait and see how many were returned.

In a letter about a second MS, Anna turned the second one down "regretfully," saying that she was "particularly sorry about this because, as you know, your last book was very successful for us."

The second book showed how promoting the French language was made the instrument for organic change; how the Charter entrenches growth of the state and undermines military discipline; how militant unions masquerade as "social movements"; how taxes could be simplified and reduced; how Canada's armed forces have been starved of funds and equipment; and the implications, territorial as well as socio-economic, of Quebec's secession.

After the usual fruitless round of the major publishers, I showed the MS to Ronald Leitch, who not only liked it but suggested to his Board that it be published as part of the work by his organization: Canadians Against Bilingualism Injustice. APEC Books Limited was formed, and 6,000 copies of *The Monstrous Trick* were printed. Once again, the book was ignored by the popular press. Reviewed by the NCC, and promoted both by NCC, CABI, and one or two other members of the Canadian underground, it topped the list of the NCC's book sales in 1999 and 2000, has sold over half the printing so far (March 2001), and is selling steadily through mail orders.

And that's about it. Serious writing is spasmodic. In 1996, when Richard Morris began his biography of Leonard Cheshire, I spent some time sending him pictures and recollections of that great man. When the book was published in 2000, Richard enclosed this note with my copy: "Dear Ken: Well, here it is. I hope you like it. You'll see that your influence looms large!" I also worked with Howard Hewer on the succession of drafts before he sent his autobiography to Stoddart, who published it as *In For A Penny, In For A Pound*, and another airman, in Nova Scotia, sent me his life story for editing.

The dozen-year correspondence with Brian Rogers in Montreal

continues to develop ideas about Canada's political evolution.

At the editor's request, I wrote an article for the Winter 2001 issue of the American quarterly *The Social Contract*. The issue was devoted to the British influence on American culture, and I was invited to give a Canadian view; a topic that stood no chance of coverage in Canada itself.

Both Martha and Peter have suggested my getting on-line, and both were generous and helpful in supervising my attempts to check it out. Stephen Harper offered the NCC's services to put me on the Net, but I'm not convinced. Yes, I'm missing stuff I might be interested in at the cost of other people's initiative, but I don't want the compulsion and prefer to make my own decisions about what to do with the time that remains.

Which brings me once again to the central theme of my modest contribution to the Canadian political scene; "scene" rather than "dialogue," because there is no dialogue—the Left has captured the sources of power. Some ten years after Friedrich Hayek's classic study of socialism was published (*The Road to Serfdom*), he wrote in a Foreword to a later edition that one of the book's main points was that:

> the most important change which extensive government control produces is a psychological change, an alteration in the character of the people. This is necessarily a slow affair, a process which extends not over a few years but perhaps over one or two generations.

In a lecture given on March 28, 1763, Adam Smith said:

> Nothing tends so much to corrupt and enervate and debase the mind as dependency, and nothing gives such noble and generous notions of probity as freedom and independency.

In an Address delivered to the Bridgnorth Institute, February 26, 1877, Lord Acton said:

> Now Liberty and good government do not exclude each other; and there are excellent reasons why they should go together; but they do not necessarily go together. Liberty is not a means to a higher political end. It is itself the highest political end.

Milton called fame "the spur that the clear spirit doth raise (that last infirmity of noble mind)"; Gibbon wrote that "Of all our passions and appetites, the love of power is of the most imperious and unsociable nature, since the pride of one man requires the submission of the multitude."

None of this registers with Canadian prime ministers rejoicing in the power of their office. In this country of paradoxes, the critical one resides in the contrast between Trudeau's declared antipathy to nationalism and his embrace of it to achieve a French Canadian takeover of Canadian institutions.

By legislating linguistic equality between English and French, he engineered the ultimate affirmative action programme; namely, the Charter's installation of preferential treatment for francophones in all the ramifications of an ever-expanding Canadian state.

At the same time, his antipathy to nationalism in general reached a peak in his antagonism to any form of sovereignty for Quebec itself, because that conflicted with his plan for Canada's conversion into a kind of enlarged Quebec.

This overarching paradox stemmed from two sources. One was Trudeau's consuming faith in making laws and constructing central agencies to solve his political problems—a system described by a senior mandarin as completely rational but deeply impractical.

The other source was in his reliance on legal solutions to political problems, heedless of people's emotions and instincts. His obsession with the idea of a homogenized world in the future blinded him to the facts of the world as it was.

It was Canada's tragedy that Trudeau's command of the English language misled English Canada into assuming that he understood it, when the fact was, as Christina McCall Newman wrote in *Grits*, "the subliminal signals Trudeau sent out, and the culture from which they were transmitted, were French."

On February 10, 1969, at the opening of Trudeau's Second Constitutional Conference, Quebec Premier Jean Jacques Bertrand, after he had made a strong plea for special consideration for Quebec in any new constitution, said this:

> Indeed, language is not only a mode of expression; first and foremost, it is a way of thinking or—better still—a way of life. The Canadian duality therefore does not come merely

from a difference in language; above all, it is due to different ways of approaching, feeling and reacting when confronted by events. A French Canadian is not the same as an English Canadian, differing only as to the tongue he speaks; *he speaks differently because he is different.*

Who can deny that French Canadians are a people, as the Scots are a people, as are the Welsh, as are the Catalonians?

At one time, notably during and immediately after the Second World War, English Canadians were a people, too. But because French Canadians were different, and were determined to preserve and capitalize on their difference, English Canadians' political leaders sought ways to accommodate them.

But accommodation soon gave way to appeasement. Lester Pearson imported Quebec's "Three Wise Men" to Ottawa, then elevated all three to positions of authority, and in 1968, English Canada was seduced into Trudeaumania.

Nevertheless, I'm hopeful. Prideful politicians like Trudeau crave permanence in their lifetime for changes they are clever enough to install. But a country, and a people, outlive prideful politicians. In 1867, when Canadian statesmen constructed The British North America Act, they did a fine thing. In 2001, voices in Alberta are following Quebec's lead in calling for Ottawa's exit from provincial jurisdictions that are laid down in Sections 92 and 93 of the Constitution. The BNA Act's distribution of powers, together with its embrace of England's common law tradition, are proving more durable than the Charter's hodgepodge of legislated entitlements that Trudeau cobbled together, and that Enoch Powell showed was incompatible with the rule of law.

The Supreme Court is starting to back away from the "judicial activism" forecast in 1981 by Madam Justice Rosalie Abella when she called the courts and legislature "partners in the exercise of law-making." Its tendency now is to defer, as it should, to legislatures.

As I have written before, man is imperfect, and the gravest harm is done by those who claim he is perfectible—if only he can be made to follow their precepts for corporate behaviour. Thus does socialism *always* lead to coercion.

Contrast Trudeau's prideful approach to constitutional reform with the views of Lord Acton.

Trudeau said of his coup de force in retrospect: "We embarked upon an exercise to change the constitution fundamentally."

In one of his addresses on *The History of Freedom*, given on February 26, 1877, Acton said:

> The example of the Hebrew nation laid down the parallel lines on which all freedom has been won—the doctrine of national tradition, and the doctrine of the higher law; the principle that a constitution grows from a root, by process of development and not of essential change; and the principle that all political authorities must be tested and reformed according to a code which was not made by man.

Amen to that.

Chapter 12

▩ 2000—2002 ▩

Most of the foregoing was written in 2000, the year of Ruth's and my sixtieth wedding anniversary, an event marked by letters of congratulation from the Queen as well as from Canada's Governor General, Ontario's Lieutenant Governor, the Prime Minister of Canada, and Ontario's Premier.

Our children mounted a splendid celebration in the house and presented us with an enlargement, on a silver base, of the wedding picture as we emerged from Collier Street United Church in Barrie, May 17, 1940.

But the years were beginning to tell. Ruth's long history of high blood pressure and high cholesterol level came to the fore after our trip to Calgary in the fall of 1998.

On October 2, 1998, Ruth suffered a mild stroke. This was followed a month later by her collapsing at night on the way to the bathroom, and a permanent condition of fibrillations.

In February, 2001, a spell of violent coughing left her with a cracked vertebra and a continuing source of pain. On August 12, she missed her footing and broke the humerus in her left arm near the shoulder. The operation was successful, but on October 4 she was diagnosed with shingles and began to suffer more pain from the new source.

All the while, our faithful family doctor, Jim Parrish, was making corrective adjustments to Ruth's medication, arranged successive readings by Holter monitor, and on January 31, 2002, examination by an internal medicine specialist whose report showed no fault other than those already being experienced.

Nevertheless, Ruth's condition continued to deteriorate. On March 18, she collapsed in the bedroom, unable to speak or write a message. At the hospital, after being given a CT scan, although the examining physician pronounced that there had been no stroke and discharged her, three days later Ruth lost her speech again.

There followed a return to the hospital, this time for a week, only to suffer more ailments at home that required hospital treatment again. It was now April 6. Further examinations revealed a hernia, leaving no choice but to operate. Two days later, after the operation, when it was found that the hernia had punctured the lower bowel, Ruth was transferred to the Intensive Care Unit, suffering from pneumonia.

Despite unremitting efforts of the ICU's dedicated staff, as well as Ruth's own inherent courage, the strain was too great for her, and she died at two p.m. on April 18.

I watched her die, watched the last laboured breath escape from the mouth already cold as I kissed it for the last time. Twenty-nine days shy of our sixty-second wedding anniversary, Ruth was no longer there.

The next morning, early, when I was sitting in the black leather armchair of this office, Ruth appeared at the door of the room, as she had so many times, but this time for a moment only—still, silent, wearing her summer housecoat and smiling at me.

Two nights later, while I was sleepless, fretting that I hadn't done enough to save her, that I should have detected the hernia sooner and got her to day surgery where my own hernia had been treated three years before, she spoke to me inside my head: "It wasn't that."

Soon after that, on another night at about three a.m., I felt the bump against the end of my bed as I had so many times when Ruth made her way to the bathroom, in the dark, not wishing to wake me by turning on a light, and grazing the end of the bed in passage.

On the night of June 7/8, I woke at two a.m., was unable to sleep, struggled through a morning meeting of the Aircrew Association, and at about four p.m., when I was dozing in the black chair, Ruth spoke to me: "It's all right," she said, meaning that wherever she was, we would be together again.

None of this should surprise me. In the thank-you notes I sent to friends who attended the Memorial Service or otherwise sympathized, I wrote that "I feel her presence every waking minute; we were, and are, very close."

Of course, there are the physical reminders: her clothes, the handbag on her desk in the kitchen, her photographs in different rooms, her bed beside mine that she grew more and more to rest on in daytime, and whose pillow I now kiss every night before getting into my own bed.

But it is the companionship, knowing that if I went to the plaza on an errand, I could phone her and share a joke—knowing that when I came back and called that I was home, she would answer.

When I wrote that I feel her presence every waking minute, it is true. It also raises questions. I am alive, it is spring, but the life can never be complete again because Ruth is not here to share it with me. Yet, the last thing she would want is for me to be sad— witness that very real appearance and her voice messages in my head. If I can come to recognize, among all the thoughts, the ones that are negative, and head them off as we both taught ourselves to do, that will leave all the more room for the positive thoughts, memories of the good times past, and anticipation of the better ones to come.

In the Preface, and in my pride, I wrote: "It may be that just as I have learned to head off and suppress negative thoughts she has come to do the same." Such thoughts were of everyday matters— not, like mine today, of the life and death that I also wrote about, and touched on in two of the poems.

I write these final words after lunch on Sunday, June 23, 2002, when I read for a while before falling into a doze, a day like many others. But this time, immediately before waking and with my eyes still closed, Ruth's dear face appeared, filling the semi-conscious screen in my head.

In a conversation with Roy Trevivian, Malcolm Muggeridge said he had

> an absolute conviction... that this life that we live in time
> and space... is not the whole story, that it is only part of a

larger story… Death is part of a larger pattern; it fits into a larger, eternal scale, not simply a time scale.

That, I tell myself, is the way to think about what has happened. If I am to feel her presence—and I know her so well that I can picture her in every day's changing circumstances—isn't that the thing for me to do? Will she not share those thoughts with me, as we shared our thoughts while she was alive?

There were so many good times. That is what we remembered when we sat on balconies looking at the sea or the woods, and that is what I remember now. How can it be otherwise for her, who is in that different state and condition we must all reach? Just as we read each other's thoughts when she was alive, when I think now of the good times we both enjoyed, does she not think of them too?

That, for me, is the resolution—to continue the sharing that made our lives together so rich, to think of the good things she brought, and still brings, to us both.

▨ INDEX ▨

219-20; CF-5, 211-3; CL-41
Tutor, 211-2, 219-221; Man-
agement style, 212-3, 219-21;
strike at, 218; Canadair 540,
204-210
Canadian Alliance Party, 247
Canadian Broadcasting
Corporation, 124, 247
Canadian Defence Forces, 213
Canadian Federation of Independ-
ent Business, 235
Canadian paradox, 253
Canadians Against Bilingualism
Injustice, 251
Canal Zone, 153
Canberra, 179, 220
Canberra, English Electric, 187,
220
Captain, the, 17, 43, 47
Cardiff, 35, 80, 132, 186
Carman, Ian, 234
Car Nicobar, 175-6
Carter, William (Nick), 121
Castro, Fidel, 13
Casualty rates, 125
Ceylon, 169, 173-4, 183, 185,
187
Changi, 170-2, 174, 178-82,
186-7, 188-90
Chapple, James, 126
Charatan's, 16, 38
Chard, 83
Charter of Rights and Freedoms,
20, 245-6, 251, 253-4
Cheshire, Leonard, 12, 16, 109,
112, 124, 129, 132-3, 162-4,
184, 251
Chesterton, G.K., 20, 38
Church, Rose, 17, 58, 141, 147
Clark Field, 174
Clarke, D.H., 78-9, 84
Clouston, A.E., 188-9

Clunies-Ross, John, 178-9
Cocos-Keeling Islands, 178-9
Cold War, 212
Collins, Doug, 238
Colombia, 207
Colombo, 45, 169
Comet, de Havilland, 183-4
Common Law, 245, 254
Common Prayer, Book of, 12
Communist Terrorists, 173-4, 182,
189
Conrad, Joseph, 46, 190
Convair, 340 series, 204
Coronel, 27
Coulson, Irene, 153, 208-9
Craig, John B., 198
Craig, John F., 92, 105, 131, 137
Craig, Lucretia, 59, 105, 137
Craig, Sylvia, 198
Craig, William, 134, 150
Crashes, 120
Croydon, 30, 36, 39, 45, 48, 143;
airport, 50, 64
Cumnor House School, 143

D

Dakota, Douglas, 140
Dart, Rolls Royce, 205
Darwin, 177
Davies, Ellen, 237
Dawn Patrol, 70
Dawson's Farm, 133-4, 233
Death by Moonlight, 247
de Havilland, 199
Delta, Northrop, 88
Demonstration flying, 206-7
Denmark, 211
Dhahran, 216
Diefenbaker, John, 210, 213
Dilworth, Clare, 17, 106-8, 115

▦ AFTERWORD ▦

I wrote the fifteen poems on pages 273–287, as well as *The Globe and Mail* article (The Mermaid Inn) and *Justice Denied— The Bomber Harris Trust Story.*

Notes to assist readers of the poems.

1. 76 and 78 were the two squadrons at Linton-on-Ouse, Yorkshire, when I was there, September 1942 to March 1943. Both were equipped with the Halifax II. In the last verse, line three, "tour" refers to a tour of operations, usually thirty sorties, after which crews who survived were posted to Operational Training Units (OTUs) or to Heavy Conversion Units (HCUs) as instructors.

2. February 23, 1979, was Ruth's sixty-third birthday. In verse three, it was in the back seat of Johnny Berven's sedan that Ruth and I first met on a blind date.

3. February 23, 1980, was her sixty-fourth birthday.

4. May 17, 1980, was our fortieth Wedding Anniversary. Kent's was the Toronto jeweller where we bought the engagement ring.

5. February 23, 1986, Ruth's seventieth birthday. Verse three, it was at a party in Marie Gendron's house that I proposed to Ruth. Bradt's in verse four was our lodging in Rivers, Manitoba.

In verse five, Mme. Trudel was the owner of the house on Bishop Street in Montreal where Ruth found us rooms while I was converting to the Hudson and Ventura at Dorval for the flight to Scotland. In verse seven, Boston Spa was where we had rooms in Mrs. Taylor's house near Marston Moor. The White Hart was one of the pubs we spent a night in while searching for a roof in Suffolk in 1945 and found Lane End Cottage. Boarding house was in Grantham-Mrs. Edwards'. In verse nine, Manor Barn was in Chesham Bois; the caravans were behind The Bull in Bracknell. "Keeping tanks full" refers to the oil stoves we installed in #22 Officers' Married Quarters at Bracknell in our efforts to keep warm.

6. May 17, 1940–1990. Our fiftieth Wedding Anniversary. Verse eight refers to the cottage at Kars, south of Ottawa.

7. The Anonymous poem, verse two. Merlin was the name of the Rolls Royce engine fitted to many operational aircraft.

UPON YOUR REACHING THE AGE OF 75

Compare thee to a summer's day?
Comparisons are odious.
It's autumn now, I hear you say.
Your voice is so melodious

To me that even in a crowd
Wherever we may be,
It comes through clear, but never loud;
A precious sound for me.

Not just the voice, I quickly add,
But everything in truth
That cheered me through the good, the bad,
Was always, always Ruth.

We reminisce, and think how well
Adjusted we are now
To life together. Who could tell
It would be thus, or how

The years, long years, in war and peace
Of this our joint endeavour
Would forge a love that cannot cease?
It must go on forever.

SEVENTY-SIX AND SEVENTY-EIGHT

The two numbered squadrons at Linton-on-Ouse
Are mirrored today in our ages.
The war is long past, though still we infuse
Its six years with those other stages

Of lives we were learning to live and embrace
As a team, like a crew of those days,
Who trusted each other with courage to face
The good and the bad; all the ways

That Life has of testing us, testing us both
To share and contribute and give
To the words of the day we plighted our troth—
'So long as ye both shall live"—

A meaning beyond all the practical things
That occupied much of our time,
Such as housing and schools and occasional flings;
Something deeper, approaching sublime,

That drew us together in ways that endure,
A team, like a crew, not faint-hearted;
For fifty-two years is more than a tour,
Beyond Life, to never be parted.

FEBRUARY 23, 1979

It's not that I didn't think of a card,
With pictures of flowers and hearts,
To remind you again of the way you have starred
In my personal horoscope's charts.

It's never once changed since I dimly perceived,
In the back of John Berven's sedan,
A face and a smile that shortly I learned
Were so perfect for me that I can,

As plainly as day nearly forty years past,
Recall and recapture the thrill
Of seeing the one I knew to be cast
At the permanent top of my bill.

So forgive me this once—though it's happened before—
For seeming to let the day slide
Without a remembrance picked up from a store;
The remembrance is here, right inside.

FEBRUARY 23, 1980

At best it would be impolite to tell your age in years,
And yet the calendar is there. For every one who fears
To add the birthdays as they pass, there must be many more
Rejoicing they have lived so long, regardless of the score.
That's how it is with us, I think. Although some times were bad
We managed to survive them, and the good times that we had
Were always better for the fact, even in English weather,
That we could take the best or worst if we were just together.
So when I look you in the eye and say you haven't changed,
That you look just the same as when the date was first arranged,
I mean it, and the reason is, the eyes that see you now
See Ruth as she was then. They conjure up exactly how
It all began those years ago when we had scarcely met.
The eyes that loved to watch you then—they love to watch you yet.

MAY 17, 1980

You'll remember in Kent's a little while back
We were able to buy a small stone
To signal the change from Ruth Craig to Ruth Mac?
It was bought with the aid of a loan.

Now, forty years later, it seems a good thought,
When credit is much more elastic,
To add some more stones to the small one we bought
With money that's sometimes called plastic.

It was only a thought, and you may not agree
With this choice that I made on my own.
But remember the choice in the house of Marie
Was another I made quite alone.

So keep this my love, or a similar ring,
As a present this bright day of May
For the girl who became the very best thing
That happened to, yours truly, K.J.

FORTY-FOUR AND A HALF YEARS ON

Once every month it used to be
The seventeenth for you and me
To celebrate the happy day
When we were married back in May

Of 1940, when the war,
And other things that were in store,
Lay far ahead and out of mind
While we began each day to find

The things from past and present life
That had prepared us, man and wife,
To share the burdens, hopes and fears,
We would encounter through the years.

The monthly date became submerged
In annual ones, for which we splurged
By dressing up in handsome rigs
And quitting the appalling digs

That postings and a lack of choice
Had dealt us. Do I hear a voice
Reminding me of times I found
Those dreadful places yet was bound

To see them through deceiving eyes
As "not too bad," and other lies
Which hid from you the awful truth
That once again a luckless Ruth

Had fallen for the tale her man,
The optimist, had spun? We can,
By pulling down a mental blind,
Dismiss the worst days from the mind,

While in their stead we take each day
As if the seventeenth of May
Was newly come. That is the test.
We still look forward to the rest.

FEBRUARY 23, 1986

When you were young and twenty-four
The world was at your gate;
The years ahead were little more
Than shadows. You could wait

With some impatience for the day,
Just twelve short weeks from then,
When you would waken up and say
"I'm going to marry Ken."

277

The years did pass, the scenes did change,
For better, oft for worse,
The rooms we occupied were strange,
We'd not much in our purse.

You braved the Bradt's, Regina too,
And overcame a shortage
By renting furniture for two
Before we left for Portage.

In Montreal you found us space
In Madame Trudel's maison,
A single bed for us to grace
Our close and fond liaison.

The ocean trip in forty-three
Was long and rough and risky,
Yet afterwards you ran to me
Along the platform, frisky

As could be. But thence did start
The saga Transatlantic.
From Boston Spa to the White Hart
The quest for digs was frantic.

A railway carriage, boarding house,
Lane End the bleakest yet,
Attested to how strong the vows
Between us had been set.

From there the outlook tended up—
A gradual improvement—
But still in Ottawa our cup
Was filled to the brim with movement.

And so it went, from Chesham Bois,
South Croydon and The Bull,
To quarters where you heard the noise
Of keeping oil tanks full,

Until the posting, last of all,
To Changi's Fairy Point,
Where you fulfilled your duty's call—
We both did, it was joint.

In fact when now mind wanders back
Across the years to Barrie
I see us sticking to the track
That moved us first to marry.

That day was yours alone to fill:
The bride of four and twenty
Was lovely then, is lovelier still,
At—dare I say it?—seventy.

ST. VALENTINE'S DAY, 1989

Will you, won't you, will you, won't you be my Valentine?
The times I've asked you now add up—you've guessed—to forty-
nine.
And you said yes, you would, you would, in spite of all the snags
You will recall from packing up and then unloading bags.

I hope you will again this time, and that you won't forget
To get my breakfast, make the beds—I know you haven't yet—
But women's lib is all about and I'd be at a loss
If you decided suddenly perhaps you were the boss.

Not that we've argued very much on that essential point,
Largely because with us the mood has usually been joint;
Which ain't too bad a parallel for men and women who
Are starting out—or lived as long—together, as we two.

And though perhaps at forty-nine I needn't tell you this—
That your face is the one for me, and yours the lips to kiss—
It's what's inside that really counts, the humour, loyalty,
That cheer the day and make me proud to live with Ruth McD.

279

BRACKNELL 1953

It was Boxing Day evening,
I was ready for bed,
When a sudden suspicion
Entered my head

That down at the bottom
Of my Bracknell sack,
In a dark little corner
Out of sight at the back

Were two little parcels
Intended for YOU!
For Peter and John
At 22 OMQ.

So I saddled the deer
With the beautiful nose
And told him there wasn't
A moment to lose

If we were to reach,
Before the next night,
The house where the children
Are *always* polite.

So off galloped Rudolph
From our north Polar home
Way down over Iceland
'Til, crossing the foam,

We saw a big aircraft
With Royal Air Force marking
And asked if up the right
Tree we were barking?

The pilot said "Yes, sir,
If it's McDonald's you're after,

Keep straight on to eastward
Until you hear laughter,

And then down below,
Through the Thames Valley mist,
You'll see the lights shining
In the house on your list."

And so we found Bracknell
And left you this present
While you were still dreaming
Of everything pleasant.

By the time you have opened them, Rudolph and I
Will be twelve hundred miles in the northernmost sky.

MAY 17, 1940–1990

I little thought when first we met
In nineteen-thirty-nine
That soon our courses would be set
Along the guiding line

Designed for those who sail the sea
Or travel in the sky,
A constant course; for constancy
Was best if we'd defy

The snags and disappointments
That marriage held in store
For us and millions like us
In those six years of war.

You sailed the sea, while I the sky;
And death was on the menu.
The rough idea was not to die
But rather seek a venue

Where we might settle near the site
Of airfields such as Grantham
In digs that looking back I quite
Don't know how you could stand them.

And then back here in forty-six
There'd surely be improvement,
But you forgot the kind of fix
That heralded each movement.

The job was mine to go ahead
And find accommodation,
A roof, some rooms, perhaps a bed
Not too far from the station.

I found the spot—'twas in the Fall—
By a streamlet of the Rideau
That rose in Spring you will recall
Half up the sitting-room window.

Undaunted still by evidence
Of failure to learn
I showed renewed incompetence—
Got us into Manor Barn;

Elizabethan, hence the name—
The walls had hollyhocks on—
And even rads; when winter came
They did for drying socks on.

Next bus and caravan behind
A Bracknell pub—The Bull—
If life to you was not yet kind,
At least it wasn't dull.

Though Singapore was quite a plum
And brought a nice promotion
We also thought the time had come
To cross that other ocean

Westward to your land of birth,
And mine so to say by marriage,
For one more try to prove my worth
With house—not railway carriage.

To leave the service was a wrench
But there were compensations.
In Montreal we soon spoke French
In dreams, not conversations.

The airplane game was hard to crack
And I could tell you tales, man,
At school they questioned Martha Mac;
"My Dad's a travelling salesman."

But TMR began to tire
When Peter, John, departed.
For house or cottage not a buyer—
The exodus had started.

It took a year; we used the chance
To travel memory lane
In England, Wales, but not to France,
Our French had slipped again.

In publishing we found a niche
The Liberal Left neglected.
And if it didn't make us rich,
That's not what we expected.

We tried instead to lend a voice
To a different view of the scene
And that we did—there's now more choice
Than if BMG hadn't been.

I started out to say a word
About my closest friend
Who stood the years of hope deferred
With that peculiar blend

Of courage, kindness, loyalty,
The sort so rarely found,
That mixed one day with royalty,
But with feet still firm on the ground.

It's not the easiest thing in the world
To do what Ruth has done
To keep the flag of the home unfurled
And stay the course—for one

Of the many gifts she brought to me,
The one that stands the test
Is what I mentioned—constancy;
There's that, and all the rest

Of fifty years of days and days,
The hopes and fears that move you,
They move me now to offer praise
And say again: I love you.

TO MY FRIEND, 17TH MAY, 1978

It's hard to remember exactly the way
I felt thirty-eight years ago.
Excited, in love, I knew that the day
Was filled with a new kind of glow.

What I couldn't have known in that previous May
Was the depth and extent of regard
That has grown with the years, of which (you might say)
The first dozen or so were quite hard.

Not nearly so hard as they might well have been
If it weren't for the wonderful bloom
I've felt then and since (as you've probably seen)
Each time you come into the room.

ST. VALENTINE'S DAY, 1990

This is the day when swains seek to lay
Claims to the innocent hearts
Of girls who they fancy might possibly say
If not yes then perhaps yes in parts

To advances less innocent, men being men,
That sooner or later might lead
Toward couch, even bedroom, and soon after then
To improving the words with a deed.

All this by the way of setting the scene
For my annual avowal of love
For the woman whose company always has been
The best when push came to shove.

Not only in February, March, April, May,
But in every month of the year
It's her smile, her voice, that brightens my day—
Her presence to me is most dear.

For the fiftieth time, in this last decade
Of twentieth-century dates,
My Valentine wish is the same as I've made
Each time for the choicest of mates.

YOU THREE 1997

To Peter, John, and Martha
On the 17th of May,
By way of thanks, or rather
Remembering the day

When Ruth and Ken together
Before assembled guests
Decided they would feather
Their own particular nests

285

Which turned out in the long run
To total twenty-nine
With one two three the last one
Of many that were fine,

And others that were less so,
Much less, to tell the truth,
A thing I wouldn't stress so
Except to point to Ruth

As keeper of the household
Through ups and many a down,
Until you left the home fold
For travels of your own.

And while it might at first appear
That we're again a twosome
It's not like that, for always here,
While laughing at the gruesome,

We also thank our lucky star
(The one that only we see)
For granting us the best by far:
That we were blessed with you three.

VALENTINE'S DAY 2000

With February the fourteenth now looming,
I can not any longer delay
The expression of joy that's consuming
Upon each and every day
When I wake to the realization
That *this* one I'm spending with you.

For the days that soon pass in procession
Are marked by a singular plus:
It consists in our mutual possession
Of love for each other, and thus

To ignore yearly signs of our aging;
They are signs of something else too.

At times it might seem like endurance
As move followed move in the past.
Yet through all of them was the assurance
That our love for each other would last.
As it has, and will surely continue,
Dear Ruth; hence this message to you.

FRIENDS IN THE AIR
(At Belleair Beach, Florida, 1990)

The best would be, along the shore,
To join the pelicans; begin the take-off run
With scurrying feet, until the wings get lift,
Drip trails of water.

Beat, beat, to gain the cruising height,
And glide, with wings outstretched,
Riding the wind not far from shore,
In echelon or line astern.

Sensing the stall, you beat again
To thirty feet, the fishing height,
And see the silver flash below the surface;
Fold wings and start

The diving turn, neck tensed,
Speed brakes in sync to slow the dive
At point of strike, and scramble,
Shrugging water, into the climb.

In dreams, no pelican, I levitate
By wishing. No wings, no engine,
Just rise, rise and hover, swoop
And rise again, above the crowd

That shows no astonishment, watches
Idly, turns away, while joy
Supports me, wingless, soaring
In a bird-free sky.

Awake, the joy fades soon,
Yet tantalizes. Death, the new dimension,
Might be like that, with friends
Who died in the air, but live.

Anonymous, submitted to *Flight Plan* by Carlyle Columbus and
published in the October 2001 issue:

I lie here still beside the hill,
Abandoned long to nature's will,
My buildings down, my people gone,
My only sounds the wild birds' song.

But my mighty birds will rise no more,
No more I hear the Merlins roar,
And never now my bosom feels
The pounding of their giant wheels.

From the ageless hill their voices cast
Thunderous echoes of the past,
And still, in lonely reverie,
Their great dark wings swept down to me.

Laughter, sorrow, hope and pain,
I shall never know these things again,
Emotions that I came to know
Of strange young men of long ago.

Who knows, as evening shadows meet,
Are they with me still, a phantom fleet,
And do my ghosts still stride unseen
Across my face so wide and green?

And in the future should structures tall
Bury me beyond recall,
I shall remember them,
My metal birds and long-dead men.

Now weeds grow high, obscure the sky.
Oh! remember me when you pass by,
For beneath this tangled leafy field,
I was your home, your friend, your shield.

Poems from John Pudney's *Ten Summers: Poems 1933–43*, Bodley Head, 1944.

For Johnny

Do not despair
For Johnny-head-in-air;
He sleeps as sound
As Johnny under ground.

Fetch out no shroud
For Johnny-in-the-cloud;
And keep your tears
For him in after years.

Better by far
For Johnny-the-bright-star,
To keep your head,
And see his children fed.

At the end of his book, *The Right of the Line* (one of the best about the RAF, and on my shelf), John Terraine quotes John Pudney's poem, "Security." It's about pre-takeoff precautions, and for me it expresses the individual tragedies in all the Bomber Command losses.

Security

Empty your pockets, Tom, Dick and Harry,
Strip your identity; leave it behind.
Lawyer, garage hand, grocer, don't tarry
With your own country, your own kind.

Leave all your letters. Suburb and township,
Green fen and grocery, slip-way and bay,
Hot-spring and prairie, smoke-stack and coal tip,
Leave in our keeping while you're away.

Tom, Dick and Harry, plain names and numbers,
Pilot, observer, and gunner depart.
Their personal litter only encumbers
Somebody's head, somebody's heart.

Extract from *Lycidas* by John Milton.

Alas! what boots it with uncessant care
To tend the homely, slighted, shepherd's trade,
And strictly meditate the thankless Muse?
Were it not better done, as others use,
To sport with Amaryllis in the shade,
Or with the tangles of Neaera's hair?
Fame is the spur that the clear spirit doth raise
(That last infirmity of noble mind)
To scorn delights and live laborious days;
But the fair guerdon when we hope to find,
And think to burst out into sudden blaze,
Comes the blind Fury with the abhorrèd shears,
And slits the thin-spun life. "But not the praise,"
Phoebus replied, and touched my trembling ears:
"Fame is no plant that grows on mortal soil,
Nor in the glistering foil
Set off to the world, nor in broad Rumour lies,
But lives and spreads aloft by those pure eyes
And perfect witness of all-judging Jove;

As he pronounces lastly on each deed
Of so much fame in Heav'n expect thy meed."

Translation from Ovid (43 B.C.–18 A.D.) quoted in *The Cunning Man* by Robertson Davies, pp. 466–7.

> Then Death, so call'd, is but old Matter dress'd
> In some new Figure, and a vary'd Vest:
> Thus all Things are but alter'd, nothing dies;
> And here and there th'unbodied Spirit flies,
> By Time, or Force, or Sickness dispossest,
> And lodges, where it lights, in Man or Beast;
> Or hunts without, till ready Limbs it finds
> And actuates those according to their kind;
> From Tenement to Tenement is toss'd;
> The Soul is still the same, the Figure only lost;
> And, as the soften'd Wax new Seals receives,
> This Face assumes, and that impression leaves;
> Now call'd by one, now by another Name;
> The Form is only chang'd, the Wax is still the same:
> So Death, so call'd, can but the Form deface,
> Th'immortal Soul flies out in empty space;
> To seek her Fortune in some other Place.

A.E. Housman (Collected Poems)

From XXXI

> The tree of man was never quiet:
> Then 'twas the Roman, now 'tis I.

HALF A MILLION WORDS LATER...

Who could forget the thrill of starting to write that first novel? Meeting the daily target, often exceeding it, pleasure mounted with the pile of pages.

Each day began with the self-indulgence of rereading, savouring the phrases, appreciating the subleties, chuckling at the humour.

Autobiographical? Well, why not? Hadn't one lived an interesting life? Could it fail to interest the readers? The thousands of readers? The hundreds of thousands?

The title was important. Short but catchy. *The Link Transaction*. Perfect. It would look well in the reviews and, later, on the billboards. International intrigue, local colour in Europe and the Middle East. A hijacking (it was during that period), an enigmatic counter-intelligence director in London (nondescript house in quiet square, "Sherry?"), love interest threaded through the plot (mature woman, hint of mystery here)—the combination was irresistible.

With the precious pages in the mail it became a question of waiting for the telephone call from the publishers: "When will you be able to come and discuss your novel?" After a month with no word it was perhaps best to phone them. You never knew with the mail. Yes, they had it. Would get back to you.

Then the letter. Incredible. "...unable to fit it into our publishing schedule." Why on earth not? Obviously the firm was poorly organized. Well, there were other publishers.

Seven (unpublished) novels later, the truth begins to sink home. Writing them was enjoyable, even stimulating. What could compare with the satisfaction of 1,000 words in the day, of typing a good chapter, of flipping back through the pages? But the talent wasn't there.

And yet, there were all those reports of the best sellers that were rejected by the first dozen publishers, by the first 18. Why not try once more? That romantic adventure, for example. Good title (*The Giant Sapphire*). Exotic setting (Singapore in the mid-1920s). No overt sex. No foul language. Just the thing, you would think, for Harlequin.

Wrong again, but what's that in *The Writer's Digest*? "Simon & Schuster, leading publisher of hardcover and paperback books, is establishing an extensive new line of contemporary romantic fiction... under the imprint of *Silhouette Romances*." Why not? It's worth the postage. Keep them moving, say the successful writers, looking back.

The most disturbing thing is to read a Murdoch, or a Powell, or a le Carré and to sit in awe of the artistry without being able to see how it's done, let alone to emulate it.

How do they make the people so real? How do they convey place and atmosphere so vividly? How, on a purely technical plane, do they move people about and keep the action going?

True, there are books on how to write fiction. Study the successful writers. Study *Treasure Island*. Study Howard Fast. But write. As one put it: "Not until you've written half a million words will you begin to get the hang of it."

Half a million words later your typing has improved. You may even be on speaking terms with some of the editors. But they're not buying.

And yet, what of that very successful woman novelist whose books your wife says have simply nothing in them? Nothing happens. They're dull, dull. But they sell, sell.

Why, you wonder, wouldn't *Finland Court* sell? Suburban setting. Interesting characters. Some politics. Some sex, some of it clandestine. What was the name of that self-contained man with the off-beat philosophy (it was your Ouspensky period)? Of course, George Sargent at No. 24. You read on, absorbed.

Later, you reread the editorial guidelines that accompanied Harlequin's rejection letter. "Harlequins... are told from the heroine's point of view... heroines have all the interests of today's women and a desire for a satisfying man/woman relationship based on love and marriage."

That's why *The Giant Sapphire* didn't suit. It was told from the hero's point of view. Maybe Harlequin will branch out in the opposite direction. Don't men have that desire, too?

What about the other titles? *The Paper Airplane*? One publisher said it never took off and glancing through it today you have to agree. *Come Home, Bill Bayley*? It had its moments, but the plot was too involved and the conversations were much too long. *Ten*

Days In Late Summer? You liked the Expo setting. No one else did.

Henry Porter's War? Now there was a stirring tale, not all imagined, either. Remembered and scared stiff all over again. But it didn't quite come off, even though one generous and kindly editor took the trouble to telephone and explain what was wrong—a rare spirit.

Is it worth another shot? That's the tantalizing thing. Five years now since you wrote the last of the magnificent seven, perhaps fiction and non-fiction don't mix after all. It has to be one or the other.

And yet, the challenge remains. You look again at Harlequin's guidelines. "Remember, a large part of being a successful writer is sending the *right* manuscript to the *right* publisher." You reach for *The Writer's Market.*

(*Airforce* magazine, Fall, 1998)

JUSTICE DENIED—THE BOMBER HARRIS TRUST STORY

Bomber Command, the RAF's offensive arm in which Canadians and Royal Canadian Air Force squadrons played a major role, was in continuous operation from September 3, 1939, until the night of May 2/3, 1945, when a force of 170 Mosquitoes attacked airfields near Kiel in advance of British and Canadian ground forces.

In a long report on World War II, *Maclean's* War Correspondent L.S.B. Shapiro wrote that "If bombing did not win the war it was certainly the outstanding factor in the victories of American, British, Canadian—yes, and Russian armies on the ground." (*Maclean's,* June 1, 1945.)

After the war, Adolf Hitler's former armaments minister Albert Speer wrote that RAF Bomber Command "opened up a second front long before the invasion of Europe" and that the bombing offensive was "the greatest lost battle on the German side." (*Spandau: The Secret Diaries.*)

None of this reached the Canadian public in 1992 when a mixture of lies, half-truths and innuendoes entitled *The Valour and the Horror,* and in particular the second episode "Death by

Moonlight: Bomber Command," was flashed on the nation's television screens by its national broadcaster, the Canadian Broadcasting Corporation.

In that episode, the CBC and its collaborators portrayed Canadian bomber crews as wanton killers of innocent German civilians, mostly women and children. A book based on the film was published by HarperCollins.

The film created an uneven contest between surviving aircrews and Canada's arts/media establishment, which closed ranks behind the film's producers' assertions in the film that "This is a true story," and "There is no fiction."

Yet since then, and since Canada's Supreme Court refused to hear the aircrews' plea for justice, the Canadian arts/media world has witnessed such an outpouring of books and videos and parades and school visits by veterans as would have seemed impossible to the producers and scriptwriters of that deceitful "docudrama."

Now it would be out of character for such a modest band of ex-aircrew as The Bomber Harris Trust to claim sole authorship of this turnabout in affairs.

But we did have something to do with it.

As did the law of unintended results. The pacifists and Brit-haters who put the thing together have seen a revival in the nation's awareness of Canada's unequalled military record that is as welcome as it is overdue.

Former Senator Jack Marshall, always a strong supporter of veterans, had the guts and patriotism to bring the "docudrama" before the Senate Sub-Committee on Veterans' Affairs; this despite efforts by CBC directors and officials to prevent the Senate hearings.

Although the Bomber Command veterans from across Canada who gave evidence at the week-long hearings were compensated, many others attended at their own expense.

Their prime concern—and later the Trust's—was to distinguish between opinions and facts, truth and falsehood. Aircrew veterans fought to preserve a way of life in which individual freedom and responsibility are paramount.

None of them dispute the right of producer Brian McKenna to express his opinions about the conduct of World War II. What they object to is his advancing such opinions as facts in a film subsidized by, and carrying the imprimatur of, the Government of

Canada, when the opinions expressed and broadcast are manifestly untrue.

The Committee's report, written by Parliamentary historians who attended its hearings, concluded that the film was "riddled with inaccuracies and biased perceptions and... the number of factual and technical errors pointed out to the Sub-Committee was astounding... [the film was] a seriously flawed assessment of the bomber offensive in the Second World War... The picture that emerges is terribly misleading."

Asked by the CBC for an independent review, its Ombudsman consulted six military historians, including three nominated by the film's producer, Brian McKenna. None of the historians supported the series as being accurate. No military historian consulted by the Senate Sub-Committee or by the Ombudsman would support the film.

Even though the Ombudsman was forced by CBC officials to revise his report from 60 pages down to 13 to reduce criticism, his report confirmed that in many instances the facts were false, taken out of context and improperly weighted. He concluded that "the thesis is unproven and the presentation misleading," further that the dramatic techniques used created serious problems and distortions that lent "the appearance of reality to hypothesis."

When CBC President Patrick Watson refused to carry out his undertaking "to take substantial corrective measures on air," aircrew veterans turned to the law, formed The Bomber Harris Trust, and sued the CBC and its collaborators for defamation.

Seeking financial assistance, the Trust made 12 separate mailings, including 8 issues of its newsletter *Flarepath*, to a list of 13,000 from all services and the merchant marine, in Canada, Britain, Australia, New Zealand, South Africa, and the USA, as well as the general public. Donations eventually reached a total of $350,000.

As if by extension of the media's stance, the Trust hit roadblocks in the courts that even now, two years after the Supreme Court refused to hear our plea, are hard to reconcile with the justice we thought we were fighting to preserve.

It still seems reasonable to us that since our reputation was damaged by a government-subsidized film that was designed to mislead the public about our contribution to victory in World War

II, the proper course was to have the matter adjudicated by representatives of the same public, namely a jury of our peers.

Chapter 39 of the 1215 version of the *Magna Carta* reads: "No free man shall be taken or imprisoned or dispossessed, or outlawed, or banished, or in any way destroyed, nor will we go upon him, nor send upon him, except by the legal judgment of his peers or by the law of the land."

We were dispossessed of reputation, were denied the right to lay evidence of the defamation before a court, and were denied the historic right to judgment by a jury, which is the normal course in actions for defamation.

A motion court judge dismissed the action because "there cannot be a libel of a group of 25,000," and because "no individual member of the group is singled out." He based this on the mistaken belief that the aircrew veterans of Bomber Command were an indeterminate group, as would be lawyers in the statement that "all lawyers are thieves," when the fact is that every individual aircrew member of Bomber Command belonged to the determinate group of aircrew who served in that Command between September 3, 1939 and May 8, 1945, and is so identified by name and service number in the record.

In short, the Learned Judge overlooked the fact that on a Motion the truth of allegations in a Statement of Claim is presumed. Instead, he watched the film, read the book, and decided that our allegations of defamation did not "bear the interpretation given to them in the Statement of Claim."

But the issue before him was not whether in his view the allegations in our Statement of Claim were borne out by his seeing the film and reading the book. The issue was whether or not, assuming the facts set out in the Statement of Claim to be true, it would be open to a jury to find defamation after evidence, cross-examination, and argument.

The Learned Judge also held that because the representative plaintiff (and an initiator of the Trust), Donald Elliott, was a POW during the time frame of the film, he could not have been libelled, when the fact is that Elliott, like everyone else who flew with Bomber Command was a member of that determinate group.

When we appealed the ruling, the Appeal Court made the curious statement that because the aircrews were heroic their reputation was secure and couldn't have been damaged by the film. This despite the almost complete lack of teaching about World War II up to that time and the fact that the aircrews were depicted as war criminals in a film aimed at the schools.

In summary, all the survivors asked was that their assertion of defamation be adjudicated by a jury which had heard all the evidence. That didn't happen. A pre-trial judgment was made, it was upheld by an Appeal Court, without any of the evidence being laid before either court—and the Supreme Court refused to hear an application for leave to appeal those rulings.

Now there is no doubt that all this has also damaged the film's credibility. The CBC has undertaken not to show it again in its original form. But this didn't stop another government corporation—and one of the film's sponsors—Telefilm Canada, from financially supporting *The Valour and the Horror* web site which broadcast "Death by Moonlight" over the History Channel several times in January 1998.

We still maintain that the CBC has a clear duty to execute Patrick Watson's undertaking "to take substantial corrective measures" by inserting as a preface to all copies of the film an appropriate disclaimer, such as "Viewer discretion advised: Many statements in this film are untrue, dramatizations are fictional, and it does not represent the official view of the Government of Canada."

After all expenses were met we were able to distribute $160,000 to aviation museums and related institutions across Canada. We sold over 4,000 copies of the Trust's book *A Battle for Truth*, many of them to libraries. Our essay contest on the topic "The Contribution of Bomber Command to the Victory in Europe," drew a strong response.

Before the 53rd anniversary of VE Day, there had been more than 10,000 visits to The Bomber Harris Trust's Home Page. It is being added to all the time, and readers of *Airforce* magazine are invited to submit new items to this modern memorial: (http://www3.sympatico.ca/jimlynch); (E-mail:achull@intranet.ca).

▣ Bibliography ▣

Acton, Lord. *The History of Freedom*. Grand Rapids: The Acton Institute, 1993.

Allison, Sam. *French Power—The Francization of Canada*. Richmond Hill: BMG Publishing Ltd., 1978.

Andrew, J.V. *Bilingual Today, French Tomorrow*. Richmond Hill: BMG Publishing Ltd., 1977.

Andrew, J.V. *Backdoor Bilingualism*. Richmond Hill: BMG Publishing Ltd., 1979.

Atrill, Verne. *HOW ALL ECONOMIES WORK*. Calgary: Dimensionless Science Publications, 1979.

Atrill, Verne. *The Freedom Manifesto*. Calgary: Dimensionless Science Publications, 1981.

Bomber Harris Trust. *A Battle for Truth*. Agincourt: Ramsay Business Systems Ltd., 1994.

Borrow, George. *Lavengro*. New York: G. P. Putnam, 1851.

Bowyer, Chaz. *History of the RAF*. London: Bison Books Ltd., 1977.

Boyd, Winnett, with Kenneth McDonald. *The National Dilemma and the Way Out*. Richmond Hill: BMG Publishing Ltd., 1975.

Cheshire, Leonard. *The Hidden World*. London and Glasgow: Collins, 1981.

Chesterton, G.K. *Ballad of the White Horse in The Collected Poems*. London: Cecil Palmer, 1927.

Clarke, D.H. *What were they like to fly?* London: Ian Allen Ltd., 1964.

Clouston, A.E. *The Dangerous Skies*. London: Cassell, 1954.

Collins, Doug. *Immigration—The Destruction of English Canada*. Richmond Hill: BMG Publishing Ltd., 1979.

Common Prayer, The Book of. London: Oxford University Press.

Davies, Robertson. *The Cunning Man*. Toronto: McClelland and Stewart Limited, 1995.

Gibbon, Edward. *The Portable Gibbon—The Decline and Fall of the Roman Empire*. New York: Viking, 1952.

Grant, George. *Lament for a Nation—The Defeat of Canadian Nationalism*. Ottawa: Carleton University Press, 1989.

Hayek, Friedrich, A. *The Road to Serfdom*. University of Chicago Press, 1976.

Hazlitt, William. *Table Talk*. London and Glasgow: Collins Clear-Type Press, 1910.

Hewer, Howard. *In For A Penny, In For A Pound*. Toronto: Stoddart, 2000.

Housman, A.E. T*he Collected Poems*. London: Jonathan Cape Ltd., 1967.

Jouvenel, Bertrand de. *The Ethics of Redistribution*. Indianapolis: Liberty Press, 1952.

Hymns Ancient and Modern. London: William Clowes & Sons Limited, 1916.

Lucas, Laddie. *Out of the Blue*. UK: Hutchinson, 1985.

McCall-Newman, Christina. *Grits—An Intimate Portrait of the Liberal Party*. Toronto: Macmillan of Canada, 1982.

McDonald, Kenneth. *Red Maple*. Richmond Hill: BMG Publishing Ltd., 1975.

McDonald, Kenneth. *Green Maple*. Richmond Hill: BMG Publishing Ltd., 1977.

McDonald, Kenneth. *Keeping Canada Together*. Agincourt: Ramsay Business Systems Ltd., 1990.

McDonald, Kenneth. *His Pride, Our Fall—Recovering from the Trudeau Revolution*. Toronto: Key Porter Books Ltd., 1995.

McDonald, Kenneth. *The Monstrous Trick*. Toronto: APEC Books Ltd., 1998.

Melville, Herman. *Moby Dick or The White Whale*. London and Glasgow: Collins, 1954.

Middlebrook, Martin, and Everett, Chris. *The Bomber Command War Diaries—An Operational Reference Book, 1939-45*. New York: Viking Penguin Inc., 1985.

Milton, John. *Six Centuries of Great Poetry—From Chaucer to Yeats*. Eds: Robert Penn Warren and Albert Erskine. New York: Dell Publishing Company Inc., 1955.

Morris, Richard. *Cheshire: The Biography of Leonard Cheshire, VC, OM*. London: Viking, 2000.

Morton, Desmond. *Canadian Social Studies*, Vol. 28, No. 2. Calgary: University of Alberta, Winter 1994.

Morton, J.B. *Vagabond*. London: Philip Allan & Co. Ltd., 1935.

Muggeridge, Malcolm. *Jesus Rediscovered*. New York: Doubleday & Company, Inc., 1969.

Ouspensky, P.D. *The Fourth Way*. London: Routledge & Kegan Paul Ltd., 1957.

Peden, Murray. *A Thousand Shall Fall*. Stittsville: Canada's Wings Inc., 1979.

Roberts, R. N. *The Halifax File*. Tonbridge: Air-Britain (Historians) Ltd., and the British Aviation Archaeological Council, 1982.

Smith, Adam. *Lectures on Jurisprudence*. Indianapolis: Liberty Classics, 1982.

Somerville, David. *Trudeau Revealed*. Richmond Hill: BMG Publishing Ltd., 1978.

Speer, Albert. *Spandau: The Secret Diaries*. London: Collins, 1976.

Stevenson, Robert Louis. *Virginibus Puerisque—Familiar Studies of Men and Books*. London: J.M. Dent & Sons Limited, 1925.

Thomas, Dylan. *A Pocket Book of Modern Verse—from Walt Whitman to Dylan* Thomas. Ed: Oscar Williams. New York: Washington Square Press, Inc., 1954.

Thorson, The Hon. J.T. *Wanted: a Single Canada—A distinguished Canadian jurist states the case against biculturalism*. Toronto: McClelland and Stewart Limited, 1973.

Tomlinson, H. M. *All Our Yesterdays*. Toronto: The Musson Book Company, Ltd., 1930.

Tomlinson, H. M. *Gallions Reach*. London & Toronto: William Heinemann Ltd., 1927.

Tomlinson, H. M. *Gifts of Fortune—with some hints for those about to travel*. London: William Heinemann, Ltd., 1926.

Vallins, G. H. *An ABC of English Usage*. Oxford University Press, 1965.

Printed in the United States
87535LV00003B/44/A